10657896

Couples Who Kill

a&b

Couples Who Kill

CAROL ANNE DAVIS

This book was published in Great Britain in 2005 by
Allison & Busby Limited
15 Charlotte Mews
London W11 4LJ
www.allisonandbusby.com

A catalogue record for this book is available from
the British Library.

10 9 8 7 6 5 4 3 2 1

ISBN 0 7490 8175 9
978-0-7490-8175-1

Printed and bound in Great Britain by
Bookmarque Ltd, Croydon, Surrey

CAROL ANNE DAVIS was born in Dundee, moved to Edinburgh in her twenties and now lives in south-west England. She left school at fifteen and was everything from an artist's model to an editorial assistant before going to university. Her Master of the Arts degree included criminology and was followed by a postgraduate diploma in Adult & Community Education.

A full time writer since graduating, her crime novels *Kiss It Away, Noise Abatement, Safe As Houses* and *Shrouded* have been described as chillingly realistic for their portrayals of dangerous sex and death. *Booklist* described *Kiss It Away* as 'a not-to-be-missed thriller by Scotland's queen of suspense' and *Kirkus Reviews* said 'Davis unveils her scariest hero yet.'

She is also the author of the bestselling *Children Who Kill: Profiles Of Preteen & Teenage Killers* and *Women Who Kill: Profiles Of Female Serial Killers*.

Carol's website is located at *www.carolannedavis.co.uk*

Also available from Allison and Busby

Children Who Kill
Women Who Kill

For Ian

Contents

Acknowledgements

I'm deeply indebted to researcher and writer Paul A Woods for his insight into serial killers Leonard Lake and Charles Ng. Paul spent hours interviewing Ng for a documentary on the Lake-Ng murders and has a unique understanding of their increasingly deadly synergy.

I was also fortunate to interview Caroline Roberts, one of Fred & Rose West's few surviving victims. Her autobiography *The Lost Girl* is one of the most honest books I've ever read.

I'm very grateful to crime correspondent Andrew Nott for answering my questions about the Trevor Hardy & Sheilagh Farrow murders. Andrew co-authored the book *Cause Of Death* with pathologist Dr Geoffrey Garrett and their writing made me aware of this particularly unusual and surprisingly little-known case.

Once again, I'm grateful to Lisa Dumond who took time out of her busy schedule to help with my American research. Lisa is especially interested in Anti-Social Personality Disorder, knowledge she incorporates in her short fiction and true crime. She's also a prolific book reviewer and a novelist.

Equal thanks to David Mulcahy for sending me his thirty-nine page document *A Case For Innocence* and various forensic statements related to his trial. Thanks also to one of Mr Mulcahy's friends for speaking to me about this controversial case.

Preface

Ask the British public about couples who kill and they'll invariably name The Moors Murderers or Fred & Rose West. Canadians also opt for a heterosexual couple, Paul Barnardo & Karla Homolka, as do the Americans who tend to cite Charles Starkweather & Caril Fugate or Bonnie & Clyde. Australia's best known deadly duo are David & Catherine Birnie whilst Daniel & Manuela Ruda recently made headlines in Germany.

But many killer couples aren't heterosexual lovers, and some have far more complex relationships - herein you'll find serial torture-killer cousins, an increasingly unbalanced mother-son duo, psychotic sisters and a cult-based brother and sister team. This isn't to suggest that most deadly duos are related: *Couples Who Kill* also profiles gay team killers and equally sadistic friends.

Most of these partnerships arose out of the individuals shared love of cruelty, others were formed through jealousy or greed. What they all have in common is their effect on the victims: duped by two opponents rather than one, they had little chance.

The serial killer who kills alone often takes time out afterwards to mentally relive the murder and regroup his defences, but deviant duos immediately discuss the homicide and move on to the next victim and then the next. As such, several of the profiled couples were responsible for a death count that was into double figures, with one duo being responsible for over thirty sexually-motivated deaths. Couples who kill only comprise twenty per cent of serial killers, but they tend to be responsible for a much larger body count than men or women who kill alone.

Even when a couple 'only' murder once or twice, the results are particularly gruesome, with the individuals often stopping partway through the assault to find out exactly how their co-killer wants to proceed. With physical strength on their side, they don't have to adopt the blitzkrieg methods of the solo attacker. Their duality also complicates matters during the subsequent trial when the jury has to ascertain who did what.

Many of these killers have similar characteristics in their backgrounds and these are summarised in the final chapter, the 'Abuse Excuse'.

1 FRIENDS REUNITED
LAWRENCE BITTAKER & ROY NORRIS

When former prison friends Bittaker and Norris were reunited in 1979, they decided to kidnap teenage girls for sexual pleasure. Within a four month period they would repeatedly rape five known victims, torture them for kicks and kill them in an especially brutal way.

Lawrence Sigmund Bittaker

Lawrence was born on 27th September 1940 to a drug-addicted single mother in Southern California. She soon put him into care, where he was moved from one home to another by families who were more interested in the foster-payment cheques than in their foster child. As such, he didn't receive the nurturing that all babies require if they are to bond with others, and if they are to ultimately care about anyone other than themselves.

Lawrence had an IQ in the top one percent of the population and also had a photographic memory. But his foster families were often Spanish so couldn't converse with him fluently even if they wanted to. He was invariably clothed in hand-me-downs, some of which were girl's clothes and shoes. Alternately ignored and laughed at, he retreated into his own little world. He literally remained on the sidelines as his foster parents fed their natural children, only giving him the leftovers. He was also sexually molested and raped by some of his so-called carers during these desperately unhappy years.

At six he was adopted by a couple who gave him their surname, Bittaker. Unfortunately it was too little too late as he was already a nascent psychopath. Young psychopaths can improve if given a consistently loving and stable environment – but George Bittaker's work as an aircraft fitter meant that the family moved around the country so the child was uprooted again and again. He attended schools in Pennsylvania, Florida, Ohio and California where he was always the new boy. It made Lawrence Bittaker feel even more of an outsider, alienated from his peers.

At seventeen he dropped out of high school and stole a car, was involved in a hit and run and fled to Long Beach to escape prosecution. But the police caught up with him and he was sent to a California Youth Authority home, where he remained until he was nineteen.

The rootless teenager now travelled to Louisiana, where the FBI charged him with a further motor theft. He was sent to a Oklahoma reformatory where he behaved so strangely that he was transferred to a Missouri medical centre. He'd later admit to forensic psychiatrist Dr Ronald Markman that he faked psychotic symptoms in order to get hospitalised. The medical centre found him to be hostile and manipulative, but he made sure that his conduct improved so that the staff believed they had cured him. As a result, he was released after a year.

The intelligent but self-destructive Lawrence now moved to Los Angeles and was arrested again almost immediately, this time for robbery. But he was let out on parole in 1963.

Lawrence Bittaker continued to cause havoc in the outside world. He again stole cars and was imprisoned, got out and burgled and was imprisoned, stabbed a shop assistant who tried to prevent him shoplifting and was arrested again. He was consequently sent to the California Men's Colony where he met Roy Lewis Norris, who had a history of sexual crime.

Roy Lewis Norris

Roy was born on 2nd February 1948 in Colorado. He was an unwanted baby, the product of a very unhappy marriage which would end in recriminations and divorce. His increasingly lonely childhood included abuse and he turned to marijuana and beer to blot out the terrible memories. By his teens he was fantasising constantly about violent sex and saw women as objects to satisfy his lust.

At seventeen he joined the Navy. He was stationed in Vietnam, though he never saw combat. But his deviant sexual desires continued to build and in November 1969 he dragged a young woman from her car and attempted to rape her. He was arrested and given bail. Whilst on bail he forced his way into another woman's flat but the police arrived before he could sexually assault her. As a result of these attacks, the Navy discharged him on mental health grounds.

Roy Norris's violence escalated and he attacked a female stranger in the street and battered her with a brick. This time he was sentenced to an indeterminate time in a mental hospital. After five years they decided that they had cured him and let him out.

Within weeks he had proved them wrong, pulling a woman into a hedge at Redondo Beach, partially strangling her and raping her. (A classic fantasist, Roy Norris would later tell an author that the woman was his girlfriend and that the sex was consensual.) He was sent to prison where he met the equally dispossessed Lawrence Bittaker.

They began to share their sexual fantasies and Lawrence suggested that when they got out they should work through the teenage years by kidnapping a girl of thirteen, one aged fourteen and so on for every year up to nineteen. They also agreed that they'd torture their victims for fun.

Freedom

In November 1978 Bittaker was given parole and found low level factory work that must have been mind-numbingly dull for a man of his intellect. Eight weeks later Norris got out and moved into his mother's trailer and began work as an electrician. The following month he received a letter from Bittaker suggesting that they meet up in a hotel.

At the meeting they discussed kidnapping and raping young girls and the various ways that they could dominate them. But they needed a place to keep their captives so Lawrence bought a van. The vehicle had a bed so it became his new abode and he kept it parked outside Roy's mother's trailer. The silver cargo van had no side windows so was ideal for keeping sex slaves. Bittaker promptly named it the 'Murder Mac'.

The next few months were the intense fantasy phase. The two men would flirt with girls on beaches and in bars and often take their photos. Some of the girls were given a lift but they weren't harmed as the men were still searching for a safe place to park the van so that their eventual torture sessions wouldn't be overheard.

Their sexual lives at this time were largely auto-erotic: Roy Norris would later admit that he could maintain an erection for hours by just staring at a girl and imagining what he'd do if he got her alone.

Finally the men found a locked fire road in the San Gabriel Mountains and, by smashing the lock, gained access. Bittaker replaced this with his own lock. They now had a secure location where no one could hear their victims' screams.

The first victim

Sixteen-year-old Cindy Schaeffer was in the wrong place at the wrong time, and became the men's first victim. The devout young Christian was coming home from church on 24th June 1979 when Lawrence Bittaker offered her a ride. The pretty young blonde refused and increased her pace but he blocked her path and Roy Norris grabbed her. Within seconds they had bundled her into the van. They gagged and bound the teenager and drove her to the mountains, where Roy Norris raped her and forced her to fellate him. Later Lawrence Bittaker took his turn. After raping her vaginally and anally numerous times, the men tired of their traumatised victim and wrapped a wire coat hanger around her neck, taking turns to pull it tightly. Afterwards they drove her body to a canyon and dumped it for the animals to devour.

Incredibly, Roy Norris now returned to his mother's trailer and went back to work. Lawrence Bittaker also went back to his day job. A fortnight later they grew tired of their day-to-day existence and succeeded in luring another victim into their mobile lair ...

The second victim

On 8th July eighteen-year-old Andrea Joy Hall was hitchhiking when Lawrence Bittaker offered her a lift. Meanwhile Roy Norris hid in the back of the van. When she voluntarily entered the vehicle, he pounced on her and tied her up, covering her mouth with tape. He raped her and, once they'd parked at the fire road, Bittaker followed suit. They continued to sexually assault and torture the teenager for the next two days, with Lawrence Bittaker even using pliers on her genitals and nipples. Roy Norris also joined in the abuse, hitting her with a hammer again and again.

Eventually Lawrence Bittaker fetched an icepick and drove it deeply into one of Andrea's ears. She screamed but didn't die so he pulled it out and drove it into her other ear. Afterwards he strangled her to death. Like the previous victim, she was disposed of on the mountain in the hope that animals would ravage her corpse.

August apparently passed without incident – leastways the killer couple aren't officially linked to any murders that month. But police believe they are responsible for up to forty-five deaths in total, especially as photographs of nineteen girls who remain missing were found in the Murder Mac van.

The third and fourth victims

In September the couple found thirteen-year-old Leah Lamp and her fifteen-year-old friend Jackie Gilliam sitting on a bench beside a bus stop. The teenagers happily accepted a lift to Hermosa Beach. But they panicked when they realised that the men were driving in the wrong direction and Leah tried to get out of the van. Roy Norris hit her with a bat and both he and Bittaker trussed up the teens and gagged them. For the first time, they had a victim each.

Noting that the struggle had alerted the attention of

people on a nearby tennis court, the two killers drove off in a hurry. They were convinced that someone would call the police. Unfortunately no one did – and the two girls went on to meet hideous deaths.

This time Bittaker used a tape recorder to keep a permanent record of their torture and rape. He again used pliers on his victims' breasts and on their genitals. They were raped and sodomised numerous times by both men. The girls' ordeal lasted for a full three days as it was Labor Day weekend and the deviant duo didn't have to go to work.

Eventually Lawrence Bittaker rammed his icepick into one of Jackie's ears then into the other, after which he strangled her till she stopped breathing. Both men turned on her younger friend Leah and strangled and battered her to death.

A raped victim escapes

The duo talked over their exploits and found further pleasure in replaying the tape. With four victims to their credit, they felt invincible. Later that same month they sprayed a woman with Mace on a Manhattan Beach street and dragged her into their van. Once she was inside the vehicle, they raped her, not bothering to drive to their isolated fire road. She escaped, reported the assault and would later identify them from police photographs.

The fifth victim

The following month – on Halloween 1979 – the couple struck again, abducting Shirley Lynette Ledford. They tied her up but decided to torture her in the van rather than drive to the deserted mountain road.

This behaviour is typical of serial killers who become wilder and more violent as their killing spree goes on. Their kills follow the law of diminishing returns so they have to murder more quickly or more cruelly in order to still feel sated. At this stage some killers will opt to kill two girls at a time (assuming they haven't done so already) or will prey upon an even more taboo victim such as a child.

In this case, the two men increased the sadism involved in the attack, with Lawrence Bittaker beating Shirley Ledford again and again, whilst urging her to scream more loudly. He also tortured her by clamping pliers around her nipples. Roy Norris joined in the atrocities, hitting her twenty-five times on the elbow with a hammer and instructing her to scream. The two men recorded part of the torture session, eighteen minutes of unendurable pain.

Two hours after they'd abducted the teenager, Bittaker strangled her with a wire coat hanger which he tightened, garrotte-style, with his pliers. They dumped the bruised and mutilated body in a random garden as Bittaker wanted to see what the press reaction would be like.

Her body, which was found the following morning, bore the numerous marks of their abuse – her arms slashed, her torso a mass of bruises. In a final act of rage they had also mutilated her most female features: her face, pubis and breasts.

A third party

The men had gotten away with at least five murders and would have gotten away with many more if Roy Norris hadn't told a fellow ex-con about the killings. He thought that the ex-con would be impressed by his daring but the man went to his lawyer who contacted the police.

Surprisingly, it's not unusual for a deadly duo to tell a third person about their crimes – Ian Brady, who killed with Myra Hindley, told teenager David Smith about their first four murders. After witnessing one such murder for himself, Smith went to the police. Diane Zamora told friends of her part in a co-killing, as did Marlene Olive. (They are profiled later in this book.)

The police now brought Roy Norris in on a parole violation charge as they had seen him selling marijuana. After all, they couldn't yet charge him with the murders as it was just one ex-con's word. Equally keen to keep Lawrence Bittaker in custody, they charged him with raping the victim who had escaped. Bittaker kept quiet in jail as he had the classic psychopathic mindset and believed he was invincible – but Norris soon began to talk.

Roy Norris's slant on the case

Norris portrayed himself as the terrified victim of his friend. He said that Lawrence Bittaker enjoyed being totally in control – and that he, Roy, was increasingly afraid of him. He allegedly feared for his life, saying that the man could strangle him at any time. Roy Norris admitted that he enjoyed the sex but said that it hadn't been part of the original plan to kill the girls, that Bittaker had insisted on this after they'd raped Cindy Schaeffer, arguing that they must not leave any witnesses. Norris claimed that he'd argued in Cindy's favour for an hour (which was remarkably brave, considering he was supposed to be terrified of Bittaker) and that he had vomited when 'forced' to help strangle the teenager. He added that he was still haunted by the victim's face.

But audiotapes were found which told a different tale.

The victims were heard begging for mercy whilst Roy Norris tortured them with a hammer, making one of them pretend to be a cousin whom he'd had sexual fantasies about. He hit one victim repeatedly with a hammer on the elbow, urging her to 'scream...keep it up, girl...scream till I say stop.' Bittaker was also heard taunting a victim as he used pliers on her nipples whilst she screamed and begged to die. Hardened detectives were so shocked at what they heard on these tapes that they couldn't stop shaking and some were sent home after becoming physically ill.

Roy Norris now talked nonstop in an effort to save his own skin. He also took detectives to sites where they'd dumped the corpses. The first two victims had disappeared, probably eaten by animals, but they found the skeletons of Jackie Gilliam and Leah Lamp. (They already had Shirley Ledford's body as it had been dumped on a suburban lawn.) Jackie Gilliam's skull still had an icepick embedded in it which backed up Norris's account.

Bittaker and Norris were now jointly charged with five counts of murder, rape and kidnapping – but Norris testified against Bittaker in return for immunity from the death penalty. When Bittaker heard his friend's confession on tape he was visibly shocked but told detectives that he had nothing to say to them. All that they could do for now was take him back to his cell. Whilst observing him there, they saw proof of his photographic memory for he could read and memorise an entire book in an hour. They also gave him the test that's given to potential prison guards and he got the highest score in the history of the tests.

Norris's sentence

Legal proceedings against Roy Norris were straight-forward as he pleaded guilty. He was given forty-five years to life which he is currently serving at the Pelican Bay Maximum Security facility in California.

Bittaker's sentence

At his trial on 5th February 1981, Lawrence Bittaker declared that Roy Norris had been the mastermind – but the tapes were played and they proved that Bittaker had been at least equally active. Incredibly, he suggested that the taped torture sessions were merely consensual rough play, in his own words 'pillow talk'. The prosecutor broke down in tears twice whilst listening to the tapes and a female court reporter ran sobbing from the courtroom. The jury was also in tears. The only person unaffected by the tapes was Lawrence Bittaker who smiled throughout.

One torture victim had screamed 'kill me' and he suggested that this was sexual role-play. There was disbelieving laughter in court at his assertion and after three days of deliberation (it took this long because there were so many charges against him) the jury recommended death. The judge agreed and Lawrence Bittaker received the death sentence on 24th March 1981. Shortly afterwards he joined several other torture-killers on California's Death Row.

The myths

The Bittaker-Norris murders are amongst the most shocking of the twentieth century, but, as with most team killing cases, they have attracted their share of myths. Several reporters have written that the victims were tortured to death on tape, creating snuff tapes. This simply isn't true – two of the victims were kept captive for three days, yet the longest torture tape lasts for eighteen minutes. None of the actual deaths were recorded on tape. Indeed, the couple tried to hide the torture evidence by recording it in the middle of music tapes, hoping that the casual listener wouldn't play the tapes to the end.

It's also been said that all of the victims were hitchhikers; in other words, perfect victims. Again, this wasn't true. Cindy Schaeffer was on her way back to her grandmother's and vehemently refused a lift from the two men. She was portrayed in one documentary as wearing tiny shorts and a close-fitting T-shirt whereas in truth she was dressed conservatively as she was on her way home from a Christian youth group. And the youngest two victims, Jackie Gilliam and Leah Lamp, had just sat down near a bus stop to have a chat.

However the most abiding myths are about which man did what – and why...

The deadly dynamics

Over the years many crime writers have portrayed Bittaker as the strong lead and Norris as his weak and reluctant follower. Superficially Bittaker was indeed the instigator in that he wrote to Norris suggesting they meet up again and it was he who bought the van. But Norris was the one with the history of sexual assaults who, as a solo rapist, didn't take no for an answer. Prior to meeting Bittaker, he had tried to enter a woman's apartment by ringing her bell and asking to use the phone but she refused him. Undaunted, he then began to batter at her lounge window, carrying out this violent act in broad daylight. By now the terrified woman had phoned the police. Meanwhile Roy Norris hurried to the rear of the house and entered through her kitchen window. Thankfully the San Diego police arrived before he could carry out a sexual assault.

He showed further brutality during the rape at Redondo Beach, pouncing on a stranger in the street and using her scarf to semi-strangle her. And he'd battered a previous female victim about the head with a stone.

In contrast, Lawrence Bittaker's criminal career was mostly theft-based though he'd hit strangers with a speeding car and had stabbed a shop assistant who tried to prevent him stealing a packet of meat.

And Roy Norris didn't immediately confess when an ex-con told the authorities of the five murders. Instead, he initially played word games with the police. It was only when he realised they knew the full story that he confessed to being a reluctant participant – and he did so to save his own life. The police noted that he showed little emotion during these interviews, even when describing exactly what the victims had endured.

The photo that is usually shown of Norris depicts a smiling, slightly boyish looking man with receding hair and a moustache – but his prison photo shows a cold-eyed man with a grim-set mouth and a shaved head. It's a face devoid of humanity, the face that his victims saw before they died.

Update

FBI agents John Douglas and Mary Ellen O'Toole interviewed Lawrence Bittaker at San Quentin and noted that, throughout the lengthy interview, he refused to make eye-contact with the female Special Agent. He wept when describing the crimes – but John Douglas believes that he was weeping for himself.

He continues to cost the taxpayer money, filing risible legal suits against the prison. One of his complaints was that he was given a soggy sandwich and that this constituted cruel and unusual punishment. On another occasion he sued after being given a broken cookie. As he's entitled to legal aid, each of these lawsuits cost the state of California thousands of dollars and untold time.

Unlikely as it may seem, both men have become pin-ups for the lost and the lonely. Lawrence Bittaker (now in his sixties) occasionally signs letters to fans with his self-chosen nickname, Pliers. A gifted artist (childhood trauma often shapes creative adults), he makes and sells intricate pop-up and personalised greeting cards. Such is the demand for serial killer memorabilia that his toenail clippings were recently offered on an internet auction site. Bittaker remains bitter and cynical, offering to sell copies of his victims' autopsy reports to the highest bidder and adding that he'll autograph them.

Not to be outdone, a dealer acting on behalf of Roy Norris has offered clippings of his hair, his handprints and his drawings on the same auction website. Roy Norris alleges he has yet to be paid by this man. Meanwhile, he tries to persuade his fans to send him videos of commercial films which include torture scenes.

Andy Kahan, the director of a crime victims division in Texas, has written eloquently about the horrors of such murderabilia, urging 'say no to killers making money off the innocent victims they brutally murdered.' But so far it remains legal for serial killers to profit from their notoriety.

It's well over twenty years since Lawrence Bittaker was sentenced to death yet he's still alive – and enjoying games of bridge with other serial killers – in San Quentin. He continues to extract money from the gullible by telling them that he'll memorise messages to their dead loved ones and take them over to 'the other side.'

Meanwhile, Roy Norris continues to perpetuate the myth that he was a good guy terrorised by a bad man, proudly telling criminologists 'I'm the one that fessed up.' He will be eligible for parole in 2010.

MOTHER KNOWS BEST
FRANCES & MARC SCHREUDER

It is rare for a middle-aged mother and her teenage son to conspire to commit a murder – especially when that murder is of the woman's septuagenarian father. But in 1978 Frances and Marc Schreuder would do just that.

Frances Bernice Schreuder

Frances was born on 6th April 1938, the fourth child of Bernice and Franklin Bradshaw. Franklin, a self-made man, had worked both hard and smart for many years so now owned thirty-one auto-part stores plus oil and gas leases. Bernice wanted them to enjoy the money but Franklin preferred to save and bought himself thrift shop clothes. He loved the Wall Street Journal but wasn't willing to pay for it so would drive to a friend's house once a week and collect free back copies. She wanted to travel but he preferred to work a sixteen-hour day.

Franklin was a Mormon who had located the family in Utah's Salt Lake City. His wife was a freethinker who resented being surrounded by what she saw as a Mormon clique. They would argue, and Franklin, who hated discord, would rush off to the warehouse and not return until his wife was in bed asleep. As they rarely saw each other, the couple were reduced to writing each other acrimonious notes. Left alone most days with her equally unhappy offspring, Bernice frequently urged them to take her side rather than their absent father's. She would later admit that she'd never wanted children and would have had all four aborted if it had been legal in those days.

Bernice had a breakdown soon after giving birth to Frances, so Frances was initially raised by one of her older sisters. She would later tell friends that she was the child that no one wanted – but her siblings felt equally cut adrift. Her older brother was diagnosed as schizophrenic and became so violent that the couple arranged for him to have a frontal lobotomy which robbed him of his personality. They put him in a state home where he was rarely visited and would die at age thirty-nine.

Frances was a prettily-dressed and intelligent child but she missed her mother. A neighbour would say that 'her eyes never smiled'. She demanded attention from everyone she met but was never satisfied.

With hindsight, it's clear that she was beginning to suffer from Narcissistic Personality Disorder, a syndrome which develops when a child is ignored by his or her parents. Such infants have been made to feel unimportant during the early months of life and this leaves them with a strong sense of injury. They have a desperate need to be recognised, to be someone, yet they retain the emotional age of a very young child.

When her mother recovered she gave Frances gifts, probably to ameliorate the guilt she felt for not being there for her during her infancy. She hoped that Frances would become a famous child ballet dancer but Frances didn't make the grade.

The little girl had increasingly strong mood-swings and temper tantrums. Onlookers would later say that her whole body looked as if it was crying out to be hugged and nurtured. Her mother still suffered from depression and Frances had to go to her dad's warehouse if she wanted to see him at all.

As a teenager, she worked briefly for him before she started college and though her co-workers were impressed at the hours she worked, they also found her very domineering and somewhat strange.

Frances went off to college where she bought endless clothes and makeup and went out to bars with friends. But an incident that has never been made public occurred at college and she was suspended. The college strongly recommended that she have psychiatric treatment but her parents hated doctors and tried to play down the situation. As an adult, she (and later her sons) would have psychiatric treatment on and off for many years.

The first marriage

On 9th January 1959 Frances married an older man named Vittorio Gentile who was a pearl magnate. The couple relocated to New York. But she was increasingly jealous about any time he spent away from the home and the marriage soon became violent on both sides. He would later admit to slapping her across the face when she went into hysterical convulsions. That summer she took an overdose, the first of many suicide attempts.

Marc Schreuder

On 6th February 1960 she gave birth to her first son, Lorenzo, who would become known as Larry. Six weeks later she was pregnant again and towards the end of December gave birth to a second son, Marco, whose name would later be shortened to Marc. He was a cute little child with blonde hair – but his increasingly disturbed and hard-hitting mother ensured that he had little to smile about.

She remained deeply unhappy and her first husband

would later note that she spent money like a maniac. Both parties accused the other of domestic violence and Frances convinced some of her relatives that she was a battered wife. After two and a half years of this marriage she scrawled swastikas on the walls of the marital home and fled with the children, setting them up in a new home. She didn't work and now had no visible means of support so asked her parents to support her until the children went to school. (In reality, her parents also had to eventually fund the children's schooling as she failed to find a job.)

Frances remained violent. She beat Larry and Marc with a belt and a hairbrush and in December 1964 she assaulted their teenage babysitter and faced legal proceedings. Her parents, who were still writing each other acrimonious notes in Salt Lake City, knew little of this.

By age four, Larry was diagnosed as having psychiatric problems and was sent to a special school. Marc looked less obviously ill – but neighbours noted that he often smelt bad as his mother hadn't bathed him. He often bore the marks of her slapping palms and scratching nails and he was sometimes seen roaming the streets for food because he hadn't been fed.

One of Frances' favourite ploys was to lock both children out of the house for hours at a time. Larry sometimes slept on the landing overnight – and Marc once had to defecate on the common stairway because he was very distressed and had no access to a toilet. He would later tell a psychiatrist that he preferred it when his mother beat him as this was better than being locked out.

Frances soon noted that Marc was easier to manipulate than Larry, so at one stage she sent the latter to her parents in Salt Lake City and he lived there for six months before asking to go home as he missed his mum. He didn't miss Marc for there was little love between the two brothers. Marc envied Larry as he seemed more capable of fending for himself during their frequent lock-outs from home.

As Marc matured, he put on weight and his nickname became Butterball. He tried to liken himself to the Incredible Hulk, but in truth he was physically weak. He was also very scruffy as his clothes were often unlaundered and unironed. It was hard to believe that he was the grandson of a multi-millionaire.

Yet he was an intelligent child who enjoyed playing chess, collecting stamps and rare coins. (Larry also collected rare coins but Frances had been known to sell them to raise money.) He grew up and went away to college, but like his mother before him, he became increasingly strange. He stole various items from his college and talked about suicide to the extent that a college friend would note that Marc was 'notably and demonstrably insane'.

Frances' second marriage

In February 1969 Frances married for a second time and took her new husband Fred's surname of Schreuder. He was nine years her senior. Both Larry and Marc liked him but before long he, too, was subject to Frances' wild mood-swings. In time, they began to have physical fights.

The family went to Brussels as Fred's firm relocated him there but it was soon apparent that Frances' mental illness was worsening. One night she was found wandering the streets in her nightdress threatening to commit suicide. She also spent so much money on designer clothes and jewels that he had to write to her parents asking them to financially help their daughter. Eventually Frances became so disturbed that she was admitted to a psychiatric institution for several weeks.

End of Frances' second marriage

In April 1973, she gave birth to her third child, Lavinia Schreuder. Ten months later Frances threw her husband Fred out of their apartment. Larry was often away at school but she now kept twelve-year-old Marc with her as her special 'friend'. She would keep him up half the night telling him about her problems. These problems were often financial but when she did have money she spent it on overpriced jewellery.

Bernice, her mother, sometimes sent gifts and cash – but Frances would keep the cash and return the gifts unused to cause upset. At times the two women wrote each other very hurtful letters. Bernice often said that she couldn't send her youngest daughter any more money – but she always backed down and found extra cash. Her husband would find out about her largesse and be enraged as he thought Frances should give up her New York socialite lifestyle and live in Utah with him.

Marc's life remained incredibly strange. On the one hand he was his mother's companion and she clearly favoured him over Larry. She even took him into her bed every night for a year for companionship. On the other hand, she often beat him, locked him out and told him that he belonged in a zoo or a mental hospital, that he was worthless. Indeed she was so obviously cruel to him that the Society For The Prevention Of Cruelty To Children became involved.

The years passed, an ugly mixture of Frances' suicide

threats, hysterical letters and emotional manipulation. She was clearly mentally ill but it seems that there was no one close enough to offer her help.

Religion

By the summer of 1977 she'd got religion and had herself baptised. That year she sent Marc and Larry to her parents in Salt Lake City and ordered them to break into their grandfather's warehouse, forge cheques and send them back to her. As usual, she wasted the money she received, spending fifty thousand dollars on one pair of designer earrings. The illicit earnings were soon spent.

She also told them to be as cruel to their grandmother as possible. And she gave them stimulants to put in the old man's oatmeal in the hope that he'd have a heart attack. Her father went very red in the face and rushed around more than usual whilst on these amphetamines but he was a very fit man and did not die. Still the two boys continued to create chaos in the household and Franklin became increasingly afraid of them. An onlooker would later say 'Frances programmed this. She created these monsters.' And Franklin's staff felt very sorry for the old man as he'd hoped, albeit belatedly, to spend time with his family but was now even further estranged from them.

Cut out of the will

At the end of this appalling summer, it was rumoured that Franklin had cut Frances out of his will. In truth, he made notes for a new will and left them lying around the warehouse, knowing that his wife and other family members would find them and that word would get back to Frances in New York.

Word did indeed get back – but if Franklin thought it would make his youngest daughter cut back on her spending spree, he was mistaken. Instead, she began to plot to kill him, ideally before he could cut her out of his will. But even if she was formally disinherited she knew that she could benefit from his death as her mother would immediately offer financial support.

Frances tried to hire a hitman, using a male friend that she'd met in church as a go-between. But the potential hitman simply took his fee and didn't kill her father.

Her hysteria increasing, Frances made it clear to Marc that she wanted her father – his grandfather – killed, that this was the solution to all of their problems. She rationalised that Franklin was old, that she could personally put all his money to better use. She warned him that they'd all end up homeless if her parents disowned her – did he really want the entire family to end up living on the streets? Frances added that if Marc didn't kill Franklin she would lock him out of her life forever, just as she'd so often locked him out of her home. But he could be her special friend again if he would only buy a gun, travel to Salt Lake City, and kill the old man…

Marc, who was now living in at college, kept saying no, but his mother phoned him several times a day and would rant at him for hours. The teenager was delighted that she wanted to talk to him, but terrified by her increasingly bizarre requests. After a year of this relentless pressure, seventeen-year-old Marc agreed to shoot his grandfather dead. He travelled to Texas and bought a .357 Magnum pistol then flew onto Salt Lake City under a false name.

The murder
On 23rd July 1978 at around 7am he arrived at his grandfather's warehouse. When the seventy-six-year-old arrived, he talked to him for fifteen to twenty minutes, asking him to provide the family with more money. When Franklin turned away for a moment, he shot the multi-millionaire once in the back. The man looked shocked as he slumped to the ground and his grandson shot him again, blowing off the lower back of his skull. Marc then went through the hard-working entrepreneur's pockets and threw some of their contents about to make it look like a robbery.

He took a plane back to his mother's house and told her that her father was dead. Francis allegedly exclaimed 'Thank God!' and kissed him and hugged him in a way that she'd never done before. She'd told him to bring the gun back with him, perhaps as a souvenir or in case she needed a weapon again in the future. She would later give the Magnum to the friend who had tried to arrange a hitman for her.

Blood money
Less than a month after her father's death, Frances asked her mother to give her three thousand dollars a month from his estate. Her mother did so. (Two years later Bernice would buy Frances a twelve room apartment in the most sought-after district of Manhattan that cost over five hundred thousand dollars.)

Larry becomes violent
Meanwhile, various acquaintances of the family told the police to look closely at Francis and Larry as possible murder suspects. They found that Frances had been in

New York at the time of the killing so couldn't have pulled the trigger. Suspicion then fell on Larry as he'd actually been staying with Franklin and Bernice on the day that his grandfather was shot dead. But Bernice claimed that he hadn't woken up until long after Franklin had left for the warehouse. As such, he had an alibi and the trail went cold.

But the following year (1979) Larry, who had become increasingly strange, attacked his college room-mate in the middle of the night, battering the innocent boy numerous times with a hammer. Other students heard the screams and intercepted nineteen-year-old Larry before he could leave the campus. Meanwhile his semi-conscious victim was taken to hospital where he had to have three operations on his head and a metal plate put in his skull. He was also temporarily paralysed down one side.

Larry claimed that alpha waves had made him do it – and his student friends testified that he'd become so odd during the previous months that they feared for their safety. He was diagnosed as being schizophrenic and it was found that in the past he'd suffered from 'burnt out child reaction' where an abused child simply can't take any more.

Larry was full of violent hate but, instead of recognising these feelings, he projected them on to others and believed he was the one who was in danger. As such, he refused to see his room-mate as the victim and showed no remorse for the horrendous attack. He was put into psychiatric care – though at one stage he escaped and went back to his mother. She promptly phoned the police and he was recaged within hours.

Ongoing hysteria

Frances now had her wonderful upmarket home and she became a patron of the arts, giving vast sums to the New York ballet. Her daughter Lavinia showed real dancing talent and was given several significant roles. But one day Frances and Lavinia arrived very late for a public performance. As a result, the ballet had had to substitute another child dancer for Lavinia and Frances became hysterical, threatening to kill the terrified child.

Frances now worried that the net was closing in on Marc so she insisted that he leave her house. The teenager obligingly booked himself into the YMCA under a false name and spent his days watching porn at the cinema and his nights with prostitutes. He would sometimes dress scruffily and go to burger joints but at other times he invented a wealthier persona for himself, dressed up and went to upmarket restaurants. He set up a post office box where he received regular cheques from his grandmother. It was a lonely and unstructured existence, but he would later say that these months of freedom were the happiest of his life.

And indeed, mother and son would have probably gotten away with the crime if Frances hadn't made herself a very bad enemy. The friend who had originally introduced her to a hitman had set up a joint account with her – and she'd taken his money. It was a tiny sum for her (but a lot of money for him) which she could have paid back but for some unfathomable reason she refused. He contacted her lawyers about the missing cash but they couldn't help so he went to one of her sisters and hinted that Frances and Marc were implicated in Franklin's death. He continued to phone the sister and eventually admitted that he was still keeping the murder weapon for Frances. The police were informed and the YMCA-based Marc Schreuder was soon tracked down.

Awaiting trial, he was suicidal as he believed he had nothing to live for. But the authorities explained that he could enrol in various educational courses from prison and his spirits revived.

Marc Schreuder's trial

Four years after he'd shot his grandfather dead, Marc went to trial in Utah where he potentially faced death by firing squad. But the jury soon heard about the mitigating circumstances, the defence explaining that his mother was completely self-centred and that her tirades at him had lasted for days. They asked for a manslaughter charge as he'd been so repeatedly badly treated and had the emotional maturity of a child.

In turn, the prosecution noted that he'd been at college so could safely ignore her threats to make him homeless. This was true – but she still influenced him hugely, phoning for up to three hours a night, demanding that he do whatever as necessary to bring her money. Sometimes his college friends heard him crying as she berated him on the phone. She said that if he didn't do what she wanted he couldn't come home that summer – or ever again.

Marc had taped her ranting at Lavinia for four hours because the child didn't understand a complex grammar lesson – and it was clear that she ranted in a similar way at Marc. A more stable teenager could perhaps have coped with such lengthy verbal onslaughts but Marc had never known stability. He was terrified of being left completely alone. It was easy for outsiders to suggest that the seventeen-year-old simply sever the connection with his mother, but she was the only parent he had and the closest thing to love that he had ever known.

That said, he was aware that he was deliberately ending the life of a man who had done him no harm, a man who had paid for much of his accommodation and schooling. And he'd shot Franklin a second time and had been sufficiently calculating to go through the dead man's pockets and scatter items about to make it look like a robbery. The jury took all of this into consideration and on 6th July 1982 he was sentenced to five years to life.

Frances Schreuder's trial

Meanwhile, having heard more and more about Frances' involvement in her father's death, the police went to her apartment to arrest her. She refused to answer the door for hours and when they did gain access they found her in bed. She said she couldn't leave the house until she'd finished writing her poetry but they insisted she come with them and she went into another room to get dressed. There she started to climb out of the sixth floor window but the police were alerted by her daughter Lavinia's screams and found the child desperately clinging to her leg.

Frances' trial opened in September 1983. The main witness against her was Marc, who'd decided to testify in order to keep her away from Lavinia. The jury heard that Frances had given money to a hitman and told him where to find her grandfather. When the hitman backed down, she'd sent Marc off to buy a gun and had ranted at him so relentlessly that she knew he'd use it. She'd told him that if he didn't kill Franklin that she would commit suicide. As she'd taken overdoses in front of him before, he knew that she was telling the truth.

Now forty-five years old, Frances opted not to take the stand in her own defence. She wore a large crucifix throughout the trial and scribbled copious notes. One witness suggested that a patron of the ballet could never encourage a murder – but more clear thinking observers noted that an appreciation of culture doesn't necessarily make a woman incapable of inciting violence.

She was found guilty of criminal homicide, murder in the first degree on 27th September 1983. Six days later she was sentenced to life imprisonment and sent to Utah State Prison. There she told the authorities that she only had one son, Larry. She had clearly disowned Marc, the fate he most feared.

Sadly, the family remained divided after the trial, with Bernice saying that Frances had been a wonderful mother but that little Marc was 'a born thief'. She blamed his and Larry's psychiatric problems on their father – but he hadn't seen them since they were toddlers. She was also enraged at one of her other daughters who had told the police about the gun.

By the time of the trial, Marc's father had come back into his life and he was very glad of his support. Meanwhile Lavinia was cared for by a nursery nurse, aided by Bernice. Larry was eventually freed from psychiatric care and set up home alone.

In 1987, film star Lee Remick played Francis Schreuder in an ABC mini series called *Nutcracker: Money, Madness, Murder*. *The Chicago Sun-Times* noted that it was 'a powerful characterisation of a woman trapped within a warped and steadily deteriorating mind – incapable of love and distant from reality,' whilst *Rivadue* said that it was 'steeped in psychotic grandeur.'

Asked to comment on Francis Schreuder, Lee Remick said 'In my view, the sickness about this woman is that she was totally narcissistic. Only her needs in this world mattered.'

Frances Schreuder's needs simply weren't met when she was a young child, a negligence for which others paid a very heavy price.

3   FATAL ATTRACTION
ALTON COLEMAN & DEBRA BROWN

Worldwide there are proportionately probably as many black serial killers as there are white – but white killers are the ones reported on at length by a largely white media. As Pat Brown of the Sexual Homicide Exchange has written, 'Minority serial killers in the United States more than likely exist at the same ratios as white serial killers for the population.' And South Africa is currently experiencing an epidemic of black serial killers. But Alton Coleman and Denise Brown are unusual in being a black male/female pairing – rather than a solo operator or male duo – who killed multiple times.

Alton (Elton) Coleman

Alton was born in 1956, the third child of an alcoholic prostitute who would go on to have another two children. She alternated between rejecting him and having sex with clients when he was in the same room. Worse, she insisted he cater to those of her clients who preferred boys. He suffered this sexual abuse throughout his formative years, repressing his fear and anger, but his disturbance showed in that he regularly wet his pants. As a result, he was teased mercilessly at school by the other children until he started to rob and assault them. By puberty he was stealing cars.

He was originally christened Elton but hated the name and changed it to Alton. As he matured and began to run with a street gang, his nickname became Big Al.

His mother died when he was thirteen, by which time he was living with his grandmother in the projects. He remained deeply disturbed and regularly sexually assaulted his girlfriends. His IQ was borderline retarded and he harboured a deep hatred for almost everyone, but as he matured he hid his rage behind a charming façade. Both men and women were initially drawn to the handsome youth with the appealing manner and winning smile. It was only when he had them alone and vulnerable that he dropped his act.

At eighteen he and a male accomplice abducted a middle-aged woman, drove her out of town, robbed her and raped her. The naked woman ran screaming from the scene and bystanders swiftly called the police. But, embarrassed and frightened, she refused to testify about the rape so Coleman was only given six years on the kidnapping and robbery charge. Two years later he was released and almost immediately raped again. He was also arrested for molesting an eight-year-old relative but it's likely that he intimidated her mother for the charges were suddenly withdrawn.

However, he was found guilty of other violent assaults and by his mid-twenties he'd spent a total of three years in prison. There, he regularly beat and sodomised younger inmates and was widely feared. He left prison and married but his wife left him after six months of sexual brutality. She had to seek police protection before she felt safe.

Coleman now raped several girls and young women but juries often found him so plausible that they returned a not guilty verdict. Other cases didn't even go to court because Coleman intimidated the victims or the witnesses.

In 1984 – aged twenty-eight – he jumped bail charges for raping a fourteen-year-old and fled to Waukegan in Illinois where he met twenty-one-year-old Debra Brown in a Waukegan bar. He was attracted to younger women with a poor sense of their own identities so she was tailor-made for him.

Debra Denise Brown

Debra was born in November 1962 in Waukegan, Illinois, the fifth of eleven children. Hunger and poverty ruled their lives. Children from large families tend to have lower IQs than children from small families but Debra was actually diagnosed as being simple. This mild retardation may have been exacerbated by a head injury she suffered as a child.

Bored, the pretty teenager dropped out of high school and took a range of menial jobs. At home she remained exceptionally quiet. Her employers noticed that she was a passive girl who was easily led.

Yet she wasn't entirely without free will, breaking off her engagement to a nice young man at age twenty-one when she met the outwardly more charismatic Alton. Her family begged her to reconsider but she fell quickly in love with Coleman who offered excitement with his tales of other cities and his flashy stolen cars.

They quickly moved in together and he introduced her to his increasingly violent brand of sex. She remained devoted to him even though he was often cruel to her, and she tolerated his need to dress in women's clothing: men who've survived life with an abusive mother often feel the need to crossdress.

But even having this willing sex slave wasn't enough for Coleman – he wanted to hurt and humiliate men, women and children just as he'd been hurt and humiliated himself.

The first murder

Alton and Debra befriended a Mrs Wheat and her nine-year-old daughter Vernita from Kenosha, introducing themselves with false names. On 29th May 1984 they took Vernita on an outing to nearby Waukegan. Her mother happily waved the trio off.

When they had the nine-year-old alone, Alton beat, raped and strangled her. (Her body wouldn't be found until 19th June, dumped in a derelict building.) When the police began to investigate the child's disappearance, Debra and Alton went on the run. She'd spend much of the next two months helping her lover to hold up and kidnap various victims for money or for sexual thrills, though, seated in the abduction car, she often stared blankly into space.

The second murder

On 17th June twenty-five-year-old Donna Williams, a beauty therapist residing in the town of Gary, became their next victim. Coleman and Brown asked her to show them her local church and she obligingly drove them in its direction. But they kidnapped her and Alton Coleman raped her and strangled her with her own tights. They drove around with her body in the boot, later dumping it in an abandoned Detroit house. (Despite an intensive search, her body wouldn't be found until the following month.)

The third murder

On 18th June, the day after murdering Donna Williams, they killed again. Seven-year-old Tamika Turks and nine-year-old Annie were on their way back from the sweet shop when Debra and Alton stopped and offered them a ride home. (Most journalists have described the girls as cousins, but nine-year-old Annie was actually Tamika's aunt.) The children had been warned not to go off with strange men but were happy to accept a lift when they saw Debra in the car.

But the couple drove to the nearby woods then bound and gagged the children. Tamika kept crying so Debra held her down and tried to suffocate her with her hand whilst Alton stamped on her face and chest. He raped her then strangled her to death with a strip of bedsheet that he'd brought from the house.

Both Debra and Alton now made nine-year-old Annie perform oral sex on them. Afterwards, Coleman raped and stabbed the child so viciously that her intestines protruded from her vagina. He beat her about the head, strangled her and believed that he'd killed her – but she revived after the couple had left and was able to identify them from police photographs.

An ongoing terror spree

The psychological peace that killing brings to the pathological mind didn't last for very long, so the lovers varied their acts of violence. Throughout the next few weeks they would commit numerous armed robberies for money and would terrorise and rape other victims in order to feel powerful and have fun. They sometimes stayed with friends for a few days, then tied them up and beat them before fleeing the area in the victim's car.

So far all of their victims had been black people killed or assaulted in black neighbourhoods where neither Coleman or Brown stood out from the crowd, therefore the police weren't hunting a deadly duo. The couple remained free to kill again and again.

The fourth and fifth murders

The duo's next victims that June were a mother and daughter. They knocked on the Temples' door, pretending they were hitchhikers who needed a place to stay. Thirty-year-old Virginia Temple felt sorry for the weary travellers and let them in and they ate and drank together but later that night the couple beat and strangled her then raped and strangled her ten-year-old daughter Rochelle. They continued to enjoy the Temples' hospitality, eventually leaving their bodies in the crawl space under the house.

The sixth murder

Reaching Indianapolis, they got talking to a fifteen-year-old girl called Tonnie Stewart and abducted her. She was repeatedly tortured. Alton Coleman sexually assaulted her, stabbed then strangled her. In yet another act of overkill, she was also shot twice. The couple dumped her body in a disused building then drove on towards Cincinnati.

The seventh murder

Two days later they killed again. The couple had started by targeting their own race but now they moved across racial lines in their desire for increasing stimulus or perhaps a subconscious desire to be caught. Both motives are equally valid for Alton would say that he enjoyed killing and Debra would concur that she 'had fun out of it' yet they were becoming increasingly underweight and malnourished through living rough.

This time they chose a middle class white couple who were selling their camper van. Harry and Marlene Waters invited the potential buyers inside, only to be violently attacked. Over the next few hours, the Cincinnati couple were beaten with a wooden candle stick, pliers, a crowbar and a knife. Marlene Waters died of her bludgeon wounds but her husband recovered – albeit permanently disabled – and was able to describe the pair to the police. Meanwhile the couple had stolen the Waters' car and they continued their victim-hunt.

The eighth murder

They drove into a car wash and realised that they could kidnap Eugene Scott, the seventy-seven-year-old owner. The unfortunate man was stabbed repeatedly and shot four times in the head. Debra Brown would still be carrying the .38 calibre pistol when she was arrested and had ammunition for it, though there are conflicting reports over whether the weapon was loaded or not.

The destructive couple dumped Eugene Scott's body in a ditch just outside Indianapolis and drove off in his car, returning to their favourite locale of Illinois. He would be their last victim in a pointless killing spree which lasted fifty-three days.

Arrest and trial

Luckily an Illinois resident now recognised Alton Coleman as he'd been on America's Most Wanted. He called the police and the couple were found watching a baseball game. Tired and unkempt, they didn't put up a struggle when arrested and taken into custody, though both gave false names.

Several trials followed. In Cincinnati in May 1985 the couple were tried separately for the murder of Marlene Waters. In court, Debra Brown said 'I killed the bitch and I don't give a damn.' Strangely, she was merely given life imprisonment for this murder whilst Alton Coleman was given the death penalty.

The following year they were taken to Indiana to face trial for the murder of Tamika Turks. Debra Brown slipped the judge a note which said 'I'm a more kind and understandable and lovable person than people think I am.' Fortunately he judged her on her trail of carnage rather than her words, and both she and her co-killer got the death sentence. Two months later they were tried separately for Tonnie Stewart's murder and both given the death sentence again. But an Ohio governor commuted one of Brown's death sentences to life imprisonment in 1991 saying that she was retarded and had been under Coleman's spell.

Moments before the Vernita Wheat trial started in January 1987, Debra signed a legal document saying that she was now Alton's common law wife and he immediately reciprocated. He was subsequently found guilty of Vernita's kidnapping and murder and sentenced to death.

They weren't tried for all eight murders as prosecutors decided to concentrate on the cases with the most damning evidence and those in states which still had the death penalty.

Update

In 1997 Debra Brown launched an appeal to get her Indiana death sentence overturned. Predictably, her cause was picked up by the feminist movement who believe she murdered eight people solely because she feared her man. But she had relatives who cared for her so wasn't completely dependent on him – and her own testimony in court suggests she enjoyed terrorising their victims, killing two of them and forcing at least one child to give her oral sex.

Throughout the Eighties and Nineties, Alton Coleman worked his way through the appeals process but on 26th April 2002 he entered the execution chamber at the Southern Ohio Correctional Facility. He asked to speak to Debra Brown but this request was refused. One of his sisters spoke to him on the telephone as his execution neared but none of his relatives were present at the prison.

So many survivors and relatives of his victims wanted to watch him being put to death that closed-circuit television had to be installed in an ante room. But, one of the survivors who got to view his death in person was Harry Waters who was accompanied by two of his son-in-laws. Mr Waters had watched his forty-four-year-old wife being bludgeoned to death by the couple – and his own head injuries have left him permanently disabled, with fragments of bone lodged in his brain.

The witnesses watched as the forty-six-year-old s erial killer was strapped down and began reciting the 23rd Psalm. At 10am the lethal cocktail of drugs was administered and at 10.13 he was pronounced dead.

Meanwhile, the nine-year-old who was beaten and sexually assaulted by Coleman & Brown still has nightmares and appalling headaches. The traumatic experiences have left her unable to trust anyone, and one of her close relatives has since attempted suicide. Anti-death-penalty supporters continue to champion Debra Brown who is currently the only woman on Death Row at the Ohio Reformatory For Women.

4 MENACE TO SOCIETY
KENNETH BIANCHI & ANGELO BUONO

Los Angeles women lived in fear after twenty-six-year-old Kenneth Bianchi moved in with his forty-four-year-old cousin Angelo Buono. Within a five month period – October 1977 to February 1978 – they would torture, sexually assault and kill ten women. Then Bianchi moved a thousand miles away and killed another two girls...

Kenneth Alessio Bianchi

Ken was born in New York on 22nd May 1951 to a teenage mother of limited intelligence and to a twenty-four-year-old father. The girl had had a very unhappy life in the juvenile care system and was a very heavy drinker. Whilst pregnant, she married a soldier who was not the father of her unborn child – and when he found out, he wanted nothing to do with the impending birth. She then set her sights on a much older man and tried to ignore her pregnancy.

Ken was a breech birth who came into the world weighing six pounds four ounces. For the first few weeks of his life his mother left him in the care of a neighbour, but the neighbour didn't want him. She, in turn, began to hand him on to other neighbours for the day. He was fed and changed but rarely held or spoken to – and such early deprivation can affect a growing child's brain, making it hard for him to bond with genuine carers at a later date.

By now a local childless couple called Frances and Nicholas Bianchi had become aware of the baby's plight. Frances had had a hysterectomy (consequently at the age of thirty she went through the menopause) so was unable to have children of her own. This deeply upset her as she came from a large religious family and had been constantly told that children were 'a gift from God'. She became a hypochondriac and called her GP so often that he refused to visit her. When a doctor suggested that she adopt, she embraced the idea with fervour, seeing this as her mission in life. She now approached Ken Bianchi's mother, asking to privately adopt the three-month-old. The mother agreed and the papers were legally drawn up by the courts.

Frances, now in her early thirties, was very much in charge of their adopted son, as her husband Nicholas was a subdued man with a speech defect. He worked at a foundry and Frances stayed at home with little Ken.

By the time he was three years old it was clear that Ken Bianchi was deeply unhappy and afraid. He often wet the bed, had sleepless nights and went down with a case of acute laryngitis. The hospital doctors who were treating him noted that his mother was highly strung and over-protective, and found that she constantly rejected their medical advice. They suggested that she bring Ken back for allergy testing but she failed to follow through.

Ken went to kindergarten but when he fell in the playground, as small children often do, his mother kept him home for the rest of the year. She would continue to keep him at home with her whenever she could.

By the time he went to Holy Family School, Ken was still wetting his pants. His mother's response was to spank him before he went to the bathroom in the hope that this would encourage him to expel all of his urine. She also took him from doctor to doctor, but rejected any suggestion that the problem might be psychological. When

Ken was checked in for tests, she insisted on accompanying him to the bathroom even though he was old enough to go by himself. When doctors suggested that she give the child some privacy, she became semi-hysterical, declaring that she would take him to the bathroom until she no longer had the energy. Hospital staff noted that Ken was no problem in the ward until his mother came to visit, at which he made numerous health complaints. In turn, his mother would rush around the various doctors, demanding that they cure the disturbed little boy.

Frances Bianchi often brought up the fact that her adopted son dribbled from his penis – and, as a result, it was frequently examined and probed by the medical staff whilst she looked on. Eventually a clinician noted that 'the relationship between these two must be considered pathological.'

The teachers noticed that Ken found it hard to concentrate at school. He developed various facial tics and his eyes would roll back in his head, signs of mild epilepsy or of tension. He fell from a climbing frame in the gym and cut his lip and as a result his mother sued the school. Sometimes he was bullied by other children – and after a bullying episode his mother would keep him at home for a month. She also kept him off school for fear that he'd get a sore throat.

Frances fostered two other children and whilst they were in the home Ken's physical and mental health improved. But social services removed the children from her care and Ken's ailments resurfaced. He was in and out of the hospital for tests after complaining of stomach and leg pains, with Frances Bianchi telling one doctor 'He's been whipped when he lies so he wouldn't lie to me.' The staff noted that Kenneth developed facial tics when talking about his mother, but he refused to say anything against her other than admitting that she shouted a lot. He said that she also shouted at his dad, who was a nice, quiet man. Unfortunately Ken hardly ever saw his father as the man had to work so hard – and when he wasn't working he liked to bet on horses, a hobby which Mrs Bianchi despised.

Financial problems

Frances had never been happy with the part of Rochester where they lived, so when Ken was eight she and her husband bought a much more expensive house in Greece, a more upmarket suburb of Rochester. As a result, Nicholas Bianchi had to work even longer hours to make ends meet. Frances got a part-time job but the family still had money problems, and Ken quickly picked up on this. Soon the Greece School District were noting that 'Mrs Bianchi is a very nervous person, easily upset. She needs to be calmed down.' But little calming took place, for Ken's mother went on to write to the school, telling them that she wanted to be informed of any injury her son suffered, however slight.

Another change of house

Within months it became clear that the family couldn't afford the payments on the new house so they moved again and Mrs Bianchi took a job with an aircraft company. Ken was now looked after by a neighbour and for a few months he blossomed. Social services noted that his disposition became much less sombre and that his bedwetting had stopped. Unfortunately his mother gave up her job through ill health and Ken's psychologically-induced medical problems started up again. By now doctors believed that Ken's illnesses were the only way for him to get his feelings out in the open, to show his adoptive mother that he was hurting. They believed that, robbed of this outlet, he might became a violent boy.

Social services had been monitoring the family for some time and when Ken was eleven the Rochester Society For The Prevention Of Cruelty To Children reported that Mrs Bianchi was 'a deeply disturbed person' with paranoid tendencies. In that same year, the staff at the local DePaul Clinic concluded that 'Kenneth is a deeply hostile boy who has extremely dependent needs which his mother fulfils. He depends upon his mother for his very survival and expends a great deal of energy keeping his hostility under control and under cover.' The insightful doctor at the clinic also noted the boy's loneliness and extreme anxiety. He ascertained that Ken's mother disapproved of his friends and that he was desperate to have other people in his life.

But Ken's unhappy home life continued. At twelve, his perfectly normal adolescent curiosity led him to leaf through a pornographic magazine – but his mother's response was to whip him with a shower hose. Clinicians who were monitoring the case noted that she seemed to spy on him, as she told them she'd seen him pulling down a six-year-old girl's pants.

Educational standards

Ken had an IQ of 116 which meant that he had a well above average intelligence but wouldn't be bright enough to eventually go to university. Unfortunately he expected to get higher grades than he was actually capable of, so he often felt frustrated at school. The one subject he excelled in was creative writing – children from unhappy households are often especially creative as they disappear inside their own heads as often as possible to avoid their external reality.

A death in the family

Ken's relationship with his father had been time-starved for many years as the man had to work so much overtime. Nevertheless he was grateful for the quiet kindness his father showed him – and when Ken was thirteen they managed to have a fishing trip together. Unfortunately, Nicholas Bianchi died a few days later at his work. Ken cried for hours when he heard the news, as did his mother, but after the funeral he rarely cried again. Social services noted that Mrs Bianchi seemed to behave provocatively in front of her teenage son, pulling down her already low-cut tops and crossing her legs suggestively. A report noted that 'this family has been known for many years to social services in many areas of the country.' Unfortunately no one stepped in to help the increasingly disturbed child.

A teenage marriage

Then the teenage Kenneth Bianchi fell in love and married shortly after he graduated from high school. Friends would later suggest that he married young to get away from home.

Sadly, the marriage was not a success. His young wife wanted to party but Ken wanted her at home with him every night. Rather than talk the situation through, he withdrew emotionally and she turned to her mother for comfort. She also started to date other men. Everyone could see that divorce was inevitable – everyone except the daydreaming Ken.

One night he came home from work to find that she'd left him, stripping the apartment of its furniture and all of her possessions. The teenage boy went into shock. When he recovered he was extremely angry and hurt: he'd tried to be a loving husband and potential family man but now had to reinvent himself.

For a while Ken tried academia, enrolling in college and taking courses in politics and in police work. But he failed to get the high grades he expected and soon dropped out. He now settled for casual work, becoming everything from a bar man to an ambulance driver. Feeling increasingly frustrated at the difference between his dreams and his reality, he flitted from job to job.

Sensing that he was desperate for a change of scene, but possibly wanting to keep him attached to the family, his mother made arrangements for him to move to Glendale, California to stay with his older cousin, Angelo Buono. He'd met Angelo occasionally when he was a young boy, but the two branches of the family had since drifted apart. In January 1976 Ken arrived in Glendale and moved into his cousin's neat little home.

Angelo (Tony) Buono

Angelo was born on 5th October 1934 to Jenny and Angelo Buono senior in Rochester, New York. (Jenny was Frances Bianchi's sister, so they had both grown up in the same impoverished family. Jenny had had to cope with an increasing number of brothers and sisters as their parents' religion forbade birth control. Eventually the Sciolino family comprised eight children and her exhausted parents found it hard to cope.) Jenny and Angelo already had a five-year-old daughter Cecelia by the time that Angelo junior came along, but the marriage was an increasingly unhappy one, with Angelo senior – a security guard – given to long, sullen silences and Jenny finding fault with everything and everyone.

When Cecelia and little Angelo were ten and five respectively, the Buonos separated and Jenny Buono took the children to Glendale. There she found poorly paid piece-work in a shoe factory. She had lots of boyfriends and would take Angelo along with her to their houses and make him wait outside whilst she had sex with them. He soon figured out what was going on and hated her for it.

It was difficult for Jenny to support all three of them on a small wage and (Angelo would later allege) she often offered sexual favours in exchange for goods and services. By his early teens he was calling his mother 'a whore and a cunt.' His early experiences ensured that he had no respect for women and by the age of fourteen he was being sadistic towards his girlfriends and made it clear that he wanted anal rather than vaginal sex.

Young Angelo couldn't control their financial problems or his mother's behaviour – but he could control how neat his surroundings were. As such, he became compulsively clean and tidy, using external order to help counter the chaos of his inner world.

An early criminal record

By sixteen Angelo – who could barely read or write – had dropped out of high school and stolen a car. He was sent to the California Youth Authority but soon escaped.

Rearrested in December 1951, he was sent to the tougher Paso Robles School For Boys. There, he heard the other boys talk avidly about gangsters, seeing them as heroes who beat the system rather than as the bullies they actually were.

Angelo's first marriage and first son

When Angelo was twenty he got his seventeen-year-old girlfriend Geraldine pregnant and reluctantly married her. But he walked out after a week and never returned. By the time of the birth he was back in prison on a further car theft charge. His son, Michael, was born on 10th January 1956, after which his young wife filed for divorce.

Five more children

In April 1957 he married for the second time. This wife, Mary (more commonly known as Candy), had already borne him an illegitimate son and over the next five years she gave him another five children – a total of five sons and one daughter – the last being born in 1962.

Angelo proved to be a cruel father and a brutal husband. He knew that his wife hated anal sex yet he regularly sodomised her. He beat and humiliated her and even raped her anally in front of the children when she tried to refuse him sex. Eventually she divorced him for cruelty after which she had to go on welfare for Angelo refused to financially support any of his brood.

Angelo fathers two more children

Shortly after separating from his second spouse, Angelo found himself a live-in lover, Nanette, who already had two children. He beat and humiliated her but she remained with him and bore him a son and a daughter. Like many insecure men, he threatened to kill her if she ever tried to leave.

By the time that his stepdaughter was fourteen, Angelo was openly fondling the girl and saying that she needed breaking in. (He'd later tell a friend that he had full sex with her.) It was the last straw for Nanette and she left the house forever, taking her desperately unhappy children to Florida.

Another marriage

After a year of dating numerous young women, Angelo married again, this time in Las Vegas. The marriage seems to have been for fun or for convenience because he didn't ever live with Debbie, his newest bride. During these sexually intense years, Angelo Buono was working as hard as he played, building a reputation as a first class auto upholsterer. He was so adept at reupholstering classic cars that some Hollywood stars brought their treasured antique vehicles to him.

Self employment

By 1975 he was able to open his own upholstery shop and it was soon thriving. So was his sex life. By now Angelo was forty but was sleeping with girls as young as thirteen. He impregnated some of these girls then arranged for them to have abortions. His trail of misery spread and spread.

But despite his bravado, he was very unhappy deep down. He developed a stomach ulcer for which he had to take regular medication. He tried to fill the lack of love in his life by adopting a stray dog and keeping rabbits and an aquarium of tropical fish. He refused to touch alcohol because he feared anything that would make him lose control.

He was still having a love-hate relationship with his mother, bringing black girlfriends to her house because he knew she was racist. One day she told him that she'd been in touch with her sister, Frances, and that his cousin, Kenneth Bianchi, was coming to Glendale to stay with him for a while.

Early violence

Many writers have given the impression that Kenneth Bianchi only became violent after moving in with Angelo Buono – but in truth most killers start with smaller destructive acts and Kenneth Bianchi was no different. In his late teens he had visited a girlfriend who refused to open the door to him, so he smashed her window and climbed through it, at which point she fled and called the police. But he was so contrite that she dropped the charges, though she refused his proposal of marriage, noting that he was immature. Bianchi was also violent to at least one stranger for, when he was working as a bouncer, he hit a man with far more force than necessary.

He may even have committed three rape-murders when he was aged twenty-one and twenty-two. Leastways, he told a girlfriend that he was responsible for the strangulation deaths of three girls which took place between 16th November 1971 and 26th November 1973. These were known as the Alphabet Murders because the victims' first and last names both began with the same letter – Carmen Colon age ten, Wanda Walkowicz and Michelle Maenza, both age eleven. Bianchi remains a suspect to this day.

A sexually liberal time

Now that he was living away from home, Kenneth Bianchi was able to enjoy some of the young girls who flocked to Angelo's apartment. But he had great emotional difficulties with these relationships as he'd been told throughout his childhood that women were either virgins or whores. On the one hand he desired the girls in their tiny shorts and halter neck tops, but when he started dating them he insisted they cover up with baggy sweaters and long skirts. He was also pathologically jealous and would fly into a rage at a party if they even danced with someone else. The weeks passed with Angelo continuing to brutalise his girlfriends and Ken increasingly joining in. The rage that he'd suppressed throughout his unhappy childhood was now coming to the surface – and someone had to pay.

Ken's common law wife

He was still having a love-hate relationship with women when he met Kelli. She was somewhat plump and tended to dress conservatively. She loved to read and fitted his image of a good girl, but she invited him to stay overnight at her house very early in the relationship, something which confused him – and shortly afterwards he realised that she'd given him venereal disease. Kelli explained that she'd been raped shortly before meeting him and must have caught the disease as a result of this. Kenneth Bianchi was still coming to terms with this news when Kelli found that she was expecting his child. Meanwhile his cousin Angelo derided Kelli as 'that fat chick' and encouraged Ken to experiment with other girls.

Prostitution

Angelo had already been prostituting some of his girlfriends but now he decided to make it into a more formal arrangement. He took in two young girls, beat and raped them repeatedly and sent them out to men who he met through his garage work. Keen to expand the business, Angelo bought a list of men who wanted a girl sent over to their homes, but when he got in touch with these men he found that they all wanted to visit a girl. As he couldn't have men turning up at his house at all hours, he'd essentially been sold a useless list. And it was a prostitute who'd sold him that list...

Angelo became further enraged when both of his callgirls escaped. He declared that he wanted to kill a prostitute. It might have been mere bravado, a way of saving face – but Ken egged him on.

Ken's own life was still in freefall at this time. He'd been turned down twice by the police department and earned so little at various menial jobs that his mother had to send him money. He had begun to beat and sodomise Angelo's many girlfriends as a way of assuaging his rage. In July he had gotten his own apartment but when he asked his next door neighbour Kristina Weckler out she sensibly turned him down. Later she would meet a hideous death at his hands.

The first murder

On 17th October 1977 the two men went out in Angelo's car and picked up a black prostitute called Yolanda Washington who they knew slightly. It's likely that they'd previously met her when she accompanied the prostitute who sold them the useless list. Yolanda was tall with long legs – but she stood no chance against two strong males. They handcuffed her then Angelo drove the car whilst Ken Bianchi stripped, raped and sodomised her on the backseat. Afterwards they changed seats and Angelo took his turn.

Ken then tried to strangle her manually but she fought back and managed to kick Angelo in the head. Angelo then held down her legs whilst Ken used a rag to strangle her to death. He removed a turquoise ring from her finger to give to Kelli, his unsuspecting common law wife.

They dumped her naked body near the Forest Lawn Cemetery. She was the only one of their victims that they murdered in the car.

The autopsy showed that semen from two men was present in her vagina and her rectum, but unfortunately the police assumed this was the result of her being a prostitute. They didn't realise she'd been raped and murdered by both these men.

Yolanda Washington was just a piece of trash to the killer cousins and to the media who remained indifferent to her murder – but she was actually the mother of a young baby whom she adored. She'd told friends that turning a few well-paying tricks allowed her to spend extra time with her little son.

The second murder

A fortnight later the men were ready to kill again. On the evening of 30th October 1977 they drove around until they espied a small, thin brunette called Judy Ann Miller. Judy had run away from her impoverished family and had turned to prostitution in order to feed herself. (Her family were all living in the one run-down hotel room, the four-year-old sleeping in a cardboard box, when the police tracked them down and informed them of her violent death.)

Aware that she might not get into a car with two men, Angelo dropped Ken off, drove up to the teenager and started chatting to her. She was hungry and happy to get in the car. Angelo drove a short distance then parked and Ken opened the passenger door, flashed a fake police badge and told the young prostitute that she was under arrest.

Ken Bianchi handcuffed her and Angelo drove them all in the direction of his house. The fifteen-year-old asked if she was being taken to the police station but they told her that they were driving to a special unit. By the time she figured that she was in Angelo's house rather than a police building, he'd found a rag and was forcing it into her mouth. He also put foam pads over her eyes and taped over them so that she couldn't see what was going on.

They uncuffed her briefly, undressed then recuffed her. Angelo raped and sodomised her, after which Ken took his turn. Before strangling her, the men put her pants back on so that she wouldn't soil the houseproud Angelo's carpet. They also tied her ankles together so that she couldn't kick out at them.

Ken sat on her legs and Angelo put a bag over her head and sealed it with a cord. He pulled the cord tighter and tighter. Within minutes the teenager's unhappy life had come to a painful and terrifying end. Ken removed the girl's bindings and her pants as he and Angelo had agreed to leave their victims nude.

At approximately midnight, the start of Halloween, they drove to the dump location which Angelo had chosen, adjacent to an ex-girlfriend's house. He deliberately left Judy on her back with her legs wide open to create maximum shock.

The third murder

On 5th November the men assembled the bindings and gag at Angelo's house then went out looking for another victim. They saw twenty-one-year-old Lissa Teresa Kastin driving home. Lissa was a dancer who'd studied ballet for many years, danced in an all-girl dance troupe and brought in enough money to live by working as a waitress. But hypoglycaemia had forced her to take a break from the group and she was thinking about going back to college to study foreign languages. It was just after 9pm as she parked close to her house.

Immediately Angelo parked behind her and Ken flashed his police ID and told her that her car had been witnessed leaving the scene of a robbery. She protested but eventually got into their car where they snapped the handcuffs on.

Back at the house, they cut off her clothes but Buono realised that he wasn't attracted to her. His sadism increasing, Ken Bianchi violated her with a beer bottle – and when she started to bleed Angelo was terrified that his pristine carpet would be soiled.

These murders – like most lust murders – were about power more than they were about sex, so the men now began to part-strangle their victim, cutting off her air supply for a moment then loosening the cord around her neck to allow her a little oxygen. They did this over and over, revelling in her terror and desperate attempts to draw breath. Eventually they continued the strangulation to the point of death and later dumped her naked body in a ditch near a Glendale country club. It was found on 6th November.

The fourth murder

On 9th November, the Hillside Stranglers killed again. A beautiful young woman called Jane King was waiting at a bus stop when Kenny joined her. He started up a conversation during which she admitted that her religion was scientology, a religion that she claimed was misunderstood by many. Ken, who had once stolen a psychology degree certificate and rented himself an office in a psychologist's suite, was able to talk about psychology and win her confidence. Jane believed that her religion gave her a sixth sense about who to trust. In this case she would be horribly wrong...

Suddenly Ken said 'There's my friend' and waved Angelo down. His cousin drew up and offered him a lift. In turn, Ken offered Jane a lift to her flat. She hesitated but when Angelo said that he was a policeman she accepted, after which they drove to Angelo's house. After they parked their vehicle in the drive both men grabbed Jane, handcuffed her and manhandled her inside.

Once there, she met the same fate as the earlier victims for they tied and blindfolded her, stripped her naked and led her to the spare room. There, Angelo raped her whilst Ken watched. Jane apparently didn't realise that she was going to die as when Ken began to mount her she said that she was hating every minute of this. Enraged, he hog-tied and sodomised her.

Angelo put the bag over her head and began to strangle her repeatedly with Ken Bianchi still inside her. He climaxed for a second time after she died.

They dumped her naked body in bushes off the Golden State Freeway. It would be a fortnight before she was found.

The fifth and sixth murders

Murder can only temporarily make the murderer feel better about him – or herself, for once the thrill wears off they are still burdened with their skewed mindset and desperately unhappy memories. As such, killers tend to up the ante in their search for emotional release. Bianchi and Buono had already done this, killing the third and fourth victims much more slowly, and hog-tied the fourth to increase her anguish. But now they decided to abduct a very young virgin, attracted to the idea of an innocent who didn't yet have pubic hair.

Twelve-year-old Dollie Cepeda and her fourteen-year-old friend Sonja Johnson walked past the Stranglers' vehicle on 14th November. The two men called them over and went into their usual police routine. The youngsters obediently got into the so-called police car and were driven to Angelo's. There they were stripped, raped and sodomised. The cousins strangled Sonja to death in the spare bedroom then went into the lounge and strangled Dollie, dumping their bodies on a trash heap where they were found on 20th November by a nine-year-old boy. Afterwards, Sonja's heartbroken father attempted to take his own life.

The seventh murder

Twenty-year-old Kristina Weckler was a brilliant art student. She was also a former neighbour of Kenneth Bianchi and had politely turned down his offer of a date. Now – an ordinary Saturday night in November 1977 – he arrived at her apartment and flashed his police badge, telling her he'd joined the force since he'd lived next door to her and that someone had crashed into her car. Kristina accompanied him to the car park where she was abducted by both men and driven to Angelo's house. Both cousins raped and sodomised Kristina then Bianchi injected her with Windex in her neck and inner arms. The drain cleaner caused convulsions, after which they bound her head to the gas outlet and gassed her for at least an hour until she died. Her body, found on 20th November, had fingerprint bruises around the breasts and rectal bleeding – and when the police first saw the injection marks they assumed that they were dealing with a drug addict. But the reality was that Kristina even disapproved of marijuana. Ironically, she hadn't gone to a party that night because she knew that the drug would be smoked.

(Much later, when he was confessing to the murders, Ken Bianchi couldn't remember how Kristina was lured to her death and surmised that she might have agreed to accompany him to a party. But she'd told a friend that he acted like a used-car salesman and that she'd never go out with him.)

The eighth murder

Later that same month, Lauren Wagner, an eighteen-year-old business studies student, drew up across the road from the home that she shared with her parents. Ken and Angelo, who had been driving behind her, came to an abrupt halt and went into their usual 'police making an arrest' routine. Lauren refused to get in their car, at which point they picked her up and carried her bodily to their vehicle. She shouted 'You won't get away with this.' The entire incident was witnessed by a neighbour who did nothing, convincing herself that she'd seen a lovers tiff. (Angelo Buono later made a threatening phone-call to her house, warning her not to say anything about what she'd seen.)

Back at the house, Lauren tried desperately to save her own life, telling the two rapists that she enjoyed sex and that she wouldn't report them. It's a tactic which can work with compensatory rapists – inadequate men who want to believe that the victim is their girlfriend. But Bianchi and Buono were sadistic misogynistic killers whose mission was to cause maximum pain and terror, not find themselves a skewed version of a date. Indifferent to her words, they raped and sodomised then tortured her by taping bare wires to her hands and administering electric shocks. Eventually they strangled her and dumped her naked corpse near the Pasadena Freeway where it was found on 29th November.

The ninth murder

The killers now upped the stakes again. On 11th December 1977 Ken Bianchi phoned an escort service and requested that they send him an attractive blonde. The service weren't supposed to accept calls from payphones so queried Ken's location, but he was so plausible that they agreed to send a girl round.

The luckless Kimberly Diane Martin was despatched to Apartment 114 at 1950 Tamarind. Unknown to her, the apartment was vacant – and both Ken and Angelo, who had forced the lock, were lurking inside. Ken opened the door to her and started up his cop routine but when she saw that the flat was in darkness and that Angelo was lurking in the shadows she turned to flee. Swiftly, the men caught her, hit her and carried her to their car, transporting her to Angelo's house. There she was doubly raped and sodomised. Afterwards they dumped her body on a hillside. This propensity for hillside locations would eventually give them their moniker of the Hillside Stranglers.

Three days after this murder, Ken went to the local police station telling them that he was interested in becoming a cop. Could he drive around with them to get a feel for the job? The cops obliged and Kenny pushed his luck, asking them to point out the Hillside Stranglers sites. He was becoming increasingly obsessed by the murders' publicity, and sometimes spent an entire day reading about the stranglings in the newspaper and watching coverage on the news.

Angelo's mother dies

The rest of December and January were victim-free as Jenny Buono was now dying of vaginal cancer. She'd had the disease for some time but was now rehospitalised. Angelo visited her every second day, occasionally stealing syringes from the wards so that he could inject future victims with drain cleaner. He still maintained his love-hate relationship with his mother but seemed genuinely grief-stricken when she died in January 1978.

Kenneth Bianchi had an equally bad December as his boss fired him. Ken, who was essentially lazy, had explained his frequent absences from work by saying that he was having chemotherapy sessions to treat cancer. He'd told Kelli the exact same thing, but his boss eventually became suspicious and checked out his story, finding it to be a lie.

Without a wage, he could no longer afford to pay his rent and had to move in with one of Kelli's brother's friends. He had no home, no job and an increasingly on-off relationship with Kelli. His rage built and built. The following month he and Angelo would kill again...

The tenth murder

16th February 1978 was Cindy Hudspeth's date with death. The beautiful young girl knew Angelo as she was a waitress at one of his favourite restaurants. She also worked nights as a telephonist to bring in extra money as she was saving up to go to college. When her new car needed floor-mats she took it to Angelo's workplace.

When she mentioned that she was saving up for her college fund, Angelo told her he had a list of employment opportunities in the house. She happily accompanied him inside where he and Ken pounced on her, stripped her and tied her, spreadeagled, to the bed. They repeatedly raped and sodomised her, strangled her, then put her body in the trunk of her Datsun and pushed it over a cliff. Her body was badly punctured and cut when found but the coroner believed that many of the injuries had occurred as the car crashed at the foot of the cliff.

Ken becomes a father

A week later Kelli gave birth to a boy whom the couple named Ryan – but it was hardly a happy families situation. Ken and Kelli had had a stand-up fight a few weeks beforehand during which he'd given her a black eye. She'd sensibly walked out and had refused to move back in with him. But now she was pleased at how loving he was towards his new son and everyone agreed that he was a doting dad.

Bianchi and Buono split up

However, the mother of one of Bianchi's girlfriends had become suspicious at how often he talked about the Strangler case, and at how strange he sometimes looked and acted. The police went round and interviewed Kenny, who was his usual plausible self. The interview only lasted for ten minutes and the police went away satisfied.

Angelo took fright when he heard that the lawmen had been round. He angrily pointed out that Kenny had deliberately drawn attention to himself by asking for rides in a police car, and by following the case so obsessively. Unknown to Angelo, he was also stealing jewellery from most of the bodies, and giving some of it to Kelli as gifts. (He was equally light-fingered at work: almost all of his employers suspected him of – or eventually fired him for – petty theft.) Angelo now told Kenny to take a hike and put down the phone whenever he called.

Angelo marries again and Ken leaves town

Angelo now wed a twenty-one-year-old Chinese woman, the marriage giving her American citizenship. Needless to say, he treated her as cruelly as his previous wives.

Meanwhile, Kelli relocated to Bellingham, north of Seattle. Soon Angelo broke his silence to persuade Ken to join her there. Shortly after his arrival in town, Ken got a new job as a security guard – but life as a husband and father is very different to life as a serial killer and he was soon restless and bored. He was taken on as a Reserve at the local Sheriff's Office and began to attend law enforcement classes, something which had long appealed to him, but he remained listless and depressed. He stole from the numerous houses that he was sent to guard, but it wasn't enough. The pressure to be powerful increased again – yet he didn't have the intellectual or emotional staying power to make himself powerful through his career.

Sex was also proving disappointing during this time as Ken didn't want to have intercourse with the woman who'd given birth to his baby. Instead, he began to masturbate compulsively, using a piece of rabbit fur because Angelo had kept rabbits and this reminded him strongly of a more exciting time. For a year, this auto-erotic sex and an active fantasy life sustained him, then he gave in to the urge to kill again...

Ken kills the eleventh and twelfth victims alone

When he was given access to an empty house through his work, he began to set his murderous plan in motion. He contacted a girl he knew, Karen Mandic, and asked her if she'd like to housesit for him. He told her to bring along her room-mate Diane Wilder. Both young women were highly intelligent students who were glad of the housesitting fee that Bianchi offered, allowing them to study and earn at the same time.

The trio arrived at the building and Ken suggested Karen accompany him in first to put the lights on. When they reached the basement he pointed his gun at her and ordered her to strip. When she was naked he tied her up and carried her to the nearest bedroom. He immediately went back to the vehicle and fetched the unsuspecting Diane, who he took to the carpeted bathroom, stripped and bound.

For an unspecified time, Bianchi went back and forward between the two girls, terrorising and raping them. He used several condoms, planning not to leave a semen trace. Then he ordered the terrified girls to re-dress, made them lie on their stomachs and strangled them with a heavy cord. His lust sated, he put both corpses in Karen's car, drove it to a nearby cul-de-sac and left the vehicle there. He hadn't been nearly as careful as his cousin, but was sure that no one would connect him to the crime.

But he was very wrong. Karen had told her boyfriend that Ken Bianchi had given her the housesitting job – and Diane had left a memo to Karen saying that Ken had phoned. So when the girls were found dead, the police searched Ken's house and found dozens of items stolen from various employers. They realised that he had previously lived in the area of the Hillside Stranglings – and further checks showed that he'd been questioned about the murders there. He even fitted the description of one of the men seen abducting Lauren Wagner – and his cousin, Angelo Buono, fitted the description of the other man. The police now took Ken Bianchi into custody and mounted a surveillance operation on his unsuspecting cousin, noting his many years of violence against his wives and girlfriends.

There was also forensic evidence against Bianchi, for, despite using a condom, his semen was found on the girls' pants. His pubic hair was also found on one victim. Moreover blonde hair from one of the girls was found on him. Diane Wilder was menstruating at the time of the murder and some of her menstrual blood had dripped onto his underwear.

At first journalists didn't know that Bianchi had used a condom, so, when it was reported that small traces of his semen had been found on the girls' clothes, they reported that he'd strangled them immediately and masturbated over their bodies. Other sources said that he'd strangled them on the stairs. But by his own account he put one girl in the bathroom and another in a bedroom and raped them before ordering them to re-dress, then strangling them. This is the same logical chain of events that was carried out again and again during the Los Angeles murders – after all, it's very difficult to dress a corpse.

A bad man did it

Facing the death penalty for up to twelve murders, Ken Bianchi looked for a surefire solution. As luck would have it, the prison television showed a film about multiple personality, reminding him of his previous reading on the subject whilst dabbling in psychology. Bianchi hinted to his psychiatrist that he was having vague feelings of being taken over. Put under hypnosis, he pretended to have a murderous alter ego called Steve. This strangler had allegedly first appeared when Ken was being abused as a child and desperately needed a friend.

Some experts on multiple personality bought Ken Bianchi's act – but another pointed out that alternate personalities had a surname and Ken obligingly provided the surname of Walker. Enquiries showed that Ken had stolen credentials from a bona fide psychology graduate called Steve Walker and had put these certificates up in his office when he was pretending to be a psychologist. The more sceptical of the doctors also told him that multiple personalities usually had at least three separate identities – and Ken quickly provided a third called Billy, a frightened child. Bianchi was well pleased with his act and began to keep a diary filled with supposedly remembered dreams and very bad poetry. Grogan, the chief detective in the case, said that Bianchi's hypnosis scam was 'a Walt Disney production from front to back.'

By now Ken was convinced that he'd do a couple of years in a mental hospital then go home to Kelli and little Ryan. He wrote to her saying that he was looking forward to walks in the park with his family and that they'd be financed by the book that he was writing. Lazy to the last, he added that he wouldn't have to write any of the book upfront – just sign a contract and accept a large advance.

Fortunately, some psychiatrists refused to buy into his multiple-personality act. One wrote perceptively that he'd been overwhelmed in childhood by a female authority (his mother) and was now killing women so that he could at last be in charge. Robbed of his Steve-did-it defence, his only hope was to make a deal with the authorities.

The deal

Bianchi had dreaded being sent to Walla Walla, one of America's most brutal prisons. So the District Attorney hinted that if he testified truthfully against his cousin he might be sent to a more amenable Californian jail. The deal included a life sentence rather than the death penalty so Bianchi grabbed it with both hands. Detectives were now allowed to interview him in prison to test his credibility. If he proved truthful, the deal would be formally signed.

Like most criminals, Bianchi didn't take responsibility for what he'd done. Instead he phrased everything in the passive tense, saying 'the bag was put over her head' rather than 'I put the bag over her head.' But he gave details of the torture-murders which were backed up by the autopsy photographs, so to that extent he was telling the truth.

The plea bargain went ahead – Ken Bianchi would plead guilty to the two Bellingham murders, for which he'd serve two consecutive life sentences. He'd also plead guilty to five of the Hillside Strangling murders, notably those of Yolanda Washington, Jane King, Kristina Weckler, Kimberley Martin and Cindy Hudspeth.

On 19th October 1979 he pleaded guilty to these seven murders and was sentenced to two life terms, with parole a possibility after twenty-six years and eight months. By now he was changing his testimony so the authorities felt no obligation to send him to a Californian facility. Instead, he was sent to Walla Walla Prison in Washington.

Buono arrested

The police were at last ready to bring Bianchi's co-killer into custody. Later that week, on 22nd October 1979, Buono was arrested at his work. The officers noted that he showed so little emotion you'd have thought they were giving him a parking ticket. Now the legal wranglings started in earnest, as the prosecution wanted to drop the murder charges against Buono, arguing that Kenneth Bianchi's conflicting statements about his cousin made their case unsound. Luckily the judge, Ronald George, refused to dismiss the charges and the case went ahead.

Buono's trial

Angelo Buono's trial finally began on the 16th November 1981. The jury heard that fibre found on Judy Miller's eyelid had probably originated in Angelo's workshop. Other fibre evidence showed that Lauren Wagner had been in Angelo's lounge. Two men fitting Angelo and Ken's descriptions had been seen abducting Lauren Wagner after she parked her car.

A flexible gas pipe had been used to gas Kristina Weckler – and Angelo had purchased such a pipe the week before her murder. There was also a cut out area in Angelo's wallet, consistent with the size of a police badge, though he'd conveniently disposed of the handcuffs which witnesses knew he had. One girl had had a lucky escape after the Hillside Stranglers approached her with their police badge scam, only to find she had a famous father. They let her go – and she was able to identify them.

There were also several sexual assault charges because he'd raped and beaten the two girls he'd kept as prostitutes. Both took the stand and told of the regular abuse they'd endured at his hands.

The defence countered that Angelo Buono was innocent, and that Ken Bianchi had committed all twelve of the murders. But Angelo had been seen helping to abduct Lauren Wagner and various incriminating fibres had been found in his home and workplace. He'd been obsessed with sodomy since he was a teenager, and almost all of the victims had been sodomised.

The defence rightly pointed out that many people enjoy bondage and anal sex, but that, of course, wasn't the point – the point was that Angelo's couplings weren't consensual. His aim had been to cause his victims maximum humiliation and pain before they died.

After two long years of listening to the evidence, the jury retired to consider their verdict. They went out on 21st October 1983 and returned the following month, on 14th November, to convict him of nine of the murders. He was found not guilty of murdering prostitute Yolanda

Washington. (Ken Bianchi had carried out the strangling during that particular crime.)

The sentencing was passed the following year, on 1st April 1984, when he was sentenced to nine life terms with no possibility of parole.

An unlikely alibi

In June 1980, Ken received a letter from a beautiful aspiring playwright called Veronica Lynn Compton. As the child of a political cartoonist, she'd had a cultured background, mixing with politicians and judges. But she'd claim that she was first sexually assaulted at the age of five and was a frequent child runaway. She married and had a child in her teens but was now divorced from her son's father. Age twenty-two, she was living in a trailer park and taking amateur acting roles, blotting out the pain of her past with an increasingly dangerous cocktail of cocaine and alcohol.

A friend suggested that she write to Ken Bianchi as he could help her with her crime writing, so she watched him on television, feeling compassion when he broke down in tears. For the next year she visited or called him daily and they were soon writing poetry to each other and declaring their undying love.

Veronica sent Ken one of her plays in which a female serial killer plants sperm in one of her victims to confuse detectives. It occurred to Ken that if she did this with *his* sperm the authorities would assume that the Bellingham killer was still out there and he'd be released. (Bizarrely, he seems to have forgotten that he'd also been found guilty of five out of the ten Hillside Strangler deaths.)

His new girlfriend agreed to the plan and smuggled out

a sample of his semen, sealed within the finger of a rubber glove and hidden in the spine of a book.

She now disguised herself with sunglasses and a wig, using a cushion under her clothes to look pregnant. She travelled to Bellingham's university campus and befriended a woman called Kim Breed in a bar. Kim kindly gave Veronica a lift back to her hotel room and Veronica begged her to come in and keep her company as she'd been deserted by the baby's father. Kim agreed to have a drink in Veronica's room. According to Veronica, she persuaded the woman to indulge in light bondage, telling her that she wanted to take photos to play a prank on a friend. The somewhat drunk young woman agreed to this too.

But Ken Bianchi's paramour suddenly took a cord from her bag and wrapped it around Kim's neck, pulling tightly. Fighting for her life, Kim managed to grab hold of the would-be killer's arms and flip her over so that she crashed to the floor. Veronica attacked her again, then broke down crying, saying that 'he' had made her do it. Kim tried to find out who 'he' was, but the younger woman simply sobbed the same phrase over again.

Kim fled, her throat bruised and her eyes bloodshot. She felt stupid for having gone drinking with a stranger, but eventually realised that it made sense to report the attempted murder to the police.

Veronica finally left the hotel room and went to the airport. There she posted three tapes to the authorities, each read by a male actor claiming to be a Hillside Strangler. She'd taken cocaine prior to the attempted murder and now acted so strangely at the airport that the staff phoned the police. They let her go after questioning but she was picked up after Kim went to the authorities.

The police searched Veronica's trailer and found a practice version of one of the tapes. In March 1981 she was sent to prison for attempted murder and became known as the Copycat Strangler.

Ken Bianchi now lost interest in her and she transferred her affections to necrophiliac Doug Clark. Veronica was soon writing him fantasies in which she cut her veins and watched him drink her blood. She also suggested that when Doug got out (it's never going to happen) they could open a mortuary together and said it would be a great honour if he made love to and dissected her corpse.

She escaped from the women's prison at Gig Harbour on 27th July 1988 but was captured a few days later whilst leaving a friend's apartment. Parole became possible in 1994 but hasn't been granted yet. Compton now says that her behaviour was due to drug-induced delusions. She has written a book, *Eating The Ashes*, which criticises the US penal system.

Update

Angelo Buono did not fare well in jail. Terrified that he'd be killed, he refused to leave his cell in California's Folsom Prison. To pass the time, he tried to make sense of the thousands of pages of his trial transcripts, a mammoth task for a man who was subliterate. He gained weight and his hair reverted to grey because he was no longer able to dye it black. Surprisingly, he still had an appeal to the ladies and married in prison in 1986 when he was fifty-two. As usual his wife was much younger, being a mere thirty-five.

Angelo Buono was subsequently moved to Calipatria State Prison. There, on 21st September 2002, he died of a heart attack in his cell. He was sixty-seven years old.

Kenneth Bianchi also gained weight and lost his boyish good looks in jail. He has spent much of his time in isolation. He changed his name by deed poll to Anthony D'Amato and then to Nicholas Fontana, hoping that newer prisoners wouldn't know who he was, but the Hillside Stranglers had become infamous and there was no escape.

Not that the serial killer has exactly kept a low profile. In 1987 he attempted to sue writer Darcy O'Brien, claiming that there was a grossly inaccurate portrait of him in O'Brien's book, *Two Of A Kind*. The author had written a wonderfully detailed account of the murders and trial – but he also painted a picture of Frances Bianchi as a devoted mother and gave the impression that Ken was simply an evil child, describing the little boy as 'a soul lost to God, rudderless on the voyage of life, a creature who caused weeping in heaven.' Yet numerous social service reports and hospital records testified to the fact that Ken Bianchi had suffered at his adopted mother's hands. But the judge threw the case out, explaining that Bianchi's name was already sullied because of his crimes. Darcy O'Brien died in 1998, but Bianchi has since attempted to sue another company for using his image on true-crime trading cards.

Happily ever after

In 1986, Ken was contacted by a true crime fan called Shirlee Joyce Book. Shirlee, aged thirty-six, was an unemployed divorcee with a teenage son who'd seen Ken on a television programme. Obsessed with reading about serial killers, she'd previously set her cap at Ted Bundy but he didn't want to know.

For the next two years, Ken and Shirlee phoned and wrote to each other and exchanged tapes, then he proposed marriage. She accepted and he sent her an engagement ring through the post. This romantic suitor had earlier told police 'When you kill a cunt, you make the world a better place.'

The couple met for the very first time on the day of their wedding. The ceremony was attended by their mothers and two convicts. Their request to consummate the marriage in a trailer in the prison grounds was denied. Shirlee, who moved to Washington to be closer to the prison, told a reporter 'I got me a good one' and said that she was sure her husband would soon be released.

But she was to be disappointed for her spouse still resides in jail where he's reverted to his adoptive mother's beliefs and become a born-again Christian, telling a reporter 'When the Lord is ready to release me to the streets, He'll open the doors. I have absolute faith in Him.'

5   THE LOST BOYS
DEAN CORLL & WAYNE HENLEY

Men who kill as a duo are often heterosexual friends or relatives – Bittaker & Norris, Bianchi & Buono, Lake & Ng. But in the following profile the men were lovers who went on to repeatedly torture and kill at least twenty-seven boys.

Dean Arnold Corll
Dean was born on 24th December 1939 to Mary and Arnold Corll in Fort Wayne, Indiana. The couple's relationship had been stormy even when they were dating, and it worsened after the marriage. But they still brought a second child, Stanley, into the world. Arnold Corll was a strict disciplinarian who would make Dean and his brother sit for hours on a chair without moving as a punishment for being boisterous. He also refused to let them play outside. He told Mary that they should be whipped but she recognised their supposed bad behaviour was just childish curiosity.

When Dean was five his parents' marriage ended. Mary Corll now had to support the family alone and took a job, leaving her sons in the nursery or with various babysitters. Stanley coped with the frequent changes of minder and went off to play with his friends but Dean stayed home and worried about everything, feeling responsible for his nuclear family. He took on a pseudo-parental role incredibly early and would fret if Mary or Stanley were a few minutes late in coming home.

He developed rheumatic fever at age six and was sent

home from school for a prolonged rest. For the next few months he stayed home with his mother. She took him to a school friend's party but when he appeared to get upset she decided that he wasn't enjoying himself and that she wouldn't take him to further social events.

Her overprotectivity heightened when he was diagnosed as having a heart condition and she rarely let him out of her sight. Admittedly this suited little Dean as he was still worrying about her and Stanley, even exhorting her not to drive too fast.

Some time after World War II ended, Mary remarried Arnold Corll and he subjected the children to increasingly harsh punishments. By now the family had moved to Houston, Texas, and were living in a trailer. All four Corlls co-existed in cramped misery. The second marriage soon went the way of the first with verbal fights and recriminations, though Arnold Corll always kept his family well provided for. He would go on to marry a third time and this marriage would be a successful one.

Alternately ignored, shouted at or punished by his father and emotionally overwhelmed by his mother, Dean retreated into himself. He was punctual, did what he could with an average intelligence but made virtually no impression on his teachers. Outwardly benign, he was probably on the cusp of developing an active fantasy life where he was masterful and cruel.

Meanwhile, he was at the mercy of adult whims. At nine he and his little brother witnessed other neighbourhood kids committing a petty act of vandalism. When the Sheriff questioned them, they described what they'd seen and were justifiably proud of having helped the local law enforcement. But their mother's response was to demand her sons be given police protection – and when this was refused she sent them away to live with relatives for the entire summer so that they wouldn't be picked on by the vandalistic boys.

When Dean was twelve his mother married for the third time so he gained a stepfather, a travelling salesman who moved the family to Vidor in Texas. The town was the birthplace of the Ku Klux Klan and was fronted by a sign which said 'Nigger, get your ass out of town by sundown.' Needless to say, the school's remit centred around sports rather than civil rights.

Dean tried to fit in with the other boys, going swimming with them in the nude and combing the woods for nuts to take home to his hard-working mother. But he fainted in church one day and his heart murmur was blamed. The doctors warned that he mustn't over-exert himself so from that day onwards he stayed home whilst the others went to the outdoor pool. He joined the school band and took great pleasure in playing the trombone, but the band leader would later be unable to remember him. The quiet boy who never gave his family any trouble was virtually invisible – but he saw and heard the constant bickering between his mother and her new husband. Casual visitors to the house quickly picked up on the terrible tension, so for a sensitive child like Dean it must have taken its toll.

By Dean's early teens, his industrious mother had set up a candy-making business from home. This took up all of the teenager's time as he collected the pecans, wrapped and boxed the candies and delivered them. There was simply no time left over for a social life. There was also no time for sexual education but his mother figured he'd watched animals copulating on his grandmother's farm and knew all he needed to know.

Meanwhile the ill-educated teenager seemed happy to work for hours after school without pay – but he eventually had enough of being ordered around by his stepfather and being told he was useless. He snapped and point blank refused to run any more errands for the ungrateful man.

Dean continued to live inside his own head. He was sufficiently nice that he didn't draw attention to himself, but not so approachable that females or older males wanted to befriend him. With his brown hair, brown eyes and neat appearance he was so ordinary that few people gave him a second glance. Those that did noted that he flirted with boys and did everything he could to keep the attractive ones close to him, behaviour that his increasingly-religious mother was quick to deny.

Dean failed his final exams at school but wasn't too worried as he was going into the family's candy business. He continued to work long hours there until he was nineteen and his grandfather died. His mother now packed him off to live with his widowed grandmother in Indiana so that she had company and someone to take her to the local Methodist church. The teenager found a job there and even sent money home to his mother. If anything, he was *too* good, a young man who seemed to live a completely selfless life.

Dean's life at this point was very similar to that of cannibal killer Jeffrey Dahmer who also lived with his grandmother and regularly accompanied her to church. The rest of the time he appeared to outsiders as completely passive. But beneath his non-person exterior, strong desires were brewing. Dahmer at first satisfied these by having auto-erotic sessions with a male mannequin, then he drugged men in bathhouses and had sex with their unconscious bodies. Finally, he had sex with men whom he'd abducted and crudely lobotomised, having further erotic encounters with them after they were dead.

At this stage Dean Corll was still getting by with an active sadistic fantasy life. But at age twenty-one he was called back home to help in the candy business as it was really taking off. By now the family had relocated to the Heights area of Houston, Texas, and for the first time the business paid him a proper wage rather than just board and lodgings. Unfortunately relations between himself and his stepfather remained mercurial.

Two candy businesses

Gradually the family split so that Mrs Corll and her children were running one candy business and her third husband – still living in the same house – was running another. They eventually separated but stalked each other for many months. Mary would later say that the split was amicable but friends said that she hated her ex-husband and was desperate for his candy enterprise to fail. Dean also loathed his former stepfather and worked even harder than before for his mother in order to make their business succeed.

Twenty-one-year-old Dean now set up a pool table on the premises and invited the local children to play there. Several boys fled after he made passes at them but others were glad of the attention as they were from broken homes.

By the time he was twenty-two, the army wanted him to

do his basic training but his mother said that she couldn't do without him. For the next two years she prevented him being shipped away, but when he was twenty-four he was drafted and attended radio-repair school. His record was spotless and he became more open about his homosexuality. For the first time he could truly be himself. But after ten months his mother contacted the Red Cross to get him back, claiming that she couldn't run the business single handed. When he returned to Houston he moved into a little trailer next to her house.

Dean kept in touch with his father at this time, visiting every second day and telling him about the family business. Friends said that he respected his dad now.

Dean eventually rented his own apartment but still worked alongside his mother on a daily basis. By now she'd married again, this time to a merchant seaman she met through a computerized dating agency. The seaman was insanely jealous of his new wife and threatened to kill her so she divorced him but bizarrely she soon married him again. The relationship remained deeply unstable and Dean had such bad fights with this man that he soon refused to visit his mother's house.

Meanwhile all the infighting at the candy company took its toll and it began to suffer losses. Mary Corll decided to give the business up so Dean trained as an electrician with the Houston Power & Lighting Company, testing relays. The work bored him but it was relatively well paid. Now his mother filed for her fifth divorce, telling her friends that her poor marriage record explained why Dean hadn't married. He was simply a bachelor boy.

The bachelor boy bought himself a powerful motorbike and gave the local boys lifts on the back of it, but he begged them not to tell his mother as she would worry excessively. When she saw the machine she did indeed worry and scolded him as if he was still a child. In turn, he scolded her for dating, but she was still an attractive woman and understandably wanted male company.

Home alone

In June 1968 a psychic told Mary that she should leave Houston. She always listened to psychics so she moved to Dallas – and twenty-eight-year-old Dean was on his own for the very first time.

He now rented a house across the road from a primary school and started to invite boys to his house to watch television. There, he'd play the handcuff game, where he'd cuff them and pretend he'd lost the keys. Homosexual serial killer John Gacy had done the exact same thing, going on to torture his cuffed victims for days before suffocating or drowning them. But for now Dean simply teased his trusting captives and let them go. Police reports would record that he had paid other boys ten dollars to indulge in oral sex with him. One such boy was David Brooks.

David Owen Brooks

David was the son of Alton Brooks, a successful paving contractor. Dean had first met David when the boy was only twelve and Dean was twenty-seven, but they lost touch when the Brooks' marriage began to disintegrate and David was moved around the country to live with various relatives.

At one stage, after stealing a stove in Louisiana, he was taken from his mother and returned to his Houston-based father whom he hadn't seen for years, but the first thing the man did was force the long-haired teenager to get a short-back-and-sides. David felt completely powerless now that even his appearance wasn't his own. All that he owned were his thoughts and as a result he began to tell his girlfriends that none of them really knew him or knew what he was thinking. They probably didn't as he had a higher IQ than most of the local children and often got good grades at school.

When living with his father didn't work out, he was sent to live with his grandfather, then his grandmother. When he was fourteen he moved back to the Heights and lived briefly with his mother. There, Dean offered him money to be his sexual partner. Brooks was heterosexual but desperate for cash to buy status symbols so he accepted the offer, rationalising that it wasn't really homosexual sex if Dean did everything to him and he didn't reciprocate. This suited Dean who liked to be the active sexual partner, the one in charge.

But during the day, the youthful David was the one in charge. The teenager could call the shots, telling Dean what to get him to drink, to eat and to get high. He also enjoyed going on fishing trips in Dean's van whilst the other local boys sat on their porches and longed for a more exciting life.

David now became best friends with a teenager called Wayne Henley who attended the same school. He started to hang around with Henley's crowd at night and his grades dropped markedly. He continued to steal, breaking into a chemists for drugs and stealing from grocery stores. He would offer these drugs for free to younger children. Luckily some told their parents who warned them off.

At fifteen the would-be drug dealer dropped out of school and began living with Dean. The teenager had grown his hair long again and gotten himself a girlfriend. He'd grown to six-foot two so presumably had little sexual appeal for the paedophile Corll, but Dean wanted to keep David around, as David was a magnet for younger boys. The fifteen-year-old had a strong personality, albeit a sadistic one, and was happy to buy a young boy a pizza then take him to Dean's house, knowing that Dean would talk him into having sex. In return for procuring these children, David got to live off Dean. As a result, Dean was frequently broke.

But the arrangement suited both parties so it continued until David Brooks returned to the house unexpectedly one day to find a naked Dean Corll sodomising two boys who he'd stripped and bound to a homemade torture board. David would later say that this didn't shock him, but that Dean was clearly shaken at having a witness to the crime. The older man untied the boys and offered to help David buy a car if he'd forget what he'd seen – and envious Heights youngsters soon saw the sixteen-year-old driving a green Corvette.

It was clear to David from the start that this wasn't consensual sadomasochistic sex as Dean had nailed a metal sheet to the inside of his door so that no one could bore their way out. The torture board was also designed for maximum restraint with holes and handcuffs in the top to hold the victim's wrists and lower holes with rope to bind the victim's feet. And, to make sure that the rape victim couldn't scream the house down, Dean bought several gags. He even wired up a security system so that he'd be alerted if anyone approached his property.

The rapes continued, with the victims – who'd happily sniffed glue or gotten drunk before the event – being set free after their ordeal. None of them reported the sexual assaults, though Dean Corll took some precaution by moving house frequently so that his victims couldn't find him. He also moved again and again when neighbours complained about him partying with boys late into the night. Once, when Brooks and Corll were in the house, neighbours were woken by a young boy screaming and banging on the wall and an older man shouting 'Stop him!' But they assumed that someone was merely tripping out on drugs.

The reality was much more ugly, for David Brooks had started procuring younger children for his friend to rape. Dean Corll terrorised and violated boy after boy but it still wasn't enough to assuage his rage. He had a lowly job which he loathed, no real friends, no creative outlet. He was approaching thirty and had nothing to show for it. His home was rented and he often had to sell his possessions to fund David Brooks' lifestyle. He still hid his sexuality from his family, so his increasingly sporadic relationship with them was built on a lie.

Now he noticed the first signs of ageing – lines around his eyes and thinning hair – but Dean Corll couldn't afford to age gracefully. After all, his persona around young boys was that of a Peter Pan. They wanted a youthful Dean who could party all night with them, not a man who resembled their dad.

Dean Corll had played at being a young boy's friend and when this hadn't brought him emotional relief he'd become a rapist. Now that too was no longer enough. He looked at the board where he'd bound his rape victims and imagined what it would be like to torture them repeatedly, to ensure they never left.

Almost thirty-one, he'd had enough of sadistic sexual fantasy and rape and was ready to put his macabre dreams into action. For the first time he'd be important, noticed, have the power to grant life or death. The obedient mother's boy and the doting sugar daddy to David Brooks was about to become a tyrant who made his helpless victims scream and beg.

The first known victim

There's some uncertainty about the fate of the two boys whom David Brooks found tied to the torture board, as at first he said Dean had let them go, but later he stated that he believed Dean had killed them. But in September 1970 a teenage male hitchhiker became Corll's first known victim. Corll gave him a lift, took him back to his flat and plied him with drink or drugs until he was semi-conscious. He was then stripped naked and strapped to the torture board.

The luckless youth was raped – and when Dean Corll was bored with raping him, the torture started. A thin glass tube was inserted into his penis and a large dildo forced into his rectum. The teenager was tightly gagged to muffle his screams. Later in the proceedings Corll would break the glass tube whilst it was still lodged inside his victim's urethra. When he tired of the boy's visible torment, he strangled him to death.

Other victims

David Brooks continued to procure boys for Dean, only now he knew that their ordeal wouldn't end with rape. He lured acquaintances to the house and remained for many of the resultant torture sessions. Some of these sessions lasted four or five days. He was, incredibly, indifferent to the victims' suffering but would later claim that he stopped short of killing any of the boys. He became more and more involved with his girlfriend so decided to take a lesser role in the proceedings: by age seventeen he would marry and have a baby. Handing on the pot of gold, he introduced Dean to his former school friend Wayne Henley, a hard drinking fifteen-year-old who he knew was desperate for cash.

Elmer Wayne Henley

Wayne – he would always be known by this, his middle name – was born in 1956 to Mary and Elmer Wayne Henley senior. The couple already had one son and after Wayne they'd go on to have two more.

He was a well-mannered little boy who was often taken to the playground by his grandmother, and he had a loving mother who welcomed his friends around. She was known as a strict and righteous woman but she loved her four sons and they loved her too.

Little Wayne initially did well at school, having an IQ between 110 and 120, which is well above average. But he often returned from class to find his father beating his mother, as when Wayne's father got drunk he became a troublemaker. He had a criminal record which stretched back years. When his marriage started to break up, he waited on the porch with a shotgun, determined to murder his wife. But the shot went wide and almost hit Wayne instead.

Wayne's parents divorced and times were hard so Wayne took two part-time jobs to help his mother. His grades fell rapidly and he dropped out of school in the ninth grade.

He was a religious boy who carried his Bible everywhere.

He hoped to join the Navy at sixteen but failed the tests and was visibly devastated. Keen to make money to impress his girlfriends – and clearly finding it easy to emulate his father's violence – he turned to crime instead. He was arrested for assault with a deadly weapon, though it was David Brooks who permanently carried a gun.

Wayne got a job laying asphalt but he was bored. At sixteen he was arrested for breaking and entering. He grew a thin moustache, smoked and drank and tried to act old before his time, almost getting engaged to one of his girlfriends. Only his thin body and teenage acne showed his true age.

The late Jack Olsen, who wrote a book about the case, would brilliantly sum up boys like Henley and Brooks in a single sentence. 'They are born, they go to school, they drop out, they get menial jobs, they reproduce others like themselves, and they die.' It's a chillingly accurate insight into people born into a poverty of expectation where life amounts to little more than a boring day job, evenings spent slumped in front of the television and alcohol used liberally to keep the boredom at bay.

Wayne Henley had led this kind of life, but now he had a benefactor in the form of Dean Corll to whom David Brooks had introduced him. Dean clearly lusted after Wayne's slender body – and Wayne was willing to go along with this, as were many of the impoverished teens living in the Heights.

Corrupted to kill

At first, Wayne thought he'd struck gold in meeting Dean. The older man ferried him and his friends around in Dean's Ford Econoline van, bought them beers and marijuana. Admittedly Wayne wasn't allowed to bring any of his girlfriends along to these drinking sessions, but that seemed a small price to pay for a free high.

But Dean soon made it clear that he wanted his new lover to lure young schoolboys to his house to rape and eventually kill them. At first, Henley said no but then his finances worsened and Dean offered him two hundred dollars, a lot of money in the Seventies. Wayne thought some more about the offer and realised that he'd not only make a lot of cash but would manage to ward off Dean's sexual advances for a few days whilst Dean enjoyed himself with his victim. Wayne wanted to see Dean as a father figure but felt ashamed of their bedroom acts.

Dean continued to ask Wayne to find him a boy and Wayne eventually caved in. He started to hang out at a fried chicken bar where the local school pupils congregated, and offered them drink and drugs if they came back to his friend Dean's house.

Boy after boy disappeared – but the police told their parents that they were runaways. This was partially corroborated when Dean Corll made them write letters to their families saying that they'd found work on a ship or in a faraway town. (Catherine Birnie, profiled in *Women Who Kill*, made her victims do the exact same thing.) One boy called his parents sounding very frightened, but before they could ascertain where he was they heard a man's voice and the line went dead.

Wayne's friends noticed that he didn't invite any of them to Dean's parties, preferring to take along boys that he hardly knew. One victim was found at the school where Wayne took his driving lessons. Another was a friend of a friend. These boys were happy to go with Wayne to Dean's house where they enjoyed cocaine and glue-sniffing sessions. They saw the thin young man and his older friend as altruists until they lost consciousness...

The victim would revive to find himself strapped, face inwards, to the specially constructed plywood board. Dean would then rape him repeatedly and violate him with the variously-sized glass tubes. Wayne also got in on the act, pulling out the boy's pubic hairs. David Brooks occasionally called round to find Corll and Henley torturing one of their prisoners, though he'd claim that he watched but didn't join in.

Cruelly, Wayne remained in touch with the parents of some missing boys and helped them distribute posters. The parents had no idea that he'd already helped to kill their sons and had buried the bodies in Dean's boat shed.

The torture worsens

But pushing an oversized dildo into a victim's rectum can't make up for more than thirty years of repression. Hearing a boy scream can't compensate for all of the years when you were emotionally scarred. As such, Dean Corll had to think up greater and greater excesses in order to assuage his blood lust – and he took to castrating his victims with a knife.

At least one victim had his testicles bitten off and it's telling that during this period Dean Corll was especially anxious about his own genitalia as he'd developed a water pocket in his scrotum which caused him increasing pain. He told a female friend that he couldn't afford to have this hydrocele treated, but it's more likely that he was fearful of the operation. He delayed until he was in agony then had the hydrocele removed.

His cruelty to his victims continued. One boy was viciously kicked to death whilst others were injured with bullets, sometimes being kept alive for several days.

The killing spree escalates

Dean Corll needed these torture murders to provide him with everything he lacked – self-esteem, the gratification he couldn't find through his boring job, revenge at those who had punished him throughout his childhood. But he found, as most serial killers do, that the good feelings lasted for a shorter and shorter time. As a result he started to encourage Wayne to bring him two victims rather than one. Some of these duos were friends, others were brothers. He would torture them repeatedly then make one of the boys watch whilst his mate or sibling was slowly killed.

Dean also began to abuse younger victims as his need for satisfaction increased: most of his prey had been in their mid-teens but now he tortured and killed a nine-year-old boy who lived across the road.

Wayne Henley noted that Dean's blood lust was up, that he now asked for more and more victims. He believed that Dean would only be happy when he brought him a new boy every day.

The men continued to kill with the utmost brutality. One day Wayne fired a gun as he entered Dean's room and it accidentally hit one of their torture-victims in the jaw. David Brooks witnessed the macabre incident. Unperturbed, Dean Corll continued to torture the badly injured boy for the rest of the day.

David Brooks leaves

By 1973, David had moved away from Dean's neighbourhood, married another teenager and impregnated her. This now left Wayne as Dean Corll's sole procurer, and the strain began to tell. In March 1973, he told his friends that he was never coming back to the Heights again and he travelled to Mount Pleasant to live with his dad, got a job in a gas station and resolved to put the past behind him. But within a month relations had soured and he returned to his mother's house, soon returning to Dean Corll's outwardly affable company.

Wayne's mother thought that Wayne treated Dean like a father, and Wayne told friends that he was more like a brother – but in reality he lurched between being sexually abused himself or finding Dean younger boys to sexually assault.

The constant killing was taking its toll on the younger man, who now begged a friend to go to Australia with him, offering to pay the friend's boat fare. He was drinking more heavily than ever and his speech was often slurred. He also asked older friends and relatives to accompany him to Dean's parties, clearly realising that the man could not kill in front of witnesses. He was sufficiently desperate to visit the local Methodist minister twice, talking about unhappy aspects of his family life.

In April he quit his job in asphalt paving and thereafter took casual employment. But he usually had money in his pocket, money provided by Dean.

Burn out

By thirty-three Dean was drinking as heavily as Wayne and had developed high blood pressure, unusual for a man of his age who was only slightly overweight and active. Acquaintances noticed that he was becoming increasingly agitated and he talked about getting married to a long-term female friend and having a child. Then he changed his mind after phoning his mother who he hadn't seen for five years. During a later phone-call he told her that he was contemplating suicide, but her religion made her believe in reincarnation and she told him that suicide was pointless as he'd have to go through the same lessons again in another life.

Deciding to teach yet another luckless boy a lesson, Dean asked Wayne to procure him a new male victim, but Wayne did the unthinkable and brought both a boy and a girl to Dean's house.

Dean is murdered

It was 8th August 1973 when Wayne brought his friends to Dean's party. Wayne fancied the girl, Rhonda, and had promised to help her run away from home. But Dean insisted on all-male parties and was so enraged at seeing the girl that he threatened to shoot them all dead.

Eventually he pretended to calm down and suggested they all sniff paint and get high. The teenagers did so, but when they lost consciousness Dean Corll tied them all up. Wayne revived to find himself strapped to the hellish plywood board. Dean was threatening to torture all three of them to death.

Wayne Henley now used all of the information he knew about Dean Corll to plead for his life. He reminded Corll of what they'd been through together and suggested the torture session would be much more inventive if two of them were doing the torturing. Eventually Dean agreed to this on the proviso that Wayne raped the still semi-conscious Rhonda – who was tied up in the bedroom – whilst the other boy was strapped to a second torture board.

Wayne said that he would and Dean untied him. But, chivalrous in his own way, Wayne was unable to rape his female friend. Enraged, Dean now began to wave a gun about.

A struggle ensued in which Wayne got hold of the pistol and Dean dared him to use it. The teenager obliged and fired six shots into Dean Corll who was dead before he hit the ground. The trembling seventeen-year-old freed the unconscious captives then called the police, saying in his singsong voice 'Y'all better come right now. Ah kilt a man.'

Investigating, the police found the torture boards and various thin white tubes plus the often-used seventeen inch dildo. They also found that Dean's van had been made into a mobile torture chamber, with manacles set in the walls and a box with airholes which had clearly been used to keep captives in.

Neighbours told the police that Dean Corll was a good man who regularly attended church. He'd pretended to them that he was a widower so they'd assumed that Wayne Henley was his son and that the younger boys who entered the house were his son's friends. But Wayne was now able to tell the police that Dean liked little boys and that he'd procured them for him. Being economical with the truth, he added that Dean had told him during their gunfight that he'd killed a few other boys.

For several hours the police did nothing with this information, assuming that Wayne Henley was hallucinating after his paint-sniffing session, but a policeman who had a young male relative missing – and who knew that other boys were missing – suggested they check out his tale.

The police asked Wayne if he knew where the burial sites were and he took them to the boat shed first and they began to dig up the floor, soon finding body after body. Each was neatly wrapped in plastic which Dean Corll had stolen from his workplace and some still had their hands tied or handcuffed behind their backs. One boy's mouth was stretched wide open in a last desperate gasp for air as he'd been strangled, whilst others had rope still tied tightly around their necks. A few were so badly decomposed that they were merely disjointed bones and skulls, but a bike found in the shed belonged to a thirteen-year-old boy who had gone missing less than a week before.

Wayne Henley was close to a nervous breakdown as the bodies were brought out so the police treated him gently, letting him phone his mother and sit in the police car to compose himself. In turn, he said that he was grateful to them for not beating him up and he began to talk. For the first time he admitted his own part in some of the murders, saying that he'd helped Dean Corll to strangle one of the victims. He added that there were more bodies at another two burial sites.

That first day, the diggers found eight corpses in the boat shed. The following day they discovered several more. Almost all of the bodies were gagged and some contained bullet wounds whilst others had cord wrapped around their throats. Sometimes the genitalia – with telltale knife wounds or teeth marks showing the means of castration – was found in a separate bag. The smallest body was that of a nine-year-old, the oldest in their teens. At the end of the day, the investigators had found another nine bodies, bringing the total to seventeen.

Wayne now led them to the second burial site, the Corll's lakeside retreat. It yielded up another two decomposing bodies. Later, further bodies were found at the Angelina National Forest, making a total of twenty-seven. Wayne said that there were more, that the total was over thirty, but investigators gave up at this stage.

The teenager was glad that his co-killer was dead and was desperate to confess further details but he shook so badly in custody that he had to be tranquillised. When asked why he did it, he said that being shot at by his own father had been pivotal. He also hinted that Dean Corll had been blackmailing him. Corll might have threatened to tell the world that he'd had sex with Wayne knowing that Wayne was outwardly fiercely heterosexual. Indeed, the teenager kept emphasising to the detectives that he'd had a girlfriend.

He also said that Dean had failed to pay him for procuring most of the boys, which suggested that he had enjoyed killing them. He admitted that two or three had been so difficult to strangle that he'd had to ask Dean to help. David Brook would also confirm this view of Wayne as someone who wanted on some level to kill, saying that Wayne had enjoyed causing the victims pain.

The abducted boys had suffered horrendously. One teenager, after being repeatedly raped, had been forced to watch his friend being strangled to death by Wayne Henley. David Brooks tried to pacify the terrified survivor, upon which Wayne shot the boy in the face. A moment later he regained consciousness and pleaded for his freedom, whereupon Wayne strangled him to death.

When the other prisoners on remand heard of what Henley had done they wanted to kill him and he had to be moved to solitary confinement for his own safety. His lawyer described him as physically and mentally ill and said that the recreational drugs and alcohol which he'd used liberally had put him into a temporarily psychotic state.

David Brooks was interviewed at length and at first denied ever seeing any cruelty taking place at Dean's house. But later he made a full statement and gave details of many of the tortures. He added that when it came to killing the boys 'It didn't bother me to see it. I saw it done many times. I just wouldn't do it myself. And I never did do it myself.'

His father proved very supportive to him when he was in custody. The older man wept as he realised that his son had procured some of these boys, knowing the atrocities which awaited them – but said he was relieved that David hadn't actually taken a life.

David Brooks was deeply involved in the deaths though, telling investigators how he'd seen boys tied to the bed and had helped carry their corpses to suitable burial sites.

Wayne Henley had initially told detectives that he'd 'be about forty when he got out' but in August 1974 he was sentenced to 594 years, a sentence that was later overturned due to legal irregularities. Tried again in June 1979, the alcoholic teenager was sentenced to life imprisonment. David Brooks also received a life sentence in March 1975 for killing one of the boys – and life in his case is liable to mean just that.

Meanwhile, Mary Corll continued to protest her dead son's innocence, describing him as asexual rather than homosexual and suggesting that he just wanted to please everyone all the time, that he didn't have a sadistic bone in his body. She said that Dean was innocent and that Wayne and David wouldn't have committed the killings if they'd gotten religion. But Dean and Wayne had both gone to church and had lured two of Dean's victims from a religious rally, and sex offenders are more likely to come from restrictive religious households than from secular ones.

Update

Wayne Elmer Henley – now in his late forties – is still in prison. He is eligible for parole consideration every three years but the authorities are considering changing this to every five years as he's such an unlikely candidate for freedom.

Wayne told a curiosity-seeker who wrote to him that he found it easiest to isolate himself in prison rather than become intimate with anyone. He expresses himself creatively and has become a respected painter of flowers and landscapes. His Houston art shows have quickly sold out and he recently featured in a documentary about people who produce or collect serial killer art.

He has undoubtedly bettered himself in prison but – given that he contributed to the deaths of up to thirty boys – it is unlikely that he'll ever be released.

6   A KIND OF LOVING
DIANE ZAMORA & DAVID GRAHAM

The murder that teenage lovers Diane Zamora & David Graham committed must be one of the most senseless in American history. During a row with Diane, the inexperienced David pretended that he'd had sex with an attractive schoolmate. Diane became hysterical and said that the other woman must die...

Diane Michelle Zamora

Diane was born on 21st January 1977 to Gloria and Carlos Zamora in Fort Worth, Texas. Her father was an electrician and her mother a shop assistant. Her grandfather was a minister so the family went to church twice weekly and enrolled Diane in the choir and Bible study group. Luckily she also managed to do some of her schoolwork there as she was desperate to excel academically.

Diane joined the Girl Scouts and excelled there as well. She was a serious child who would start studying at six in the morning. By the time she was twelve her parents had produced three more children who she'd babysit at night. At twelve she joined the choir and sang along with her mother. The family were Hispanic so she learned numerous Biblical verses in Spanish and in English. She was pretty and petite but seemed old before her time.

By thirteen she'd joined the Civil Air Patrol. She hated all the marching and authoritarianism but stayed with it as she'd heard it was a good way to get into the Air Force. She was taking on an increasingly heavy academic and social workload, working as hard as her impoverished parents were.

With four children to feed, Gloria and Carlos Zamora had to work full time. Gloria decided to go to nursing college in order to better herself and also sold cosmetics to bring in extra money. They were commendable decisions but left her little time to spend with Diane whom a relative would later describe as 'starved of love.'

Meanwhile Carlos Zamora had found a new love at church and started a torrid affair. He left Gloria and the children twice for his mistress. Worse, the extended family knew about his indiscretions. Gloria and fourteen-year-old Diane talked about the situation far into the night. Diane even confronted her father after finding him in bed with his mistress, telling him in no uncertain terms what a cad he was.

To make matters worse, Carlos lost his job and the family filed for bankruptcy and lost their home. They lost another home and would ultimately file for bankruptcy four times. Sometimes the electricity was cut off for non-payment and Diane would do her studying by candlelight. On other occasions they were evicted from their home and lived with Gloria's dad. By now Diane had begun to self-harm, cutting her arms as a way of relieving emotional pressure. Outwardly however she was still the controlled teenager who was in the top ten percent of her class.

Gloria decided to confront Connie, the mistress, and took Diane along with her. The pair saw Connie's car parked outside an apartment, entered and ransacked the place before realising that they were in the wrong house. By then, they'd unwittingly terrorised the apartment's elderly bedridden occupant. They fled but not before taking several expensive items from Connie's car.

Police involvement with the Zamoras continued after

Gloria made a series of phone-calls to Connie. The other woman filed for harassment. The next day Gloria counter-sued her husband's mistress, claiming that Connie was the nuisance caller. Diane was learning at first-hand that a wronged wife should blame the other woman and take revenge.

To make matters worse, she originally hated her senior officer at the cadet programme, David Graham. He was secretly attracted to her but had no way of showing it as he was hopelessly awkward around girls. He shouted at Diane and criticised her marching, dress code and attitude. In turn she told other cadets that he was a pig.

David Christopher Graham

David was born on 2nd November 1977. Like Diane, he was from a family of four but in his case he was the youngest. His father Jerry was a school principal whom author Peter Meyer (in an interesting book on the case) would describe as 'passive and pleasant.' His mother Janice was 'the tightly wound mover and shaker of the family', who stayed at home until her children moved into their teens. AW Gray, who wrote an equally gripping study of the cadet murder, noted that Janet was the family disciplinarian. David's father was twenty years older than his mother, an age gap which – along with arguments about disciplining David – would eventually strain the partnership to breaking point.

The family's life revolved around the Southern Baptist Church and they attended church every Wednesday and twice on a Sunday. David also attended a religious summer school and studied the Bible at night.

Janice (who would later train to be a teacher) taught

him at home for his first few years and many people described them as close, but he would later tell Diane that he came from a violent family and that his mother had stabbed him in the elbow with a fork for putting his elbows on the table. He'd also tell her that he developed into a violent boy who murdered the family dog. Whatever the real story, all of the Grahams were academically gifted and his siblings graduated with flying colours and got top jobs, one becoming a lawyer. David too did brilliantly in his early exams and was expected to go far.

When he was still a little boy his father took him to an airshow and he became obsessed with becoming a pilot. He made increasingly sophisticated and detailed drawings of planes for the next few years and was desperate to become old enough to take to the air. And he succeeded in his goal, signing up for the Civil Air Patrol at age thirteen and gaining his pilot's licence by fourteen, a remarkable feat. Deferential and dedicated, he became one of their most decorated cadets. With his short hair, immaculately pressed clothes and insistence on calling everyone sir or ma'am he was an old-fashioned boy who was mocked by his school's more streetwise kids.

The girls largely ignored him and the boys thought that he hated females, but he was just desperately shy in their company. By age sixteen he was making up stories about his sexual prowess, stories which no one believed. He also stole his father's credit card and bought thousands of dollars of stereo equipment, perhaps in an effort to look adult to his peers or to cheer himself up.

By now he and his parents were having regular screaming matches where he was beginning to stand up for himself.

He was becoming a young man rather than a child and had grown to six-foot three. With his hazel brown eyes and neat appearance, he was reasonably attractive. But he was still nervous and awkward around females and must have inwardly despaired of ever finding a girl to love.

His luck was to change when he went on an exchange visit to Ottawa. There he was the highly decorated air cadet, rather than the geeky schoolboy who still went to church with his mother. He revelled in the attention of a Canadian girl and lost his virginity to her at the age of seventeen.

By the time he returned to the states his imagination had gone into overdrive and he suggested that he'd had sex with *two* girls and that they'd virtually performed the Kama Sutra on him. However, this loss of virginity does seem to have been genuine, and he wrote to the girl until the long-term romance reached a natural end.

Sadly, his parents' marriage was also coming to a natural end and Janice Graham walked out one day leaving a note on the kitchen table, a note which David found when he came home from school. It said that she was leaving because David's father refused to discipline him. There were rumours that she'd left because of David's violence and other rumours that she wanted to start a new life. By now David's father had resigned as school principal and had become a driving instructor so it was a time of change for the unhappy seventeen-year-old.

He began to flirt with Diane Zamora and, much to everyone's surprise, she reciprocated. Soon they were going steady. It was against the rules for seniors to date juniors, but love has never been a respecter of rules.

The love object

Diane had seen her father leave her mother twice (albeit briefly) and David had seen his mother leave for good, so both teenagers were particularly motivated to make their own affair permanent. They began to spend all of their spare time together, forming a relationship that others thought suffocating but which was probably relatively normal for their age. First love is always an incredibly powerful state of mind – and before meeting David, Diane had only been on three dates.

Teenagers have an enormous influence on each other, and Zamora and Graham were no exception. He began to act more like a normal teenager, growing his hair longer and wearing T-shirts with anarchic logos. In turn, she became more disciplined at the cadet academy, deciding that the marching, canned foods and survival routines weren't so bad.

The couple got engaged though they knew it would be five years until they could marry, choosing a date in August 2000 when they'd both have graduated. Diane now gave David her virginity. Her parents' religion forbade this and afterwards she felt guilty and told her mother. But she convinced herself that everything was fine because David was *The One*.

The teenagers, who attended schools twelve miles apart, continued their intense affair but it also became increasingly violent. She hit him and he stabbed her in the knee. They bit and kicked each other and on another occasion he tried to strangle her with a belt. But they always made up after these terrible fights and were so over-protective that visiting relatives couldn't get close.

Their own closeness deepened after Diane was driving

David's car and had an accident where she almost lost her left hand. Surgeons worked tirelessly to save her fingers but three of them would never open properly again. Both Zamoras were devastated by the fact that they could have lost their beautiful daughter. Carlos, aware that she needed transport of her own, bought her a car.

A complex confession

The seventeen-year-olds' troubled relationship continued. Diane was constantly asking David about his previous girlfriends and how much they'd meant to him. One day she thought that he was looking particularly troubled and asked him what was wrong. In truth, he was withdrawn because he was in serious trouble at his cadet patrol for dating Diane and for neglecting his duties. But, perhaps in a bid to feel popular or free to do as he chose, he told Diane that he'd given another student called Adrianne Jones a lift home from a track event in his station wagon and that they'd made love in the back seat.

Upon hearing this, Diane Zamora went berserk. She attacked him with a brass bar then began to batter her head off the walls, screaming hysterically for a full hour. She kept begging him to 'kill her' (meaning the other woman) and eventually he said yes. He was unwilling to admit that he'd invented the adulterous union – or perhaps he knew that the obsessively jealous Diane wouldn't believe him if he now told the truth. The teenagers' love hadn't made them as happy as they'd hoped. How could it, when they had so many unresolved issues from their difficult childhoods? But now they could blame a third party and convince themselves that killing her would restore the purity of their love.

The murder

On 3rd December 1995 David put a rope, barbells and his pistol in a bag, phoned Adrianne and asked her to sneak out of her house to meet him after her parents had gone to bed. (Adrianne often sneaked out late to meet friends.) Shortly after midnight she did just that. They drove off together to the lake, Adrianne still in her gym wear as she'd earlier worked out with her mother. The luckless sixteen-year-old had no idea that he planned to kill her and that an equally vengeful Diane Zamora was in the trunk of the car. The plan was to break Adrianne's neck then weigh her body down with the barbells and put it in the lake but David got lost and couldn't find the water, so he parked in a quiet lane instead.

At the same time he signalled to Diane to leave the trunk and slide into the back seat. When she did, he grabbed Adrianne by the neck and she started screaming, asking what he was doing. Her neck was becoming bruised but it didn't snap.

Diane now struck her rival on the back of the head with one of the weights and struck her again, shattering her skull and driving pieces of bone deep into her brain. Adrianne's left hand was also smashed when she raised it to deflect another blow.

Somehow she managed to push herself backwards out of the car window, stumble away from her tormentors and climb over a barbed wire fence, collapsing on the other side of it.

David followed then ran back to Diane and said that she was dead – but Diane told him to play safe and shoot her. So David Graham went back with his pistol and shot the badly injured teenager twice in the face at close range.

Shortly afterwards, they noticed Adrianne's blood all over the car. David became nauseous but Diane remained controlled enough to clean it up, then the trembling killers made their way to one of David's friends and swore him to secrecy about their visit. They were blood-spattered and obviously upset as they hurried into the shower. The friend assumed they'd been in a motor accident and helped out as best he could. Now it was Diane's turn to go to pieces, and she lay there in the friend's bedroom, crying and shaking. Both teens expected to be arrested at any moment so for the next few days they were unnaturally quiet.

The investigation

Police knew that Adrianne had talked to someone called David on the phone late the night she was killed so they asked David Graham for his alibi. He replied truthfully that he'd been with his fiancée, Diane. The police had also heard that Adrianne had been kind to a troubled young teenager who used to hang about the fast food outlet where she had an after-school job. After a couple of interviews, they battered down his parents' door in the early hours of the morning and took him into custody. The innocent seventeen-year-old, who was on medication for a bi-polar condition, was sick twice on his way to the station and his parents were in shock.

Meanwhile Diane and David kept going to church and praying for forgiveness. But their religion didn't prick their consciences sufficiently for them to tell police that they'd jailed the wrong boy.

The boy spent the next three weeks in jail, being held in squalid conditions. But at the end of the third week he was polygraphed, passed with flying colours and was released.

By now the strain of being murderers was beginning to tell on Diane and David, who continued to hit each other. He told his friends not to mention other girls in her presence. They both applied for afterschool jobs but when only he was accepted she persuaded him not to take up the post.

Diane found it impossible to keep the murder secret and told one of her schoolfriends, but the teenager kept her counsel. It's also rumoured that she told several of her relatives.

A new beginning

A few months later the star-crossed lovers went off to their respective colleges, she to the Naval Academy and he to the United States Air Force Academy. Interviewed about her success, she said that she attributed much of it to David and added 'I owe so much to God.'

But on a more earthly plane, she had crying jags whenever David didn't answer her emails. She found the physical arduousness of her new course difficult and soon forged an increasingly strong friendship with another man. She swore him to secrecy then told him that her fiancé David had killed a girl. Unsure whether or not to believe her, he didn't pass her confession on to the authorities.

Increasing mind games

Diane now told David about her new friend and he tried to get the young man charged with sexual harassment. In turn, David invented a girl at the airforce base who he claimed fancied him. When she heard about this supposed new threat, Diane sent back an email referring obliquely to

Adrianne's murder, reminding him of 'the secret they shared.'

When David didn't hear from Diane for a few hours he'd begin to pace the room. Eventually his weary room-mate asked for a transfer. Both Diane's room-mates also found her impossible to live with as she talked about David constantly and kept hinting that he'd killed a girl. Unsurprisingly, she went through several changes of room-mates in a matter of months.

Arrest and trial

But Diane continued to talk, eventually telling her third set of room-mates that 'someone is dead because of me.' The next day the worried teenagers went to the chaplain and the police were called in.

Incredibly Diane was given a plane ticket home – but she swapped it for one which took her to the airforce base where David was stationed. The young couple then spent three days together, days in which it seems they rehearsed their stories which would then sound almost identical. She then flew back to her parents' house but they'd been evicted so she moved in with them at her grandfather's home.

David and Diane were arrested separately on 6th September 1996, nine months after battering and shooting Adrianne. Diane now retracted her story, claiming that she'd made it up to impress her room-mates – but she had a motive of sorts and so did her boyfriend David Graham.

He initially denied the murder and said that he'd never heard of Adrianne Jones. Only after he took a polygraph and failed spectacularly did he admit to killing her because 'no one could stand between me and Diane.' Ironically, no one *was* standing between him and Diane. Both were their own worst enemies. Their pathological jealousy had caused them to invent an enemy and brutally slaughter her.

Diane also admitted to the crime, saying that she and David were jointly responsible. She showed no remorse for the pointless killing, and spent her nineteenth birthday in the county jail.

Celluloid couple

Inevitably the couple's story was turned into an entertaining film, *Swearing Allegiance*. But the film gave the impression that Diane's motive for wanting Adrianne dead was all about restoring the purity of Diane and David's love. Though that was certainly a motive, the fear of others finding out was probably far stronger. Diane had seen her mother shamed through her father's infidelity and she'd told everyone at school how perfect she and David were, so she risked a loss of face if he publicly admitted being attracted to Adrianne.

Both teenagers shared a fear of splitting up. Their families were disintegrating and Graham had lost the respect of his peers and superiors at the Cadet Air Patrol because he spent so much time with Diane Zamora. They literally only had each other. The right thing to do would have been to forge new friendships and build themselves a new peer group – but they opted not to do the right thing.

As usual, the media portrayed them as the 'perfect couple' and said that the murder was completely out of character. But the reality is that both teenagers were deeply troubled before they met and their relationship was increasingly violent. They simply looked for a scapegoat and took their confused rage out on her.

A death wish

Hours after being found guilty, Diane Zamora allegedly slashed her arm with a razor in prison. She told a psychologist that it wasn't an attempt to take her own life, but the prison played safe and placed her on suicide watch for twenty-four hours.

In her cell she wrote David endless letters, read her Bible and sang hymns. She wrote that 'God has forgiven us' and that 'everything that happens, happens for a reason.' She seemed incapable of recognising that the murder had happened because she battered Adrianne's skull in and David shot her dead.

Meanwhile David's lawyers said that he'd only confessed after thirty hours of interrogation and that the confession might be unsafe. When a reporter asked him if he had a message for Diane he said that he loved her and he made it clear to his legal team that he still expected to marry her.

David also wrote to a friend quoting Biblical tenets and adding 'God forgives people for anything.' He told his friend that he was optimistic about the trial and asked him to hold onto his gear.

Sentencing

But David was unduly optimistic – for in February 1998 Diane Zamora blamed David Graham at her trial, saying that he had manipulated her into helping kidnap Adrianne. The jury found her guilty and she was given life imprisonment. She now works as a clerk in the prison warehouse and is regularly visited by her family.

Five months later David Graham went on trial. It then transpired that he hadn't had sex with Adrianne Jones after the track meet as he'd claimed: indeed, another youth had given her a lift home from that particular event. David and Adrianne knew each other from their cross country runs but they hadn't had the full sex that he'd told Diane had taken place.

David's separated parents were very supportive of him and jointly paid for his defence. Diane briefly took the stand at his trial but only to say that she was taking the Fifth Amendment and would not testify. He was subsequently sentenced to life. He has since become co-editor of a prison newspaper, ironic as his initial statement about loving Diane was described by reporters as 'pure Mills and Boon.'

Under Texas law both killers will serve forty years before they can be considered for parole. Unless this is changed by a later appeal they will both be over sixty when they get out.

Update

Diane had lost David through testifying against him so the love affair that she'd sworn would last 'forever' was over. In early 2003 she petitioned to marry a prisoner called Steve Mora. The couple had become close through exchanging letters but had never met. Steve had served previous sentences for auto theft and burglary and was on the last few months of a four year stretch for threatening someone involved in one of his previous crimes.

On 17th June 2003 the marriage took place in a double-proxy ceremony, with Diane's mother standing in for Diane and a male friend standing in for Steve Mora. A judge in San Antonio performed the ceremony. Meanwhile the happy couple remained in their respective jails, Steve at Texas's Ramsey Unit and Diane at the Mountain View

Unit of the maximum security Texas Department of Criminal Justice.

It's unlikely that the couple will live happily ever after as Steve was due for release within months of the marriage whereas Diane won't be free until 2038. A criminal justice professor commented that 'They're kind of naïve about realities. That's really not surprising. If they were realistic, they probably wouldn't be where they are.'

Male-male couples who kill tend to be more sadistic than male-female or female-female partnerships. But Lake & Ng plumbed new depths of depravity in killing babies as well as adults, and by the end of their lethal partnership at least sixteen people had died appalling deaths. Leonard Lake managed to convince himself that he was kidnapping women whom he could breed with and create a post-Holocaust society, but his true motivation was a combination of lust and rage.

Leonard Thomas Lake

Leonard was born on 29th October 1945 to Gloria and Elgin Lake. His father was in the Navy and the family resided in San Francisco. Unfortunately it was a poor marriage during which Elgin Lake anaesthetised himself with drink. Five years after Leonard the Lakes had a daughter and a year after that they had another son.

But the family remained in discord and shortly after the birth of this third child, Elgin left the marriage and Gloria understandably found it difficult to cope with three young children. The fatherless family now moved to the projects and were constantly hungry, frightened and cold. Leonard would later recall that he had no toys and would fantasise that he'd been sent to an orphanage instead.

When Leonard was six, his mother decided to follow her ex-husband to Seattle and ask for a second chance. Leonard apparently said that he didn't want to go, and as he was settled at nursery school she decided to leave him with his grandparents. But at the railway station he changed his mind and clung hysterically to her skirt. She had only booked places for her other children so had to leave him – and he would never forgive her for this.

Yet his life improved dramatically when he moved in with his grandparents, for he was no longer hungry, had pocket money and his own room. He was also allowed to breed pet mice.

Within a year his mother, brother and sister returned to San Francisco but Leonard remained with his grandparents. He was polite to his mother but no longer close to her. When he was eleven she remarried and asked him to live with her, but he said no, though he was civil to the two daughters she subsequently had.

Leonard didn't just have misgivings about his mother but also about his younger brother Donald who had been hit by a train and suffered brain damage. The older boy despised his younger sibling who he saw as a burden on their mother and on the state. He would retain this viewpoint throughout his life, being openly contemptuous of anyone who needed welfare aid.

In his teens, the boy who wanted revenge on his mother became erotically charged by John Fowles' classic book *The Collector*. The novel explores the life of a dull man who kidnaps a girl for sexual pleasure. Fantasies in which young women were debased and kept captive began to dominate his masturbatory dreams. He hadn't been able to control the first woman in his life, but could endlessly control his fantasy lovers. They always did exactly what he said.

Bored with living at his grandparents and already possessed of a prodigious sexual appetite, he joined the US

Marine Corps on 27th January 1964. He was eighteen years old, six-foot tall and fighting fit, but his mental health was somewhat less robust than his physical health, something which became apparent as his love life and military life progressed ...

Marriage and mental illness

Leonard became fascinated with guns whilst in the marines, a fascination which would remain with him. For the next six years he learned field survival techniques and aircraft radar technology. He travelled throughout the states and to Asia with the marines and won four medals – two for good conduct, the others for exemplary service whilst on a tour of duty in Vietnam.

When he was twenty-four he married a young woman, Karen, in California whilst home on leave, and almost immediately began to dominate her. He also joked constantly in front of his friends about selling her to them.

The following year he returned to Vietnam but soon began to crack up, becoming paranoid that his wife was being unfaithful. He also talked of having killed numerous Vietnamese, but as a radar technician he hadn't seen active service. Eventually he asked to speak to a psychiatrist who thought that he was on the verge of schizophrenia. Sent home after only a month of this second tour of duty, he continued to act strangely and was discharged on mental health grounds in January 1971.

Often out of work or doing menial driving jobs, Leonard Lake now had time on his hands and became increasingly obsessed with sex, and for him that meant control-based activities. He persuaded Karen Lake to take a job in a topless bar and to meet with other couples to discuss partner swapping. He also met with other women and took nude photos of them. He started to beat his wife – and when she left him he continued to stalk her. From Leonard Lake's point of view, he had now been deserted by the first two women in his life.

Numerous failed relationships

Later that same year he began a love affair with a young woman he met through a contact ad. Again, he followed the same pattern that he had with his spouse, being incredibly sweet and attentive throughout the early dates and lovemaking. Only when his new girlfriend was deeply in love with him did he ask her to become a prostitute and start taking numerous nude photographs of her in bondage sex. He dropped the mister nice guy act and began to dominate every facet of her daily life, expecting her to account for all of her time and give him all of her money. When this verbal abuse turned to violence she, too, left.

Lake moved to a rural retreat 130 miles from San Francisco known as The Ranch. His new house was surrounded by miles of woodland: this inspired his already active survivalist fantasies. But, though he enjoyed his own company, he also wanted sexual partners and started relationships with various local woman. He was still an attractive man and an interesting one, but in time each of these girlfriends left him due to his controlling behaviour and overwhelming misogyny. He had so little sense of appropriate boundaries that he suggested a friend's ten-year-old daughter pose nude for him – and he dated a fifteen-year-old until her parents sent her away to boarding school.

Perhaps fuelled by these numerous failed relationships,

the thirty-five-year-old made a videotape of his feelings in October 1980, stating 'what I want is an off-the-shelf sex partner... And when I'm tired or satiated or bored or not interested I simply want to put her away.' He was, in short, describing prostitution and many men in his position would simply have paid for the occasional callgirl. But Lake wanted to enjoy 'girls as young as twelve' and women who would literally be enslaved to him, doing all of his household chores as well as attending to his sexual desires. He'd decided to satisfy these requirements by kidnapping a young woman and training her 'by a combination of painful punishments...and minor rewards' to do exactly as he asked.

During these fantasy-based years, Leonard remained obsessed with guns and it's likely that he was responsible for many local break-ins where weapons and dynamite were stolen. In his fantasies he was the survivor of a holocaust – but in actuality he only held down menial jobs.

Blocking out reality, he turned more and more to sexual fantasies in which he was king, and when he met Claralyn Balaz, invariably known by her nickname of Cricket, he was able to make this fantasy a reality for a while. Cricket, a teacher's assistant, shared his love of domination and submission and the two enjoyed an orgasmic sadomasochistic relationship. Cricket was also bisexual so Lake got to photograph her and him with other women in bed. She enjoyed being whipped and he enjoyed doing the whipping so it was the perfect sexual relationship.

In other areas, though, the two weren't an exact match as Lake was much brighter and better travelled. Cricket was also very much her own person so couldn't be psychologically dominated – yet psychological domination was crucial to Leonard Lake.

Nevertheless, she soon joined him at The Ranch and they continued to live together, albeit arguing frequently, until he was caught stealing from his employer. The pair of them sold up and fled the area, relocating to a tiny hamlet in California, where Lake became a volunteer fireman.

A second marriage

In September 1981 Leonard married Cricket, the marriage witnessed by a female friend whom they'd both had sex with. Shortly afterwards the friend, who had been living with them, moved out, unable to endure the couple's constant immature bickering. In the same time period, November 1981, Leonard was contacted by one of his survivalist acquaintances. The acquaintance told him about a young man who was on the run from the marines. If they caught the twenty-year-old youth he'd be facing a court martial so he needed someplace reclusive to stay.

Lake agreed that the marine could live with himself and Cricket and do all of their chores in return for bed and board. He welcomed the slender, five foot seven Oriental. Their new lodger was surprisingly strong, keen to help out, and interested in survivalism. His name was Charles Ng.

Charles Chitat Ng

Charles was born on 24th December 1960 to Oi Ping and Kenneth Ng in Hong Kong. (The surname is pronounced Ing.) The couple already had two daughters, Alice and Betty. Kenneth's two-bedroomed house accommodated his immediate family plus both grandmothers and two aunts.

Kenneth Ng was a camera salesman who worked long hours to provide for his children. He fed them well and took them on social outings. Unfortunately he also demanded that they excel academically. He punished all three when they failed to meet his lofty expectations but Charles was the least interested in his schoolwork so his father beat him frequently with a stick and a cane. The child tried to run away to escape the torment, but his father merely tied him up and continued the abuse. Even his wife tried to intervene, but Kenneth Ng was determined to beat intelligence and conformity into his only son. He was a Christian who had managed to persuade a Catholic school to take his children so he felt especially vulnerable when Charles got low grades, fearing he might be expelled.

Failed by the humans in his life, Charles turned to animals for comfort. But his relatives eventually killed his pet chicken and ate it for dinner. They also gave away his pet turtle, complaining that it smelled. He had doted on both creatures and was desolate to lose their love.

The sensitive little boy was desperate for some kind of release. He found this briefly at age ten by stealing explosive chemicals from the school chemistry lab and setting it on fire. As a result, he was sent to a behavioural psychologist. The psychologist noted that the boy was an arsonist and school bully. He was also an embryonic sex offender, having written obscene letters to one of his female teachers. The hurt that he had internalised throughout his junior years was beginning to turn outwards, seeking revenge. In real life Charles had absolutely no power – he wasn't even allowed to choose his preferred style of haircut. But in his fantasies he could rule supreme.

Charles Ng began to draw pictures of women being ill-treated and he hit and mocked other children, copying the abuses inflicted on him at home.

At age fifteen, he was expelled for stealing from another pupil and his parents briefly sent him to school in England. There he resided with an uncle. But (according to Charles's mother) the man didn't feed the boy well, his room was cold and he was visibly afraid. Noticing all of this on a visit, his mother took him back to Hong Kong. From there, the family sent him to San Francisco to live with another relative and complete his schooling. Bored and unable to make friends with the other students, he quit college at eighteen.

The increasingly immoral teenager was driving erratically one day when he hit a telephone pole. Rather than report the incident, he fled from the scene and was subsequently arrested. But the charges were dropped when he joined the Marines on 12th October 1979.

Charles remained a solitary figure who was sometimes picked on by the marine corps racists, but he made some acquaintances who shared his love of martial arts and weaponry. Unfortunately after two years service, he stole a cache of weapons worth eleven thousand dollars, was caught and faced a court martial. He was determined to escape but was kept under heavy guard.

Ng now deliberately injured his leg in order to get moved to the hospital. When his guard fell asleep, Ng left the building. Early the following morning he made his way to Leonard Lake's remote home.

He now assumed the name of Charlie Lee, probably after Bruce Lee, his childhood hero. (One of the most prolific teenage killers profiled in *Children Who Kill* changed his name to Bruce Lee as he was equally in awe of the martial-arts-trained actor and his films.)

For the next few weeks Lake and Ng talked about survivalist methods and about their shared love of weapons. Charles did most of the cooking and they shot rabbits for the pot. He saw Lake as a father figure and was impressed by his invented tales about active service in Vietnam, but Charles continued to steal for kicks, getting caught whilst taking a bed sheet from a department store. Cricket, whom he genuinely seemed to care about, bailed him out.

Arrest and divorce

After six months of living with Leonard and Cricket, Charles Ng was re-arrested for his military crime. The police also arrested Leonard Lake because of his illegal store of weapons. Out on bail, Lake fled the area before his case could go to court. He now moved from one cheap motel room to another, funding himself through petty theft and by selling recreational drugs, primarily marijuana. But Cricket was unwilling to live as a fugitive so moved back to her parents' house. She would continue to sleep with her husband – but, as usual, he also slept with other women. The marriage quickly disintegrated and Cricket asked for a divorce, which was finalised in November 1982.

Donald is murdered

Distraught at the loss of his friend and his wife, Leonard Lake may have looked for an easy target to take his anger out on. He invited his brother Donald, whom he'd always hated and frequently talked of killing, to stay. He shot the brain-damaged man – who he believed was his mother's favourite – through the head whilst he was asleep, then used his driving licence and other personal papers as fake ID.

Leonard continued to have a sexual relationship with his ex-wife. Chillingly, she shared in some of his confidences about acquiring sex slaves. In a video they took of themselves in March 1983, they discussed luring female victims to Lake's house. (Karla Homolka did the same thing with her lover Paul Barnardo before and after killing their sexual slaves.)

By now Cricket was working as a teaching assistant at juvenile hall and pictures of young girls who had been photographed there would later be found on Leonard Lake's walls.

Lake also kept a diary which showed his deteriorating mental health, writing that he planned to build a network of bunkers stocked with food, weapons and unconsenting women. He added 'After the nuclear bombs have rained from the sky, these women will become breeders. The future of the race is in my loins.' It's telling that those who see themselves as the great white hope for the future are always under-achievers like Leonard Lake rather than modern Einsteins...

Yet Lake wasn't all bad, writing in his diary that he was disgusted when his former friend, Charles Gunnar, whipped one of his children. Lake later looked after these children for a while and appears to have treated them well.

Murdering a friend

1983 is also the year that Leonard Lake is believed to have murdered Charles Gunnar. He'd grown tired of his former friend who was now grossly overweight and cruel to his family. Lake shot him dead in May, recording the murder in his diary as 'Operation Fish'. Later, in an unusual act of generosity, he returned Charles Gunnar's car to his wife – he'd keep or sell his subsequent victims' belongings. He would take on Charles's identity for a time, telling strangers that his name was Charles Gunnar and proffering the bearded man's ID.

Plans for a chamber

Leonard Lake also filled up some of his time in 1983 and 1984 by writing letters to Charles Ng. The young marine was now serving an eighteen- month sentence at Fort Leavensworth's high security prison for his earlier weapons theft. Leonard sent Charles numerous photographs of nude women and the artistically-gifted Ng responded by sending sketches of animals.

Then Leonard Lake upped the ante by sending details of a bunker with an inbuilt torture chamber that he wanted to build for imprisoning unwilling females. This inflamed Ng's already sadistic fantasy life and he told another prisoner of what he and Lake would like to do.

Still a fugitive, Lake now moved to Humboldt County, rented a rural retreat and began to actually build his fantasy bunker. Then he decided that the area wasn't secure enough and moved house again, this time to Blue Mountain Road, Wilseyville in the Sierra Nevada foothills. He was still sleeping with Cricket and with various other women – but consensual sex would never be enough for him.

Reunited

Bored and increasingly dissatisfied with making a modest living from drug selling and theft, Leonard was delighted when Charles Ng reached the end of his military sentence.

In July 1984 the younger man joined him and they prepared to turn their vicious fantasies into reality.

Perhaps because he'd successfully shared his cruel thoughts with Leonard Lake, Charles tried them out on his new co-workers when he found employment. He often made comments like 'no kill, no thrill' and 'daddy dies, mommy cries, baby fries.' As a result his co-workers wanted nothing to do with him and he was left out of social events.

But he and Leonard continued to socialise and to seek out control-based sex. Lake even hired an escort girl – but when she entered his hotel room, she found a naked Charles Ng there. Ng raped her whilst stabbing his knife into the pillow beside her head. Meanwhile Leonard Lake took photographs of the sexual assault, telling her afterwards that he and his friend usually killed their victims, but that he liked her so would let her live.

Strangely, it may be that Ng's first known homicide victim was male, as a man matching Ng's description answered a contact ad from a gay man. The slim Oriental promptly shot the man dead. He also shot the man's flatmate whom he encountered as he fled the apartment, but the wounded man lived. Perhaps this was a rehearsal for the family they were about to abduct, for Ng must have known that the local police were less interested in gay murders than in heterosexual homicides...

A family of victims

Later that same month, on 24th July 1984, Lake or Ng phoned to answer an ad from a camera man called Harvey Dubs who was selling duplicating and recording equipment. They arranged a time when one of the men would call and Harvey's wife, Deborah Dubs, answered the door. It's most likely that Charles Ng pointed a gun at their one-year-old baby Sean and abducted the child in a travel bag, warning the couple to do as he said. Leastways, witnesses saw Ng struggling with two heavy bags as he left the house, got into a car driven by Leonard Lake and was hurriedly driven away. Presumably he left the adults tied up and gagged, returning for them when the coast was clear. The following day the deadly duo returned for the Dubs' valuables, ignoring neighbours who tried to talk to them as they left the house laden with bags.

What followed has been pieced together from bones and torture apparatus found at the scene and from comments previously made by Charles Ng. It's likely that Lake shot Harvey Dubs then imprisoned his wife in Lake's house for his and Charles Ng's sexual pleasure. She was almost certainly bound and repeatedly raped, just as the men's future female victims would be. Eventually, when the couple tired of her, she was probably shot or strangled. Ng later told a prisoner that he'd strangled one-year-old Sean himself, but he'd subsequently tell the court that the babies were murdered by Leonard Lake.

A male victim

Four months later, on 14th November 1984, the men located their next known victim, thirty-nine-year-old Paul Cosner. Paul was selling his car and told his girlfriend that he'd found a 'funny looking' potential buyer. He left the house to meet this buyer and was most likely shot dead in the car – the front seat was later found to be splattered with blood and there were bullet-holes at head height in the upholstery.

Soon Leonard Lake was seen driving the vehicle and it was later found on his property, as was Paul's identification. Both men were bearded so looked vaguely similar, and Lake was always looking for new identities in order to stay one step ahead of the law. Paul's glasses were eventually found buried on Lake's land.

Another three victims

Leonard celebrated Christmas 1984 with several members of his family, videoing himself telling them about survivalism as he served the sprouts. But by 5th January he was hunting for humans whose possessions he could steal. That day he went to a hotel he'd previously stayed at and hired several workers to help out on his property, namely twenty-six-year-old Cheryl Okoro, thirty-eight-year-old Maurice Rock and thirty-five-year-old Randy Jacobson. None of them would ever be seen alive again. It's unclear exactly how Cheryl and Maurice met their deaths, but the police later found a photo of Cheryl in handcuffs taken at Lake's house. Only parts of her neck bone and a partial leg bone were found at the property.

Maurice Rock's skull was found in the vicinity, as was Randy Jacobson's corpse, which had been encased in lime. Some reports state that he was killed by ingesting cyanide, whilst others suggest that the Vietnam veteran died of a gunshot to the head.

Another two male victims

Two weeks elapsed, then on 19th January 1985, Ng asked his co-worker Cliff Peranteau if he wanted to earn some extra money during a trip to Tahoe. Cliff agreed to go with him. The two had argued earlier about work and Cliff had called Ng a 'godamn Chinaman.' Ng would later allegedly tell a prison friend that he held a gun to the weeping man's head, making him chant Chinaman again and again before he shot him dead.

Cliff's belongings were later found at Ng's apartment and at Leonard Lake's remote house. Whilst Ng was at work, Lake removed Cliff's motorbike from his property and subsequently sold it, and Ng or Lake wrote to a friend asking them to send on his paycheck to a PO box address, a box which belonged to Leonard Lake. As Leonard didn't work, he used his victims' cash and belongings to fund his lifestyle. In contrast, Charles Ng had a reasonably paid job with a removal firm and saw killing as recreation, as fun.

Five weeks later Charles Ng was ready to kill again. This time his victim was co-worker Jeffrey Gerald. On 24th February, Charles phoned twenty-five-year-old Jeff several times, asking him to help a friend in Stockton move house. The pay was good and Jeff took a bus to meet Charles. He was never seen alive again.

Three days later someone took most of Jeff's belongings from his apartment. One of his books was later found at Ng's apartment whilst his guitar was found at Lake's house.

Another family of victims

For the next few weeks, Leonard Lake was busy building his concrete bunker to contain future female victims. When it was finished in mid-April 1985, he casually asked his nearest neighbour, nineteen-year-old Brenda O'Connor, and her boyfriend Lonnie Bond to come over for a meal. She hesitated so Leonard sent Charles Ng over to ask them more formally. They then said yes.

Lake and Ng probably killed Lonnie Bond senior early on in the proceedings, despatching him with a single shot to the head. His corpse would later be found buried on the property, gagged and bound. Lonnie and Brenda's baby, also called Lonnie, probably perished at Charles Ng's hands.

Leonard Lake videoed Brenda not long after her abduction, her hands cuffed behind her back. He tells her that he's given her baby away to a family, then hints that the infant may be dead and also suggests that she'll never see her boyfriend again. He tells her 'You will work for us, you will wash for us, you will fuck for us.'

There's a great deal of emotional cruelty when he says that the baby will have to live without her, that she wasn't a fit mother, that he's gone to a better home.

Seconds later the sexual threats begin as he says 'Jeans off. Panties off and everything else. Shove them down.' When he was doing this consensually with Cricket it was erotic, a consensual powerplay fantasy – but now it's an ugly criminal act.

Ng rips open her blouse then produces a knife and cuts her bra off. He tells her that he and Leonard Lake now own her. She explains that she feels nauseous but Lake's only response is to show her a whip. Later he softens slightly and tells Ng to bring her a glass of water. He explains that he's about to rape her but that his friend Charles is going to shower with her first. Ng adds 'Make sure you're clean before we fuck you. That's the house rule.'

The men persuade her to remove the rest of her clothes then she's seen walking dejectedly to the shower. As usual, they benefited financially out of the abduction, stealing Brenda's boyfriend's car, wallet and worldly goods.

Another male victim

With Brenda imprisoned (or already murdered) and Lonnie dead, it was easy for Lake and Ng to lure Brenda's lodger, Robin Scott Stapley – always known as Scott – to the property. We may never know the exact sequence of events, but it's likely that they gave him a headstart then hunted him down like a deer. Leastways, the pathologist speculated that he'd been shot in the shoulder and the leg whilst running, and then shot again through the head and the mouth at much closer range. The pistol had been shoved down his throat so viciously that it had broken all of his teeth. He was gagged, his hands cuffed behind his back and his ankles tied with rope before being buried inside a sleeping bag. Ng would later claim that this bondage was added after death to make it look like a biker kill.

Both Lake and Ng dug his grave, and his still-bound body would later be found buried at the property in Blue Mountain Road. Lake and Ng then went to Scott's house and took all of his clothes and various other possessions. Lake would offer up Scott's driving licence when he was finally arrested by the police, and Scott's camera was in Charles Ng's bag when he was eventually overpowered by security guards in Canada.

In early May, a blood-covered Leonard Lake answered the door to an insistent gas meter reader. He told the startled man that he was butchering an animal, but it's more likely that he was sawing up a body, for many of the bones later found on his land were sawn through.

Further victims

Twenty-three-year-old Mike Carroll was one of the next victims to disappear. He'd spent time in prison with

Charles Ng so was happy to receive a telephone call from his former acquaintance. But afterwards he vanished from work and home. Then his girlfriend Kathy Allen, whom he'd been living with, received a phone-call at the supermarket where she worked. She left hurriedly and would never again be seen alive in the outside world.

But she was kept alive at Leonard Lake's retreat for several days as he videoed himself and Charles Ng abusing her. On the first film they shot, they tell her that her boyfriend is dead. This is doubtless true as Mike's bullet-ridden body would later be found buried on Lake's property.

Lake and Ng soon went to Mike's house and removed his belongings. By now they had pots of coins hidden all over the property, but they were endlessly greedy for more. Both men were possessed of a criminal mindset where they'd rather steal even when they could afford to buy.

Meanwhile Kathy was videoed in bondage, stripping at the men's command. Charles Ng helps to remove her clothes then pushes her into the shower.

In another scene she's seen rubbing lotion into Charles Ng whilst he tells her 'don't forget to...get my ass, too.' Two other videos show her putting on lingerie which Lake has chosen. He tells her 'I'm having a little war within myself between what I want to do and what I think I should do.' He admits that he wants to whip her. Later, according to cartoons drawn by Charles Ng, he would.

Suicide
The men had benefited financially from their numerous kills, but greedy as always, they now went out on another stealing mission. They drove to a large hardware outlet in

southern San Francisco on Sunday 2nd June 1985. Despite the heat, Charles Ng wore a parka. He used its bulk to hide a vice while stealing it from the store.

But a clerk had seen the theft and Ng was apprehended in the car park. He fled, leaving Leonard Lake behind. Lake gave a false name and offered to pay for the vice but the manager called the police.

Interviewed in the car park, Leonard Lake said that his name was Robin Scott Stapley, but a quick check showed that Robin (officially missing) was twenty-six whilst Lake was clearly in his forties. A search of Lake's car revealed identification belonging to Charles Gunnar, Lonnie Bond and Paul Cosner, the latter also reported missing. Lake was handcuffed and taken into custody.

Realising that the police would return to his house and find the bodies, he asked for a glass of water. He wrote a note to Cricket saying that he loved her and forgave her, then took out the cyanide capsule he kept hidden about his person and swallowed it.

Leonard Lake swiftly slid into unconsciousness. Taken to hospital he remained in a coma. His mother rushed to his side. The police also informed Cricket that her ex-husband was on the critical list – but her first response was to go to the house and remove various items. She and Leonard's mother also cleaned the place up. She'd later tell police that she'd removed a dozen videos of herself in sex scenes with Leonard Lake, and they were able to verify this.

Lake remained on a life support for three days but it was apparent that he was brain-dead so his mother gave permission for the hospital to switch the support machine off. Charles Ng was now left to face the music alone.

The body farm

At Lake's retreat, the police soon found the bunker with its soundproofed chamber. On the wall was a list of instructions that the captive slaves must follow to avoid punishment. They located the video of Kathy Allen and Brenda O'Connor being mentally tortured, stripped and threatened with rape. Kathy was also shown lying on a bed on her stomach wearing only denim shorts. Lake referred to these women as the M Ladies after Operation Miranda in John Fowles' *The Collector*, his favourite novel since adolescence. The police found a copy of the classic text at the house.

In the videos both Lake and Ng threatened their captives with death so the authorities began to dig up the property. Almost immediately they found a male corpse which was never identified and other male corpses which were. Several had been gagged with ball gags, handcuffed and tied up then shot. Some also had plastic bags tied tightly around their heads. One had been strangled with a rope whilst another had been poisoned with cyanide, the poison with which Lake had killed himself.

Charred internal organs were believed to come from a child aged three who was never identified. They also found badly burnt handcuffs – and Charles Ng had drawn screaming men being dropped into a fire.

The horror continued when pieces of Kathy Allen's and Brenda O'Connor's teeth were found. Another woman – Cheryl Okoro – was identified through DNA taken from a single bone, all that remained.

The main house also held its share of horrors, with bindings attached to all four corners of the bed. The dressing table was filled with bloodstained lingerie and there were blood spatter patterns on the walls and bullet-holes in the plasterboard. There were further bullet-holes in the living room ceiling and in the kitchen floor. Visitors had entered the house having been offered refreshments, only to suddenly face the worst horror of all.

Arrest

Charles Ng now phoned Cricket and told her what had happened and she drove him to the airport. He immediately fled to Canada where he had relatives. But it was clear that the FBI and Canadian Mountain Police were after him so he couldn't stay with them. Instead, he fashioned himself a survivalist's retreat in a campsite and was based there for the next five weeks.

But again shoplifting was to be his undoing, as on 6th July 1985 he was seen stealing a large quantity of tinned food and biscuits from a supermarket. A security guard tried to arrest him and Ng promptly shot him in the hand. He was overpowered and taken into custody where he lost control of his bowels, tried to hang himself with his soiled underpants and was put on suicide watch.

When interviewed, Charles Ng began to talk but his comments were unsurprisingly self-serving. He said that Lake had murdered various men (some of whom were Ng's co-workers, men who Ng hated) and that Lake had also murdered baby Lonnie Bond. Ng said that Lake had done so by strangling the child, with Ng exhorting him not to let the baby suffer. But the police had drawings that Ng had made of babies held above woks or being put into microwaves and they knew that one of Ng's favourite comments was 'baby fries'. Ng had also told a friend that he had 'roasted a sucker' (his word for a child or baby) and that Lake had released some of the adult victims into the forest then tracked them down like prey, but Charles Ng had allegedly told his friend that he'd done most of the executions as Leonard didn't enjoy that side of things.

Trials and tribulations

The only known crime which Charles Ng had committed in Canada was the shoplifting and wounding charge. For these he was sentenced to four and a half years in a Canadian prison. America now fought desperately to get him extradited so that he could face a multiple murder charge. Meanwhile some of the other prisoners shoved their waste products under his door and made it clear that he was beneath their contempt.

But officially Canada didn't want the alleged torture-murderer to die, the radio announcer who broke the story stating 'We Canadians feel strongly enough about barbaric state-sanctioned executions to have outlawed them in our own country.' Meanwhile the American public were left to reflect on the barbaric executions which Charles Ng had allegedly carried out...

Ng spent his time in a Prince Albert penitentiary studying law, knowing that he might face extradition. He also practiced his martial arts and was so good that he terrified the other prisoners. He told one that he would kill a guard in order to remain in Canada and he told another that he liked to torture women with pliers.

Numerous legal hearings took place but eventually, six years after his arrest, the Canadian government agreed to send Ng back to California. The date was 26th September 1991. He then stayed in Folsom prison in Sacramento to await trial. There, Ng did what Lawrence Bittaker had done, filing endless complaints against the prison and legal system. He also asked to represent himself then changed his mind and tried to sue his legal team for malpractice. Incredibly, these legal arguments kept the system busy for another seven years and it was 26th October 1998 before his trial began.

The prosecutor opened with the words 'Leonard Lake and Charles Ng turned Blue Mountain Road into a mass graveyard, a killing field.' She showed the videos of Kathy Allen and Brenda O'Connor being psychologically tortured and stripped. The defence countered with 'He is charged with murder, not cutting off people's clothes, as offensive as that might be.'

On trial for twelve murders

But Ng wasn't just on trial for the murders of Brenda O'Connor and Kathy Allen. He was also the defendant in the murders of Harvey Dubs, Deborah Dubs and their one-year-old son Sean Dubs, Paul Cosner, Jeffrey Gerald, Michael Carroll, Lonnie Bond senior and his baby Lonnie Bond junior, Robin (known as Scott) Stapley and Clifford Peranteau.

The court heard that he'd been unexpectedly absent from work during the first three days of Kathy's captivity. He'd worked alongside victims Jeffrey Gerald and Clifford Peranteau who'd left town to meet him and immediately disappeared. And, after stealing from the military, he'd spent time in prison with Mike Carroll. Documents and electrical goods belonging to many of the victims had been found at Ng's apartment. Moreover, he had admitted to helping his friend bury Robin Scott Stapley and Lonnie Bond, though he'd suggested Lake had done the actual killing. Ironically, Robin had been a founding Guardian Angel, trained to peaceably end trouble whenever possible – but he'd had no chance against the gun-toting survivalists Lake and Ng.

Ng denied that he'd had sex with Brenda O'Connor, saying that he felt sorry for her. He added 'I tell Lake this is getting too far.' But he couldn't explain why he stayed with Lake if the man's actions were so repugnant to him. At another point in the trial he said that he loved Leonard and Cricket, that his family had been unable to show him closeness and that the couple were the family he'd never had.

Charles Ng's earlier military theft was also brought to light. An investigator for the marines had asked him why he stole the weapons and he'd replied 'I feel I am a born fighter and I like to...perform clandestine operations... My main feeling is just to prove that I can do something nobody did before.'

Immunity

Some of the evidence against Charles Ng was circumstantial, so in an effort to find out more from Cricket, the authorities gave her immunity. She then took the stand and admitted that she'd gone along with Lake's capture-a-sex-slave fantasies (and had even suggested that a woman she'd fallen out with would make a suitable victim) but had never believed he'd put them into practice. She'd given him several hundred dollars to help build his bunker but apparently didn't believe he would put it to use. She added disingenuously 'I guess it just got out of control' rather than accepting that she'd had some choice in the matter. She had taken police to the burial site of one of the bodies, a man that Leonard Lake was believed to have killed.

Changing face of a killer

At the pre-trial hearing, Ng mainly presented himself as the subdued houseboy of the dominant Leonard Lake. Ng, who had been a slender but strong young man at the time of the murders, had now put on several stone in weight and looked passive, but the authorities knew that the martial arts expert could still be dangerous and they transported him from one venue to another in a cage inside a van. During the trial itself he was attached to a stun-gun so that he could be temporarily disabled if he attacked anyone in court. It was a fitting irony as he'd been shown in one of the videos threatening a captive with such a gun.

The evidence

Charles Ng presented himself as a harmless submissive to the court, but the prosecution pointed out the numerous links between him and many of the male murder victims, and the fact that he'd been seen using their documentation and belongings. He'd also been seen leaving the Dubs' family home after their disappearance and he'd made sadistic drawings of them.

The defence countered that Leonard Lake had harboured a deep hatred of women – and that he could have carried out the murders with Cricket helping him. Lake also had a motive for killing the men as he needed their documents to help him remain a fugitive.

It was certainly true that Ng hadn't murdered all twenty-six of the named victims. (He was only being charged with twelve.) He'd been in jail when Lake's friend Charles Gunnar had disappeared – and Lake had admitted in his diary to the murder. He'd similarly been out of the picture when Leonard murdered his own brother, Donald, the sibling he'd always loathed.

But there was a suspicion that Ng had killed other victims that weren't included in the known Lake-Ng deaths. He'd told Cricket about murdering a gay taxi driver and a Hawaiian woman. And he was heard on the tape to Brenda O'Connor saying 'You can cry like the rest of them.'

The court heard that thousands of bone fragments had been found, but that the bodies had been so extensively smashed up and burned that it was impossible to identify their source.

Charles Ng insisted on taking the stand in his own defence, explaining that he'd liked and admired Lake, who he saw as a patriot. He said that he'd gleaned victim details from the newspapers in order to draw the sadistic cartoons. He denied that he'd told another prisoner that he'd killed Deborah Dubs and her baby Sean, that he felt strange about killing the latter. He denied strangling Deborah whilst anally raping her. He also denied repeatedly sodomizing Kathy Allen at knifepoint and penetrating her vagina with a gun, all things that he'd allegedly told a prison friend. He denied hammering nails into Paul Cosner's hands and using a chainsaw on his genitals.

But he admitted to seeing the dead bodies of Robin Scott Stapley and Lonnie Bond, stating that Leonard had killed them. Ng claimed to have merely helped tie them up and had put a ball gag in the men's mouths so that they would look like biker murders. He'd also helped to bury them.

Ng's take on the crimes was that he'd done everything to please Leonard Lake but that he'd had no idea that anyone was going to be murdered. He said that the statement the prisoner in the next cell had made was all lies. But the prisoner had known that Kathy was dressed only in tights with the crotch cut out, information which wasn't made public and that only Ng could have passed on.

The verdict

The jury retired on 8th February 1999, returning on 24th February with their verdict. They found Ng guilty of eleven of the twelve murders. He wasn't charged with the murder of Paul Cosner as there was insufficient evidence. (Lake almost definitely killed Paul Cosner for his ID and his vehicle, but there was no way of proving that Charles Ng had played a part.) Ng immediately tried to fire his lawyers, claiming that they'd misrepresented him. His own legal work, plus the level of caution shown by the courts, made his trial the most expensive in American history.

Formative experiences

Prior to the penalty phase, the court heard that Ng's frequent beatings from his father had left him with a dependent personality, that he was totally in Leonard Lake's thrall.

Ng's father took the stand and admitted viciously beating him – but unlike most heavy-handed parents he said that he now recognised that this was wrong, that in his day they hadn't understood the dangers of corporal punishment. Throughout his father's entire testimony, Charles looked away. Ng hoped that the jury would accept that he had a dependent personality disorder, that he had been led astray by the more sexually experienced Leonard Lake. But the jury returned with the verdict that the victims' relatives longed for – death.

Charles Ng swiftly returned to his legal books and instructed his lawyers to file motion after motion. Still protesting his innocence, he was moved to San Quentin's Death Row.

An archaic system

It had taken thirteen years and over sixteen million dollars to bring Charles Ng to justice, years in which he'd mocked America's archaic legal system. Harrington & Burger, who wrote a book about the delays in the case, *Justice Denied*, noted that 'it is an extreme demonstration of the absurdities of our present justice system.' They explain that US lawyers and judges are 'victims of a protocol that rewards delay and punishes change' and recommend the French system which is swifter and has shorter sentences, uncomplicated by the possibility of parole.

Remembering the victims

Because the media concentrated on the videos showing Kathy Allen and Brenda O'Connor and knew that a similar fate had befallen Cheryl Okoro and Deborah Dubs, the Lake-Ng murders have largely been seen as sex murders. But the male victims also deserve to be remembered – namely Donald Lake, Charles Gunner, Maurice Rock, Randy Jacobson, Harvey Dubs, Sean Dubs, Paul Costner, Cliff Peranteau, Jeffrey Green, Lonnie Bond senior, Lonnie Bond junior and Robin Scott Stapley. A seventeenth body, that of an African male, was also found at the property and has never been identified. Nor has the three-year-old child whose burnt internal organs were found buried on the property.

Culpability

Charles Chitat Ng will never be paroled, but debate still continues as to his role in the Wilseyville murders. Many people have assumed that Leonard Lake was the cruellest of the duo, probably because Lake kept a misogynistic diary and built the concrete bunker. But Ng commented that Lake didn't enjoy the killing – and Lake himself admits on video that the better part of him balked at being cruel. In contrast, the teenage Charles Ng bullied younger children and, after becoming Lake's best friend, he produced increasingly sadistic cartoons.

A law enforcement agent who profiled both men noted that Leonard Lake wanted 'psychological domination' and enjoyed playing mind-games. In contrast, Charles Ng had an 'intense need to physically abuse as well as dominate females' and was 'considered to be the executioner.'

Journey into evil

In August 2000 Britain's Channel Five broadcast a documentary about the Lake-Ng murders called *Journey Into Evil*. The documentary said that by age seventeen Leonard Lake was suffering from 'retarded sexual development.' It discussed how Ng committed the murders 'for his amusement', the bodies being 'dismembered, burnt, crushed.' Police had spent eight weeks sifting through the ashes and bone fragments, their discoveries including baby teeth.

Psychologist Patrick Callahan acknowledged that Ng's father had been physically abusive whilst Ng's lawyer, Bill Kelley, said that if other adults asserted themselves, Charles would go into his shell and become almost childlike.

Ng had alleged that Leonard Lake gave Ng's name to the police in order to give Cricket time to escape or hide vital evidence. The documentary showed brief footage of Cricket in one of Lake's home videos saying that she'd like to 'do interesting things' with cute fourteen-year-old girls.

One of Lake's sisters courageously spoke on camera, admitting that Cricket had a lower IQ than Leonard Lake and was not particularly pretty. But Lake had such low self-esteem that he'd felt lucky to have her in his life, and 'he had no power in the relationship.'

Paul Cosner's sister Sharon was also interviewed and it transpired that her determination to find out what happened to her missing brother had helped crack the case. Paul had disappeared after placing an advert to sell his car but when his sister went to the police she was told that they wouldn't search for a missing adult, only for a stolen vehicle. Consequently, Sharon re-reported the car as stolen every month. (She also distributed flyers around the area and searched tirelessly for Paul.) When Leonard Lake was found driving Paul's stolen car – at the ironmongers when Charles Ng stole the vice – it ensured that the police arrested him. The rest is history.

Meeting Charles Ng

In February and March 2004, I interviewed Paul A Woods, a London-based researcher and writer. Paul was the originator of the *Journey Into Evil* documentary about the Lake-Ng murders. He provided me with some of the details found earlier in this profile including material which hasn't been broadcast before. Paul interviewed Charles Ng by phone in December 1998 and March 1999. In April 1999 he went to California to interview Charles in person, visiting him three times whilst he was on remand in Santa Ana, Orange County. Paul also interviewed forensic psychologist Dr Patrick Callahan and Assistant Public Defender Bill Kelley and met some of the victims' families.

He got close to the ranch house where Lake lived – it's now inhabited by a new owner who understandably wants his privacy. The bunker where the captives were held has been destroyed.

So what made Charles Ng talk to a British researcher in the visitor's enclosure at Orange County? 'He'd heard that there were these liberal English people around who were concerned about a British subject receiving the death penalty,' Paul says, adding that the director and producer of the documentary were opposed to capital punishment. And it's clear that Ng was desperate. 'He was literally fighting for his life over the weeks that we spoke.'

Paul's initial impression of Ng was that he was a quiet, almost submissive individual. He didn't feel at all threatened by him. Bloated through years of prison food and lack of exercise, he was a far cry from the powerful young man trained in martial arts whose favourite saying was 'no kill, no thrill.' Paul even found him quite personable – but Ng's occasional flashes of violent anger revealed that he still has a dangerous side.

'I appreciated the hours of his time he took to speak to me and his courtesy and politeness, apart from the occasional manic outbursts,' says Paul. But he has no illusions about the killer, adding 'His agenda was to spin-doctor the most horrific evidence as being something other than what most people assumed it was. To a large degree he succeeded in showing himself as a self-absorbed individual whose self-pity was far more real to him than the suffering of the victims.'

As the interview progressed, Ng talked about his childhood. Paul says 'He described being tied up by his wrists to a windowsill so that he couldn't move, and beaten with a bamboo cane. But he didn't make a great deal out of it.' He believes this is because Charles disagreed with his defence counsel who wanted to use his father's brutality in the penalty phase as a mitigating circumstance for the murders – but Charles Ng's stance was to deny responsibility for the murders and suggest that his childhood suffering hadn't helped turn him into a sadistic killer. He had to admit that he was guilty of kidnapping and torture but said that he'd only done this to please the only white man he'd ever liked, Leonard Lake.

Paul continues 'But the defence described him as a morbidly shy child who, during his early Hong Kong schooldays, would be beaten with a cane by his father when his teachers complained he didn't speak up in class – he was debased, devalued, told he was stupid.' This emotional cruelty continued for many years – Charles's sister Betty told the court that her father had thrown the boy's favourite toy in the rubbish bin, a doll that he loved as much as his sisters. Betty also admitted that Kenneth Ng had brutally disciplined them.

Paul adds 'Charles described how, after the first few beatings, he resolved not to cry. He reached a point, like many kids who suffer cruelty, when he wanted to become calloused, and to feel that no one could ever hurt him again.'

The prisoner, however, was mainly respectful when discussing his father, though he seemed to blame him for his disastrous deference to the wrong people (principally Lake) in later life, citing how he was never allowed to make any decisions for himself when he was at home.

The researcher found that Ng became a bully as he matured, occasionally picking on weaker kids and lashing out at them. 'But as for cruelty in its purest form, the way that we usually perceive it denotes sadistic tendencies, I don't believe there's any evidence of that in his early life.'

When his parents decided he'd brought shame on them and shipped him out to relatives in the West, he felt totally adrift, Paul explains. 'He's admitted at various times that he didn't get on with white people, and felt very much alone.' The seventeen-year-old was miserable in Yorkshire, even though he was accompanied by his sisters. 'I think it compounded the defensiveness and hostility he already felt. He was expelled for stealing from a classmate, and arrested for shoplifting from a department store in Lancaster.'

The researcher sees this as symbolic of the young Charles Ng. 'He was an unhappy kid who reacted to this sense of entitlement, this feeling that he should be a lot happier than he was, by stealing anything that he fancied. That was a constant throughout his life, and it's ironic that, given the enormity of the crimes he was convicted of, it should be his track record as a compulsive and very unsuccessful thief that brought him down.'

Some of the interview with Paul A Woods comprised of Charles Ng negating his reputation as a violent and dangerous prisoner and emphasizing his supposed deference to more dominant figures. 'He kept talking about the incontrovertible evidence of the case, but trying to put his own spin on it. I think it's emblematic of years of building up false hope in Canada, and that Ng will probably be trying to file appeals against his conviction up until the day he dies.'

Ng claimed that he took the rap for what Lake had done, telling Paul in his broken English 'Basically what happened is after Leonard Lake died, I think they try to build a case on the evidence that was left behind by him – the circumstantial evidence – and his wife, his ex-wife. You know, even though she didn't know much about the situation, because I believe Lake essentially compartmentalized all these things that he's doing during the time that we associate with him. And the fact that his wife is scared, and his lawyer, his criminal lawyer is probably try to encourage her to co-operate with the police in the sense of thinking that she'll have something to offer, to give that information to prosecute me... So that's the scapegoat. They want to blame me for everything Leonard Lake had done.'

Charles Ng continued: 'Even she had property where Leonard Lake was residing, and where the bodies and remains were found. And also equally, victims' property were found in her possession, in her house. That she was not charged with the crime and yet they used the same rationale – well, they turned it around, and used the same evidence essentially in my case, in my situation, and charged me with it...I'd say during that period of time between 1984-85 when – June when I was arrested – she was there for at least ten or twelve times.'

Despite Ng's protestations that he isn't violent, the items sequestered from his San Francisco apartment by the police in 1985 included rice flails (heavy batons joined by a chain), kung fu stars, a hollowed-out book with a gun compartment, a 9mm Walther PPK and Chinese-made ammunition. Equally damning was his obsession with sadistic cartoons.

Paul Woods, who has some of Charles's cartoons, notes 'there's a strong homoerotic element, an obsession with and simultaneous disdain for gay sex...and a strong element of pederasty.' (It's very likely that Ng shot dead a gay taxi driver who had fellated Lake when he was in his sexual experimentation phase. Leastways, an Asian answering Ng's description was seen to shoot the taxi driver at his home before fleeing from the property.)

Outwardly, both Lake and Ng were macho men who saw themselves as fugitives and survivalists. They lived off the land whenever possible and Lake's property included numerous DIY tools. So does Paul think that Ng took the vice for carpentry purposes or to use as an implement of torture, given that he told a prisoner he used pliers on his victims' genitals?

'I think that the intended use for the vice would have been a purely secondary matter to Charlie at the time he was stealing it,' the researcher says, 'Bearing in mind what a compulsive thief he was, he was probably just conforming to Leonard Lake's edict that "You never pay for anything unless you have to." But there's little doubt in my mind that all DIY implements at Ranch Apocalypse were used for torture.'

He believes that it's likely that Lake and Ng were in the South San Francisco area to procure another victim, but also stresses that the sex slaves were only a small proportion of the victims. 'Leonard was quite happy to commit murder over small amounts of money or to steal ID cards, and to torture the male victims when it might be used to obtain credit card or bank account information.'

Paul recollects some of the male victims' fates: 'Randy Jacobson – a thirty-five-year-old homeless Vietnam veteran from the Haight Ashbury area of San Francisco, and an acquaintance of Lake, paid for knowledge of the Blue Mountain Road bunker with his life. Shot through the head execution-style with a .22 handgun, his death probably prefigured the ultimate end faced by most of Lake's victims. As Ng was in military prison at the time, no one could ever stand trial for Jacobson's murder once Lake committed suicide.'

'Ditto two unidentified workers from the black area of San Francisco – perversely recruited despite Lake's overt racism from a barbershop frequented by black men. They were found decomposing in a trench near the bunker, below the bodies of Scott Stapley and Lonnie Bond (both of whom later died, along with his baby son, so that Lonnie's common-law wife Brenda O'Connor could be made a sex slave.) They were also probably shot dead to erase their knowledge of Lake's private sanctum.'

He also remembers some of Ng's likely victims. 'Cliff Peranteau and Jeff Gerald – mid-twenties workmates of Charlie Ng at the Dennis Moving Company, not seen since 19th January/24th February 1985 respectively. Though neither body was ever recovered, evidence that links them with Blue Mountain Road suggests they may have been lured in order to obtain their cash and bank account numbers – presumably obtained under torture – by the promise of payment for maintenance work and possibly by the lure of Leonard's homegrown marijuana.'

Ng had allegedly admitted to fellow prisoner Laberge that he had murdered Scott Stapley by smashing a handgun through his teeth and firing. Needless to say, it's a charge that the convicted murderer now denies.

This author had assumed that Leonard Lake alone murdered Paul Cosner, as Mr Cosner had told his girlfriend that he was going to meet a 'funny looking man' and if he'd been going to meet Ng he'd surely have said 'an Asian man.' But Paul Woods found evidence to suggest that more than one killer was involved. 'There were bullet-holes found in the front passenger seat of his car suggesting he was shot from behind while someone else drove. Charlie couldn't drive – literally every attempt he every made to learn ended in a minor crash. It suggests there were probably two other people in the car when Cosner was murdered.' He adds that, in this case there's no conclusive forensic evidence as his body has never been found.

So, if Paul hadn't known of the mutilated male bodies that *were* found on Lake's property and if he hadn't seen part of the M Ladies tape, would he have believed that Charles Ng, the soft-spoken man sitting across from him in the prison visitor's enclosure, was capable of so many torture-killings?

'I can only answer in the words of one of my old drinking buddies, the great noir novelist Derek Raymond: "One does not describe evil by giving it six fingers." In other words, assess people by their actions rather than their outward demeanour or whatever opinion they have of themselves.'

But he's aware that others are understandably more swayed by appearances. 'One of the jurors in the Ng trial was torn by mixed emotions. She was traumatised by the M Ladies tape, and Brenda O'Connor's pleading for her baby, but found it difficult to reconcile the chubby, docile Charles Ng in the courtroom with the vicious young man on the video monitor. But of course, Ng dispelled any residual sympathy she might feel when he violated her sense of security by telephoning her at home, shortly before the jury returned their recommendation of death.'

Paul adds: 'I think Ng, who seems to have a short fuse since his abused childhood, certainly had a proclivity toward crime, although he would never have made a successful criminal. He was also violent, and it's quite possible he committed murders of his own accord that were acts of male-on-male aggression. But in terms of the wholesale mass murder and sex murder that Lake initiated, I think Charlie was an associate. Dr Callahan called him *the sorcerer's apprentice.*'

He continues: 'Ng lacked the cruelty to pets which so many embryonic serial killers display, and Leonard Lake mocked him for being unable to discipline the household's new puppy. Ng was actually sentimental toward animals, in a manner that I've often found with men who are violent but not necessarily sadistic.' He believes that Leonard Lake gave Charles Ng the freedom to become more cruel and that Ng's actions 'echo the pessimistic findings of Harvard University psychological researcher Stanley Milgram and his 37% of those experimental participants in the late 1960s who refused, when confronted with disturbing faked evidence, to participate further in inflicting pain on human subjects. The majority (63%) continued to inflict staged but seemingly authentic electrical shocks.' He adds 'Whereas I don't feel Charlie Ng was predisposed toward sex murder, I believe he allowed himself to learn to like it under Leonard's tuition.'

Ng has used the excuse that 'I just have that personality that facilitates ...allowing him to dominate me in certain areas.' In reality, individuals who are dominated by one person often go on to dominate others. For example, Rose West was terrorised by her violent father – but she, in turn, went on to sexually abuse and beat her children. We can see this pattern in many violent families where the father beats the mother, the mother beats the children, the oldest children beat their younger siblings and the youngest child beats the family dog.

As Ng alleged he had no interest in the sex slaves, the former marine found it hard to explain why he'd waited in the cabin for more than six hours while Lake drove to San Jose to kidnap Kathy Allen. 'He told me to stay and wait,' he said weakly, 'So I did.' He added 'My relationship with Mr Lake is essentially one of respect and loyalty and looking after him.' He adds that he 'worried about him.'

Paul isn't convinced that Leonard reciprocated Charles's feelings. 'I don't think there's any doubt that Ng was regarded as a mere lackey by the man he believed to be his closest friend.'

The researcher thinks this is a classic case of *folie à deux* 'with both parties – particularly the shy socially-backwards Charlie Ng, whose formative environments had been all male – capable of more extreme criminal acts than if they acted alone.' He's aware that 'in Lake's case this was more a question of logistics than psychology.'

Despite the changing dynamics of their relationship, there's no doubt that Charles Ng became violent in his own right and remained so after Lake's death – after all, he shot the security guard who tried to prevent him leaving the Calgary supermarket with stolen goods. Paul notes that Ng skirted around this issue. 'If memory is correct, he may have tried to sell Dr Callahan the line that his pulling the gun was actually a form of attempted suicide.' The researcher found that 'Charlie could be very aggressive in the way he asserted that he was a passive compliant person.' In Ng's own words 'I become an easy scapegoat because I'm an associate of Leonard and because I'm an Asian, I just think they throw in all these stereotypes, you know – a general kamikaze type.'

He manages to ignore the fact that his kamikaze reputation began after he crashed his car, fled from a military prison hospital, terrorised kidnapped women on tape and drew incredibly sadistic cartoons.

But were the bondage cartoons which Ng drew in prison representative of the horrors carried out at Wilseyville? Paul's not convinced. 'Ng insisted to me that his cartoons were obvious satire and I basically concur. Which is not to say that I don't think he's a sexual sadist – that, by gradual degree in his case, and by personal inclination in Leonard's case, was a large part of what the Lake-Ng partnership was all about.'

He adds 'There's no doubt that these drawings have a strong sadistic element, in emotional as much as in sexual terms. But I think it's also true that, as Ng says, he was drawing them as a crude satire of the charges against him. What we can also observe, and what Ng would dispute perhaps until his dying day, is that they also exhibit a form of gloating over the victims and their bereaved families.'

'When Ng took the stand in his trial, his dismissive reference to the more savage examples of his cartoon art inadvertently allowed the prosecution to show further pieces to the jury. While Ng claimed they had "no basis in reality", and that he was "goaded" into drawing them for another prisoner, the darkly satirical images of Lake and Ng frying babies in a wok, microwaving them in an oven or smashing them against a wall inside a pillowcase contradicted his statement that the two prisoners never discussed the accusations of child murder against Ng.'

Paul thinks it likely that the babies were murdered – but not tortured, to gain their parents compliance – as soon as their mothers were seized by Lake and Ng. 'To reinforce this, there are also the partial confessions that Charlie made to the FBI when he was collared in Canada in 1985. These are relatively little known as they were ruled inadmissible at trial due to the fact that Ng started spieling before his legal aid attorney turned up and told him to button it. When questioned about the babies, he said that Leonard murdered them by holding them between his legs and breaking their necks with the flat palm of his hand. It's a hideous image, but it has the ring of truth. Ng claimed to play no active role in the child murders, but his admission to being present makes him at very least complicit in the murders of the Dubs and Bond families.'

And the cartoons hinted at further child deaths. 'Perhaps most ominously, one of the cartoons suppressed in court features Ng being decorated by the French Foreign Legion for "snuffing out" American babies, with four small coffins in the background. Ng was convicted of the murders of two children. He's never been linked with any other child murders, which is presumably why the defence argued against admission of this particular drawing. However, at Blue Mountain Road, the human remains included a liver identified as that of a three-year-old child. (Sean Dubs and Lonnie Bond Jr were both around a year old.) There was also a little girl's embroidered satchel buried in the dirt with other incriminating possessions.'

Perhaps remembering the full horror of his acts is what made Charles Ng's body break out all over in psoriasis sores after he was jailed – but it's more likely to be a result of stress from being kept caged and shackled in a moveable restraint.

So what are Paul's final thoughts about Charles Ng? 'Though I don't think he'll ever confess the full extent of what he personally did or didn't do, we know that Charlie must have committed some of the worst acts that a human being can. As a consequence, he's in the worst trouble that a human being can be in.'

He's aware that Ng still sees himself as a victim rather than a predator, for Ng has said 'You feel like a battered wife in a burning house because you're totally powerless to do anything.' He has also likened himself to a terminal cancer patient, desperate to try any potential cure – or, in Ng's case, make yet another legal appeal.

'There's no doubt that Charlie exercised moral choice in allowing himself to be dominated by a psychopath. Leonard took him where he wanted to go.' He notes that 'under California's definition of *common cause and plan*, Ng is an equal partner to Lake.'

Charles Ng was recently diagnosed as having hepatitis C, so it's a moot point as to whether the disease or his execution date will get him first.

8 ABSOLUTE BEGINNERS
MARLENE OLIVE & CHARLES RILEY

Children who kill invariably have appalling childhoods, often being physically and emotionally abused by their parents or primary caregivers. The following case is typical in that relatives, social services and friends knew that Marlene was going through hell and that she increasingly wanted to strike back. Failed by the adults in her life, she finally found a lethal weapon in the form of her lovestruck teenage boyfriend, who was willing to die – or kill – for her...

Marlene Louise Olive
Marlene was born on 15th January 1959 to Jeanette Ellen Etheridge, a nineteen-year-old socialite from an upmarket American family. Jeanette lived with her parents in Norfolk, Virginia and became pregnant by a Scandinavian sailor whilst he was on shore leave. The family worked hard to keep the pregnancy secret and when Marlene was one day old she was adopted by Naomi and Jim Olive.

Baby Marlene spent her first few months in Virginia. She saw little of her well-meaning overworked father but was overwhelmed by the attentions of her mentally ill mother. Naomi was so terrified of Marlene becoming ill that she wore a mask every time she approached the infant and hardly every took her out. Even when a neighbour invited them to dinner, Naomi took her baby daughter into a bedroom and kept her away from the other guests.

It was a theme which continued as Marlene grew up. Naomi would lock herself in the house, keeping her adopted daughter with her. As a result, Marlene missed out on all of the neighbourhood children's parties. At other times Naomi passed out from too much drink or prescription drugs, leaving Marlene alone with her thoughts for hour after hour. The only companionship in her day was when her exhausted father came home from work. Jim doted on Marlene, and the feeling was mutual. He brought her back gifts from every one of his work-based trips.

But Jim Olive's work was a bone of contention, as he lost job after job through working in unstable fields such as advertising, oil, and sales. He even attempted to become a novelist. Some of these jobs took him all around the country – from Miami to New Mexico – whilst Naomi stayed home with Marlene and became increasingly neurotic and insecure.

In 1964, when the Olives were living in Ecuador, Naomi was diagnosed as being schizophrenic and paranoid. Jim's response was to ignore the situation, simply telling five-year-old Marlene to be nicer to her mother. The child did what she could to cope with the unstable adult, but the strain took its toll and Marlene frequently wet the bed. Neighbours noted that Naomi didn't know how to show her love for her adopted daughter and treated her like a cross between a paid companion and a pet. By eight the little girl had become asthmatic and would often have difficulty breathing after Naomi berated her for coming home from school late or bringing home a friend.

Marlene turned more and more to the family's two maids for affection (domestic labour was inexpensive in Ecuador so most families were able to afford them) though she was assured of her father's love and attention when he finally got home from another long day at work.

Meanwhile Jim Olive put a brave face on things, writing upbeat letters to friends and relatives around the country and attending the 8am mass every Sunday at his Episcopal church. Occasionally he took Marlene with him but he was never accompanied by his wife who rarely left the house. She had now begun to drink whisky in large quantities and kept obsessively buying – and counting – towels, convinced that the maids were stealing them.

At ten Marlene discovered that she was adopted and wondered aloud if that was why Naomi didn't love her. At eleven she admitted in class that she hated her mother – but the response was merely a shocked silence. That year she took part in a confirmation ceremony to please her parents but there was nothing heavenly about her life.

Naomi hated her daughter having any freedom, and once, when she did go to a friend's house, she sent the Ecuadorian militia to bring her home. On other occasions she'd start telephoning friends in a panic when the eleven-year-old was three minutes late.

Marlene's relationship with her adoring father was also increasingly unhealthy. He and Naomi had separate rooms, and Marlene would sneak into her dad's bed at night for a cuddle. He began to take her to work-related social events (he was a brilliant networker) where he introduced her jokingly as 'his other girlfriend.' A colleague referred to Marlene as 'his little mistress' and Marlene herself echoed this idea in her poetry, writing 'Long brown hair could entice any man/And her green eyes could light the night/Daddy couldn't have chosen any better.' There was nothing incestuous about Jim's love for his child, but by making her roleplay the part of his spouse he stole her childhood and contributed to her feelings of being overwhelmed by life.

On the upside, Marlene was sent to a private school in Ecuador and she had designer clothes and a beautiful home. She also had two cats and a dog to lavish love on. Denied normal friendships, at thirteen she played for hours with her dolls. She also wore her father's clothes when he was away on business trips, her confused way of remaining close to him.

Jim Olive was still convinced that he'd make a million, telling his friends that selling could lead to untold riches, or as he put it 'pie in the sky!' But his latest business venture failed, leaving the Olives close to bankruptcy. They said goodbye to their lovely house and servants and returned to the States.

Further upheaval

Now the teenage Marlene was enrolled at a state school in Terra Linda, California, where she looked totally out of place in her designer dresses and lacy cardigans. She was too shy to make eye-contact with the other teenagers, was bullied mercilessly, and simply didn't fit in. She was homesick for Ecuador and also desperate to escape her unstable mother, who had now begun to stockpile food. Marlene started to overeat and was teased for being plump – but with her green eyes and long brown hair she was still beautiful. She was also a gifted poetess, writing heartfelt lines such as: A broken sound/Cries out in pain/People hear/But they don't listen.' Her teachers saw that she was academically gifted but alternately angry and sad.

But to Naomi the teenager was a no good whore, and she told her so virtually every day. She shoved Marlene into a window, cutting her arm. On another occasion she threw a hot iron at the girl, scalding her wrist. During one argument, where Naomi insisted that Marlene was cutting celery 'the wrong way', Marlene retaliated, throwing the vegetable knife at her mother. Naomi's response was to tell Marlene that her natural mother had been a promiscuous girl who had given her away.

Physical symptoms

The emotional stress continued to take its physical toll and fourteen-year-old Marlene had stomach aches by day and was insomniacal by night. She developed a duodenal ulcer for which her GP prescribed sleeping pills and tranquillisers. For the first time, Marlene had a crutch to get her through the day, albeit one which ignored the reasons for her symptoms. She began to take the mood pills in increasingly dangerous quantities.

She turned to Buddhism in a desperate bid to escape reality, and when that didn't help, she experimented with the occult. Like many children from abusive homes she hoped to find a gateway to a better life than the one she currently endured.

But there was no escape and her hellish home life continued. Social workers recognised that Naomi was an alcoholic and that Jim's solution was to ignore Marlene's misery. They strongly advocated family therapy – but Naomi's own mother had spent most of her adult life in a mental hospital, leaving Naomi terrified of psychiatry. She started to have arguments with herself, taking the parts of four or five relatives. She would argue loudly like this every night, keeping Marlene from sleep.

Fostered

Marlene now asked to be fostered out, and social services found her an older couple who wanted a babysitter for their grandchildren. The first week went well, but by the second week Marlene sometimes didn't show up for her babysitting duties. On the third week she stayed out all night at a rock concert, and the foster parents returned her to the Olives. Marlene was in floods of tears.

An astute family worker noted 'Marlene is angry at her parents – legitimately so. She has a disturbed mother and an ineffective father.' Marlene's probation officer also recognised the family's problems, writing a pre-vacation report which warned 'This one could blow up while I'm gone.'

Marlene ran away on her sixteenth birthday and stayed with friends for several days. She spent most of this time in bed with stress-related stomach pains and cried constantly. Eventually the police brought her back. By now her father was so involved in his latest business venture that he didn't have the energy to mediate between mother and daughter so he took Naomi's side to keep the peace.

Marlene was devastated, then angry. For years he'd been her only ally, an island of sanity in a home wrecked by schizophrenia and alcoholism. Now he'd chosen a mad woman over her and Marlene wanted revenge.

Murderous fantasies

Her resources stretched to breaking point, the sixteen-year-old began to tell her friends that she longed to kill her parents, especially her mother. She half-heartedly put her prescription drugs in Naomi's lunch but Naomi noted that the food tasted bitter and refused it. Marlene then fantasized out loud about hitting her with a rolling pin. When she acquired a boyfriend, Chuck Riley, she told him she wanted to kill her mother but he hoped that it was just angry talk.

Charles 'Chuck' David Riley

Charles David Riley (known as Chuck) was born on 2nd May 1955 in Marin County, California, to Joanne and Oscar Riley. He came along within a year of their marriage and was their first son. Two years later the couple had another son and four years after that a daughter completed their brood.

Oscar had a business qualification and had originally taken blue collar work as an interim measure, but when he and Joanne started a family she had to give up work so Oscar retained his supermarket job. He worked hard to provide for his family and hoped that they'd grow up to have better employment opportunities than himself.

Chuck was initially a happy child who enjoyed going to the zoo with his siblings, going fishing with his dad or playing with his trucks in the backyard. He was an animal lover who kept an increasingly large number of rabbits and several types of pet bird.

When he started school, his mother went back to work as a nurse's aide and this helped the family finances. When Chuck was eight they moved to a bigger house in Arkansas, but the family weren't happy there and by the time Chuck was nine they'd moved back to California.

Unfortunately Oscar found it difficult to show his oldest son love -author Richard M Levine, who got to like the family, admitted that Oscar was 'rigid and authoritarian' – so Chuck became increasingly withdrawn.

Oscar would point out San Quentin prison to his children when they annoyed him and warn that they'd end up there if they didn't mend their ways.

Ironically, Chuck would indeed end up there, just as Marlene would end up becoming a whore, the label her adoptive mother gave to her. It's a pattern that crime authors see again and again. A dysfunctional parent constantly tells a child that he or she is potentially criminal, and the child grows up to believe he or she is bad and commits bad acts. Robert Thompson (who killed alongside Jon Venables and is profiled in *Children Who Kill*) was often shown a juvenile hall by his abusive father and told he'd end up in a similar establishment. At age ten he did.

Oscar continued, in a well-meaning but disastrous way, to discipline his children and Joanne tried to lighten the atmosphere by giving the children extra food.

By the age of four Chuck was piling on the pounds and by ten he was so overweight that his mother asked for medical help. But the doctor discovered that there was no biochemical reason for the boy's obesity – he was simply eating too much. He was given a diet sheet but found it difficult to adhere to, especially when Oscar (now driving a truck for a bakery outlet) brought home lots of cut-price baked goods.

Chuck also began to fail academically and his parents decided he should repeat third grade. He lost his friends and felt humiliated. A follower rather than a leader, he didn't know what to do with his days.

As he entered his teens his life improved when he became a paperboy. Unfailingly polite and dutiful, he won the regional paperboy of the year award several times. His prizes included statuettes, a trip to Disneyland and his photo in the local paper. He saved up his money from this part-time job, knowing that he'd eventually be able to buy an inexpensive car. Meanwhile Chuck plastered his bedroom walls with pictures of Corvettes, a symbol of freedom. In real life he was mocked at school for his obesity – but in his dreams he sped through the local streets in a sports car, winning everyone's respect.

By fifteen Chuck weighed over three hundred pounds and was described by Richard M Levine as 'an affection starved fat boy.' His doctor prescribed Dexedrine for weight loss but Chuck quickly began using it to give him more energy, a much-needed high. He began to experiment with other drugs, taking pot and coke and angel dust. He found that if he sold some of this on at a profit he could fund his own supply.

Desperate to make friends, Chuck sometimes gave his drugs away at cost or even for nothing. This gained him male associates but he remained a virgin, unable to get a girlfriend.

Still failing at school, the obese teenager increasingly played truant. He spent his days on a piece of scrubland, dirt-bike riding and target shooting. Guns made him feel powerful, in control. He also used drugs whilst out on the scrubland, snorting, smoking and mainlining them.

When Chuck quit school he made a living through selling marijuana and coke. Though still a shy, gentle boy he tried to adopt the persona of a tough drug dealer, boasting to friends that he supplied the country's top rock groups with whichever drugs they wanted, and at sixteen he fulfilled one of his dreams by buying an inexpensive second-hand car.

Chuck was trading outside the high school one day when he saw Marlene sitting crying on the grass, lost in the middle of her first bad acid trip. For the lonely and inadequate boy, it was love at first sight.

The love slave

Marlene wasn't impressed by Chuck's looks or personality – but she loved the drugs that he could offer. For the first few months of their relationship she used him as an unpaid driver, drug supplier and a companion to take her to rock concerts. Meanwhile Chuck at last had the motive to lose weight. He slimmed right down, bought some fashionable clothes and treated himself to a good haircut. Marlene began to see him in a less embarrassing light. Their relationship would never be healthy as she was too damaged by her upbringing to maintain a quality relationship, seeing people as users or objects to be used.

It was immediately obvious that Chuck fell into the latter category, as he told Marlene he was happy to be her slave. She took him at his word, and would bite him during arguments. She also continued to bite herself when her fights with her increasingly disturbed mother got especially bad.

Marlene took Chuck home to meet her parents and their initial impression of the polite boy was understandably favourable. Chuck honoured Marlene's embarrassingly early curfew and talked to Jim Olive about the older man's work.

For the first time, the sixteen-year-old girl had an ally that she was allowed to bring home – but she was a child who'd grown up with discord. She now recreated it by going on numerous shoplifting binges, during which she would drop items into Chuck's pockets or bags. Soon he was impressing her by walking out of the region's top boutiques with several outfits in his arms. The couple wore some of the clothes they stole but left others in their wrappers in the boot of Chuck's car, the main reason for their spree being a combined need for excitement and an adolescent cry for help.

Juvenile hall

Inevitably, the couple were caught and sent to juvenile hall. Chuck was swiftly released (to be sentenced at a later date) but when the social workers saw the extent of Naomi Olive's mental illness, they wanted to keep Marlene in the hall for her own wellbeing. Marlene, though, was homesick and begged to go home. Meanwhile the police had discovered a sawn-off shotgun in Chuck's bedroom so he was also charged with possessing an illegal weapon. His law-abiding parents were shocked.

As is often the case, both families blamed the other. The Olives told the authorities that Marlene had been fine until she met Chuck. It was a lie as Marlene had been wetting the bed and self-harming for years, and had asked to go into foster care before she even met Chuck. Similarly, the Rileys said that Chuck's problems stemmed from being in love with Marlene – but Chuck was addicted to food and drugs and had dropped out of school before he even met his first girlfriend.

Naomi now made it clear that Chuck wasn't good enough for her daughter because his mother was a nurse's aid and his father drove a truck. (This was ironic as the Rileys were industrious whereas Naomi had spent most of her life watching television in her bedroom.) The Olives banned the working-class youth from their home and when he tried to sneak in to spend time with Marlene, Jim Olive threatened to kill him. The teenage boy believed the threats and stayed away.

Sometimes Marlene sided with her parents and finished with Chuck. On two of these occasions he tried to commit suicide by overdosing. On both occasions he slept for twenty-four hours but suffered no other harmful effects.

Grounded at home, Marlene's life became even smaller than before. Determined to have some freedom, she started playing truant from school in order to see Chuck. Often they rented a motel room and Chuck was so lovesick that he kept every motel room key as a souvenir.

For the first time, sixteen-year-old Marlene had control over someone, a sense of power. She masturbated with Chuck's hunting knife, acted out bondage and rape fantasies and even shared him sexually with another girl. Each act drove her previously-virgin boyfriend into paroxysms of desire. Chuck's love for her intensified and he told everyone that he would do *anything* for Marlene.

He even believed her when she said that she was a witch who had special powers. She gave him a bracelet through which she could allegedly communicate with him, and talked about casting spells.

A fatal argument
But the spells made no difference to her unendurable home life. Naomi continued to shuffle about in an alcoholic daze during the day, calling Marlene a whore whenever the teenager wore fashionable clothes. Jim's response was still a curt 'try harder to support your mother.' Marlene continued to steal, was arrested again and faced spending

the summer in juvenile hall. Worse, her father said he was going to send her away to boarding school and that she'd never see Chuck again. The tension escalated and her father began to shove and slap her, whilst Marlene alternately wept and shoved him back. When she became so desperate that she spoke to a counsellor, Jim Olive berated her for washing their dirty linen in public. He dressed neatly for work and went to church every Sunday, determined to give the impression of an orderly life.

On the final day of Naomi Olive's life – Saturday 21st June 1975 – she argued again with Marlene, calling her adoptive daughter a tramp and telling her that her biological mother was a slut, that the apple hadn't fallen far from the tree. Moments later, the familiar insults still ringing in her ears, Marlene phoned Chuck and told him that it was time to shoot Naomi dead.

Chuck went off to collect his Ruger which he'd lent to a friend. Meanwhile Marlene fetched a hammer and stood over her sleeping father, but she couldn't bring herself to kill him. Instead, she waited until he woke up then agreed to accompany him on a supermarket shopping trip. She left the door unlocked, knowing that Chuck would sneak in to kill her sleeping mother. Leastways, that's the statement he originally gave to the police...

What's certain is that someone battered a hammer into the woman's skull, blood spurting everywhere. The hammer cut so deeply into the bone that it was hard to get it out. Naomi was still alive so her attacker stabbed a steak knife into her chest, but the badly injured woman continued to gasp for breath so her killer picked up the pillow and began to smother her.

Meanwhile Marlene's father returned to the house and

found his dead or dying wife in the bedroom and Chuck trying to hide behind the furniture. He lunged at Chuck – and Chuck raised his pistol and fired four times at the man in what he later claimed was self-defence. Chuck then apologised to Jim Olive's corpse and attempted to shoot himself but Marlene knocked the gun from his hand.

Afterwards, the nineteen-year-old was in shock – Naomi's death rattle was still audible – but sixteen-year-old Marlene reassured him and gave him beer and Valium. They made love then took her parents' jewellery and credit cards. Both teenagers scrubbed the blood from the walls, Chuck still feeling shaken but Marlene triumphant. For the first time in her life, she was free.

The lovers went shopping, briefly visiting Chuck's brother at the shop where he worked as an assistant. Chuck was incredibly pale and Marlene didn't say a word.

After a Chinese meal and a trip to the cinema they returned to the death house, put Naomi and Jim's corpses in the family car and drove to the nearby China Camp State Park. The couple then set the bodies alight in a barbeque pit, returning hours later to restart the fire until there were only ashes and small pieces of leg bone remaining. Ironically, the double homicide would become known as The Barbeque Murders, reduced to a sense of place. The location would eventually be listed jokily in tourism articles, the moniker giving no clue to the murders' desperately sad cause and effect.

For the next week Marlene and Chuck led a schizophrenic life. She frequently phoned home and half-expected her father to answer. When business colleagues called for him, she dutifully wrote down their messages. But on one occasion she left the house at a run, convinced that she was in the presence of her mother's 'ghost'. Chuck also managed to blank out the horrors of the double murder, taking a job in a waterbed factory. His employers were incredibly impressed by his dedication which went beyond his allocated assembly-worker tasks and extended into impromptu customer sales. The teenager talked endlessly to his family about the merits of waterbeds and no one had any idea that he and Marlene were responsible for two ugly deaths.

But after a week of relative normality, one of Jim's colleagues reported him missing. Marlene was taken into police custody and told the police that she'd had visions of her parents' deaths, that they'd been killed by burglars. Later she decided the murderers were hired gunmen or Hell's Angels. Later still she decided they'd simply gone on holiday. A child psychiatrist found her neurotic but sane, intelligent but deeply troubled. Eventually one of her friends told of the woodside cremation and led them to the remains.

Meanwhile Marlene appeared completely remorseless for the crime, writing a note to Chuck which said 'I have no guilt feelings about my folks. None. Neither should you. Relax...'

But Chuck couldn't relax. When he heard that Marlene's friend had led police to the Olive's ashes, he blurted out 'I did it...Marlene made me do it. She kept begging me and begging me for months, telling me to do it or she wouldn't love me any more.' He wrote her letters, telling her how much he cared for her and signing them 'your slave'. He spent hours reading his Bible, his father telling him that there would be an ultimate judgement in an afterlife.

In turn, Marlene – who also remained fixated on the

supernatural – reaffirmed her love for Chuck. Like most damaged people she loved the *idea* of love and found that absence made the heart grow fonder. She read the tarot and they showed her that she'd marry Chuck and have his children. 'You're my man for the future' she wrote to him.

Sentencing

But Marlene was sent to juvenile hall where she soon reinvented the past, referring to Chuck as 'the man who killed my parents...broke my heart.' She soon found herself a new boyfriend. At other times she cried for hours, wailing 'I want my daddy' and she wrote poems for her parents as she still believed in life after death. She had nightmares, spoke in her sleep and continued to wet the bed. She also lost her puppy fat and increasingly relied on her sexuality to make friends.

Chuck, for his part, remained in love with Marlene for many months. Meanwhile his heartbroken father tried desperately to support him, visiting often and writing his oldest son long, supportive letters. Oscar couldn't believe that Chuck had battered Naomi's skull in with a hammer, as the image didn't fit with the gentle, animal-loving boy he knew. He – and Chuck's friends – suggested to Chuck again and again that he was covering up for Marlene. Eventually the easily-led boy seems to have believed their version and he decided to publicly revise events.

Chuck now said that Marlene might have killed Naomi so his lawyers arranged for him to be hypnotised and he told a story of finding the older woman close to death. He said that he'd walked into the room to find a bloodspattered Naomi with a hammer embedded in her skull so he'd pulled the hammer out to spare her further pain, whereupon he'd heard Jim Olive walking down the hall. Panicking – after all, Jim had previously threatened to kill him – the teenager had attempted to hide but had been confronted by the horrified husband. He'd then shot Jim Olive dead in self-defence.

Chuck told this story several times under hypnosis and also passed a lie detector test. The implication was that Marlene had killed her mother and Chuck had killed her father – but the jury found him guilty of the double homicide and he was put on San Quentin's Death Row.

The case will always have unanswered questions. Why did a boy who was a first class shooter kill Naomi Olive with a hammer rather than with his gun? But it's unlikely that Marlene carried out the murder as she returned from a visit to the supermarket with her father to find Chuck in the house as planned. Marlene would have had to bludgeon Naomi then immediately accompany her father on his shopping trip – but she had no blood on her and witnesses said that she looked glum but not traumatised.

Update

In December 1977 Chuck Riley's death sentence was commuted to life imprisonment. He's still incarcerated at the California Men's Colony in San Luis Obispo, where he spends most of his time keeping fit, telling author Richard M Levine that he 'takes one day at a time.' He has been turned down for parole ten times, his chances hampered because he claims to have only killed Marlene's father rather than both of her parents. The hypnosis may have fixed this second version of events in his mind and he genuinely believes it to be true.

Chuck has led an exemplary life in prison and has been

made a clerk, a job which has various privileges. Nevertheless he admits the regime is still very dull. He jogs and lifts weights to help pass the time and is determined to leave prison in a healthier state than when he went in.

Marlene escaped from the California Youth Authority to be with another female juvenile offender, recently released, with whom she'd fallen in love. But the relationship soon ended and Marlene fled to New York where she acquired a pimp and became a high class callgirl. As she herself once said, she was called a whore so often by her adoptive mother that it felt the right 'career' move for her. She was captured a few months later and served out the rest of her sentence, being released in 1980 at the age of twenty-one.

She visited Chuck once in prison and they spoke for five hours, but the fact that he was bettering himself by studying psychology and keeping fit seemed to unnerve her. In contrast, she lacked goals and her life was continuing to go downhill.

For the next few years she injected heroin and used speed, sometimes supporting herself through prostitution, then in 1986 she was arrested on suspicion of being part of a San Fernando Valley counterfeiting ring. Found guilty, she was sentenced to five years in jail.

In 1992 she was sent back to prison for Los Angeles-based financial fraud, and in 1995 she was convicted in Santa Monica for possessing a forged driving licence. Then in February 2003 she was arrested in Bakersfield for passing bad cheques, being in possession of stolen property and being under the influence of drugs.

In October 2003 she was found guilty of these charges and sentenced to another seven years, namely two years for cheque forgery, two years for having two prior strikes and one year each for three prior convictions. The girl originally sent to juvenile hall as a troubled teenager will be middle-aged when she is next released.

9   THE MISFITS
LUCAS SALMON & GEORGE WOLDT

Lucas Salmon was a sexually repressed timebomb and George Woldt a wife-beating misogynist with a rape fantasy. Separately they were bad news. But together they were twice as dangerous, and an innocent girl died a terrible death at their hands.

Lucas Salmon

Lucas was born on 9th February 1976 to Robert and Gail Salmon. He was their third child and they swiftly went on to have two more. Both Christian Fundamentalists, they named their children after Biblical characters and believed in the maxim of spare the rod and spoil the child. They beat the boys with a paddle whenever they thought that they weren't living up to the ideal of the perfect family. Lucas grew up awkward and shy.

When he was around age seven, his fifteen-year-old babysitter alleged that Lucas's father had performed oral sex on her. Robert Salmon didn't deny the charge and the babysitter declined to take the matter further but rumours of sexual inappropriateness spread throughout the small Californian town where they lived. Shortly afterwards Robert allegedly had inappropriate contact with another teenage babysitter. At this stage he decided to leave Gail and start a new life. He left the family but often attended church with them on Sundays so that his peers wouldn't know that he was separated and seeking a divorce.

When Lucas was eight, his father remarried and moved

to Oregon amidst rumours that he'd sexually harassed a local woman. Lucas retreated further into his shell and, though academically capable, he was an outsider in the playground. Meanwhile his mother increasingly suffered from depression and withdrew into herself.

When he was twelve, he and one of his brothers went to live in Oregon with his father. By now his father's relationship with his second wife was failing and Bob was dating another woman. When Lucas was fifteen, his father announced that he planned to divorce for the second time.

Two years later he uprooted the family again, moving them to Colorado Springs. Bizarrely, he wanted to be near a Fundamentalist Christian programme which believed that marriage was for life no matter how unhappy. Ironically, his mother and her second husband had also moved to the area.

Seventeen-year-old Lucas attended yet another school and kept up with numerous church activities. He was told that sex before marriage was wrong and that everything in life is predestined. When he questioned this he was given the anti-intellectual reply 'ours not to question why.'

The unhappy schoolboy took an after-school job at a telemarketing firm. Employees noticed that he stared hungrily at the women and that he was difficult to talk to. But he got on well with one equally strange telemarketer, George Woldt.

George Woldt

George was born on 8th November 1976 to Song-Hui and Bill Woldt. Song-Hui was Korean and the family spent the first few years in Korea, living near the American army base where Bill worked. Two years later the couple had a second son, but by then the marriage was already a troubled one.

Song-Hui loved both of her sons in her own way, but she became obsessed with little George's appearance and would groom him for hours. If his posture didn't look quite right to her, she would hit him and shout at him. Bill also beat both children and was twice investigated for child abuse.

His work eventually took him away from Korea and the Woldts moved to Germany and then to the States, eventually ending up in Colorado. His wife's mental health continued to deteriorate and Bill Woldt coped by turning to drink. By now George was ten and was standing up to his mother, telling her that her punches and slaps no longer hurt.

George was an exceptionally intelligent child, but his unhappy home life eventually led to a deteriorating academic performance. Other pupils and teachers noted that – like many abused children – he sometimes went into a fugue state.

He moved into his teens and his compulsions increased: he feared germs and cleaned obsessively. He also screamed back at his parents and was becoming as violent as them.

Psychotic

When George was fifteen, his mother was sectioned under the mental health act and diagnosed as suffering from clinical depression and psychosis. It was noted that his father's side of the family included schizophrenia. George was now so enraged at his treatment that he told friends he wanted to kill his mother, and said that all women were bitches who were only to be used for sex.

At seventeen, after one beating from his father too many, George went to the police but they decided not to take his complaint any further. He also told his teachers about the beatings but again nothing was done.

Obsessive compulsive disorder

Lacking control of his external surroundings, George Woldt became desperate to control his appearance and spent hours grooming his hair and fingernails. Steve Jackson, who wrote an insightful book on the subject, *Partners In Evil*, noted that George was so desperate to look symmetrical that if he had a sticking plaster on his right hand he felt compelled to put another on his left.

He left school and got a job in a telemarketing company which is where he met his eventual co-killer Lucas Salmon. Lucas saw George as sexually experienced and worldly and George saw in Lucas a friend he could both easily impress and dominate.

For the next three years, Salmon and Woldt would meet up whenever Salmon was in Colorado and would sometimes share a house, albeit usually with one of Woldt's many girlfriends. The rest of the time Lucas was away at Christian college or doing missionary work overseas.

Marriage

In February 1997 George married his latest girlfriend Bonnie who by now was six months pregnant. She already had a three-year-old son from a previous marriage which had ended in violence. The three of them lived together in Colorado Springs.

A lethal combination

Soon Lucas moved in with George and his wife, and the two men began to sit up at night watching violent pornography together. Christianity forbids sex before marriage, so at twenty-one Lucas was still a virgin. It also forbids masturbation so he was incredibly frustrated, and he couldn't repress his desires with alcohol as fundamentalism forbids that too. Like most people who try to be 'too good' he eventually rebounded in the opposite direction and began to make obscene comments to female workers. He was promptly fired.

But his misogyny continued. One night when George got into an argument with a teenage girl, Lucas Salmon screamed that she was a bitch. He watched George have sex with a woman who he wasn't married to and doubtless wished that it was him.

Eventually he broke his religious code and masturbated into a pair of woman's shoes, having bought several pairs to feed his fetish. He also began to fantasize about having sex with girls age nine and ten.

By now George Woldt was equally adrift as he'd been fired from his work for making nuisance phone-calls. His marriage was unhappy and he was sometimes so threatening towards his wife that she feared for her safety. Neighbours heard him hitting her throughout her pregnancy. He got another job in a store but was fired for poor timekeeping. He was increasingly lost and full of rage. He began to hint to various male acquaintances that they should abduct, rape and kill a female. Some thought that he was joking, but others realised that he was serious and they kept away. But when he talked to Lucas Salmon about his plans, Lucas didn't appear quite as shocked or recriminatory. Rather, he stayed close to George who he now thought of as his best friend. Over the ensuing weeks, George elaborated on the abduction scenario until Lucas agreed to join in.

Several practice runs

The young men began to stop their car for various females, offering them a lift. All refused and hurried away. But it was enough to keep their fantasy going. They elaborated on how they would rape and sodomise a girl – then kill her so that she couldn't tell. Lucas kept a knife in the front seat of his car in order to subdue any suitable female. He also kept his Bible in the back.

On the afternoon of 29th April 1997 they went out driving with George at the wheel. He deliberately knocked a young woman off her bicycle then rushed out of the vehicle to help her. Lucas followed and they asked her how she was. George offered to drive her to hospital but she sensibly declined, an offer that probably saved her life. Lucas Salmon kept the woman's sunglasses as a masturbatory trophy. They would later be found in his chest of drawers.

Immediately afterwards the men relived the fantasy, knowing how close they'd come to finding a teenage victim. Next time, they decided, they'd strike in a quieter area after dark.

Rape and murder

That night they succeeded in their obscene plan, driving around until they spotted a car driven by a lone female. They followed her a short distance until she drew up close to a block of flats and parked. Jacine Gielinski, a twenty-two-year-old student, was going to her boyfriend's flat for a meal and was only a few yards from his apartment block when the deviant duo pounced.

One of the men grabbed her around the waist and the other took hold of her legs and started carrying her towards their vehicle. They tried to gag her with a hand but she freed her mouth and began to scream.

Jacine did everything right, fighting to stay in the street rather than be taken away to a quiet location. She also made lots of noise, attracting several onlookers – but none were close enough to physically intervene in time. As they raced towards the scene, the twenty-two-year-old was still holding onto the car door, trying to prevent being pushed inside it. But Lucas Salmon battered her arms, George Woldt punched her in the face and they forced her into the back seat, whereupon Salmon drove away at speed. An alert witness was able to jot down their car licence plate and reported it to the police.

Within the hour the authorities knew that the abduction victim was Jacine, as her handbag containing her identification had fallen to the ground during the struggle. They also ran checks and found that the car she'd been kidnapped in belonged to Lucas Salmon. The registered address was Lucas's dad, who was able to give them George Woldt's address.

Meanwhile, Salmon & Woldt took their weeping victim to a car park and George Woldt raped her on the back seat. He then traded places with Lucas Salmon who also raped her. Then they pushed their naked victim to the ground and discussed who would stab her first.

They decided that Salmon should make the first incision so he cut her throat then Woldt cut equally deeply into the same area. As Jacine was still breathing, they discussed how to hasten her death. Salmon stabbed her in the chest and she screamed. He handed the knife to Woldt who stabbed her near the heart, but she kept moving. They each stabbed her again, noting dispassionately that she was automatically lifting her hands to cover the wounds.

Finally, Salmon attempted to smother her with her own shirt whilst Woldt cut one of her wrists twice. The unfortunate young woman was still gasping for breath so George Woldt stamped on her stomach to force the air out of her. Her combined rape and murder had lasted for a horrifying hour.

Woldt now suggested removing her vagina and hiding it so that there wouldn't be a forensic trail, but Salmon came up with the idea of forcing earth into her vulva. They'd hoped to contaminate their semen – but some viable traces remained.

Afterwards they drove around for a while, smoking cigarettes and talking about the crime. Both believed that a place called hell existed and they decided they were destined to go there when they died.

Confession

By the time law enforcement arrived at George Woldt's house, the men had returned and gone to bed. When woken, they at first said they'd been playing pool till late but after further discussion Salmon reluctantly allowed them to search his car. The officers found his Bible plus a blood-spattered shirt which had belonged to Jacine. The men had used the garment to wipe blood from their hands and had unthinkingly thrown it into the boot. They also found the blood-stained murder weapon which had bent under the strain of the multiple thrusts. Confronted with the evidence, Lucas Salmon admitted that he and George had stabbed a girl and left her naked body under a car in a parking lot.

Formally interviewed, it was apparent that both men were psychopaths. Neither seemed aware of the enormity of what they'd done and they had no interest in the victim. Rather, their response veered between indifferent (they ate heartily at the police station) and self-pitying.

Lucas Salmon later told his psychologist that 'it was God's will for Jacine to die...Everybody dies. It's not right to question God.' His victim was now 'with God' he said, and stated that he too would be in time.

Salmon's trial

In February 1999 Lucas Salmon pleaded guilty to kidnapping, sexual assault and murder. The jury listened with horror to details of the double rape, throat-slashing, multiple stab wounds and suffocation attempt.

The defence said that Lucas suffered from Dependent Personality Disorder and that he had the maturity of a five-year-old. They didn't add that Lucas was only easily led in directions which suited him – if George Woldt had told him to jump off a cliff, he'd doubtless have refused. He *wanted* to lose his virginity, and had admitted to others that murder had become part of the men's shared rape-fantasy.

The court heard that Lucas had been devastated when his father's name was sexually linked with several teenage babysitters. He was being told to lead a celibate life (or a married one, for the Bible says it's better to marry than to burn) yet was seeing other religious adults have sex outwith marriage. The anger had built in him until he took it out on an entirely innocent girl. He'd now reinterpreted the rape so that he referred to it as 'having sex' and he told his psychologist that he still felt sexual pleasure when reliving the act.

His parents were very supportive throughout the trial. His father said he partly blamed himself and his mother said she was praying that the jury would make a just decision.

Lucas Salmon was found guilty of all the charges against him, but one of the judges said that he didn't fit the profile of the usual killer on death row, so his life was spared and he was sentenced to life imprisonment without the possibility of parole. In truth, Salmon shared many killer traits – he'd been subjected to harsh corporal punishment throughout his childhood, had had a repressive upbringing, had various stepmothers and stepfathers and was moved around geographically.

Woldt's trial

Three years after the murder, on 3rd February 2000, George Woldt eventually went to trial. The jury heard that he was an embryonic sexual sadist with psychopathic tendencies. The defence countered by saying that he wasn't responsible as he had calcium deposits on his brain, alternately described as a bleeding lesion. He also had scars on his back from the numerous childhood beatings he'd received.

But apparently a bleeding lesion doesn't necessarily result in violent acts – and many of us survive abusive childhoods without going on to murder as adults. (Abused children who kill are, of course, much less culpable and so are more deserving of help rather than further punishment.) George was a twenty-year-old married man and killing Jacine Gielinski was a choice he made.

The court wanted to hear Lucas Salmon testify as to whether George Woldt had appeared mentally ill that night, but Salmon refused to take the stand. He was given an additional six months for contempt of court.

Incredibly, the defence suggested that Woldt had gone into a disassociative state during the rape and believed that the victim was mounting him. This made no sense as the crime wasn't a momentary mental lapse – Salmon and Woldt had planned for weeks to rape and kill, had even had practice runs at it. They knew exactly what they were doing and why.

Woldt had already believed that there was a deity when he carried out the rape and murder, but in jail he got religion big time. He told the jury that, if they spared his life, he would 'honour God.' He was subsequently sentenced to death.

Update

On death row, George Woldt lost weight and his boyish good looks began to fade. But his lawyers argued that his death sentence was invalid because it had been imposed by the trial jury rather than by the judge, something which has retrospectively been deemed unconstitutional. The Supreme Court agreed in February 2003 and his sentence was commuted to life imprisonment.

Lucas Salmon is also serving out his life sentence, though his defence team now argue that he is suffering from high-functioning autism and only killed because he mimicked the murderous actions of George Woldt. But

Lucas chose who to mimic – he could equally have copied the acts of a charity worker or a selfless carer. Instead, he copied a misogynistic rapist and took part in a cruel sex act which he admits he enjoyed.

Salmon may now pose a danger to gay prisoners. Whilst on the outside, he belonged to a Christian organisation which abhorred alternative sexual lifestyles and focused on helping gay people see 'the error' of their ways and 'convert' to heterosexuality. He still considers all forms of sex outwith heterosexual marriage to be a mortal sin.

JAMES DAVEGGIO & MICHELLE MICHAUD

Most of us read about torture killers and cringe at man's inhumanity to man – but the following couple were turned on by reading about the exploits of killer team Charlene & Gerald Gallego. Charlene, who helped her husband lure ten young victims to their deaths, is profiled in my book on female serial killers, *Women Who Kill*.

James Daveggio & Michelle Michaud didn't murder as many victims as the Gallegos, but they sexually assaulted seventeen females, one of whom was only twelve years old.

James Anthony Daveggio
James was born on 27th July 1960, the second son of Darlene and Jim Daveggio. He was born with additional tissue on his larynx, a congenital condition which would ensure that he'd have a husky voice throughout his life.

Darlene was only nineteen when James was born, but his twenty-three-year-old father had been married before and had deserted the three children from that previous marriage. It was a pattern which his father would repeat again and again. The four Daveggios lived in poor quality housing in San Francisco. Jim drove a truck for a living and money was scarce.

Shortly after James's birth, the couple moved to Santa Rosa and Darlene became pregnant again. But before their daughter was born, the Daveggios had split up. Jim swiftly remarried and started his third family – and James wouldn't see his father again until he was twelve.

When James was three and a half his mother moved her

three toddlers to Nevada and remarried, but their lives remained precarious. James almost died at age four when he set himself on fire whilst playing with matches, having to undergo extensive skin grafts to his shoulders and back.

Darlene's second husband found a job with a supermarket chain and the family moved frequently, living in four different parts of San Francisco in the next two years. Darlene contributed to the family by working nights in a biker bar. She was much more aggressive than her second husband, who just wanted a quiet life. When the marriage finally broke down, he would file for divorce citing 'extreme cruelty.'

By now James had started school but he didn't enjoy reading and wasn't particularly bright. He found lessons a chore and often ignored his homework. The teachers noted that he didn't try very hard – but his blonde hair and big blue eyes meant he was easy to forgive.

Troubled

James remained a deeply unhappy boy. One of his sisters would later tell author Carlton Smith that she'd heard her mother 'criticise Jimmy viciously, telling him to his face that he was worthless; but let anyone else say anything bad about Jimmy and she'd be all over them.' As a result, she always made excuses for him when he got into trouble at school.

One of the neighbours, an incest survivor who understood abuse patterns, would later become convinced that James was traumatised, either by abuse or by a parent withdrawing their love at a critical stage. He'd eventually show all four of the symptoms – not knowing right from wrong, hurting others, abusing alcohol and/or drugs and self-mutilation. James's sister noted that the more he was punished, the wilder he became. This is a common response to corporal punishment as violence never calms anyone down.

When he was eleven, the family moved again, this time to Union City, so James had another new school to cope with and new friends to make. At thirteen he led an eleven-year-old girl into the bushes and had sex with her – from this time on he was rarely without a sexual partner. By fourteen he had a twelve-year-old girlfriend, Cassie Riley, but within a fortnight the couple had broken up.

Six months later, Cassie – now thirteen – was found murdered. She'd been grabbed around the throat from behind, punched, stripped to the waist and held under water until she drowned. James was questioned by the police as were the rest of his class, but he said that he now felt indifferent towards Cassie, and he didn't particularly stand out as most of his classmates also claimed to have dated the unfortunate girl.

James's teenage years were as chaotic as his earlier ones. He dated constantly, getting at least one of his girlfriends pregnant. Darlene took the teenager to the clinic to get an abortion. On another occasion he stole a car from a girlfriend's mum to go joyriding.

His mother decided he might fare better living with his dad and managed to track the man down to an address in Pacifica. Sixteen-year-old James was sent to live there. His father got him an after-school job in a burger restaurant but he stole from his employer. Fired from that job, he began stealing from his father's house. He was sent back home but not to Union City, as whilst he was away the family had relocated to Pleasanton.

Strangely, James continued to idolise his dad yet the man wasn't an ideal role model – he'd marry at least four times and father eight children, abandoning several of them.

By age seventeen the troubled youth was playing truant along with some of the tougher guys in town. He began to steal cigarettes and the local police noted that he was easily led. He also increasingly loathed authority, and was suspended from school for calling one of the administrators 'a baldheaded mother-fucker.' He now upped the ante and was the driver in an armed robbery.

This time even his mother couldn't save him and he was sent to a juvenile detention centre in Almeda County. Afterwards he attended a continuation school in a middle class area where he felt increasingly inadequate.

A first marriage

When the going gets tough, the weak tend to procreate. At nineteen, Daveggio got his girlfriend pregnant and married her, becoming a father seven months after the wedding. But, too young to settle, he kept going out with his drinking buddies at night, cheating again and again on his teenage bride. He also faced charges of burglary and receiving stolen goods, charges which would later be dropped for lack of evidence.

A year later, whilst officially separated, the Daveggios had a second daughter. Now his mother stepped in and persuaded him to join the army, hoping that military training would straighten him out. The result was a disaster. Twenty-one-year-old James was naturally lazy and hated authority. Whilst at boot camp he deliberately stared at the sun until he temporarily blinded himself, knowing that this would obtain him a medical discharge. His army career had lasted three months.

A second marriage

The following year, now age twenty-two, James married for the second time. The couple had lived with his mother and stepfather whilst they were dating, and continued to do so after the wedding. James's new wife noted that he expected her to do everything for him – and that his mother encouraged his chauvinistic approach.

Eventually the couple got an apartment of their own, and James made money from burglary. He remained troubled and violent, starting numerous fights in bars in which he lost teeth and had his nose broken. He frequently added to his tattoos: many heavily tattooed men are psychopaths. He certainly fitted the profile, lying, abusing others and being unable to maintain a relationship.

Sexual assault

In the summer of 1984, whilst still married to his second wife, he followed a drunken woman out of a bar, brandished a pistol at her and demanded that she fellate him. The terrified woman complied then fled to the police but the alcohol had made her so hazy that she couldn't give them a coherent picture of events, and eventually charges against Daveggio were dropped.

Another child

By the following year – July 1985 – Daveggio's second wife was pregnant. This put him in a foul mood as he couldn't afford the children he already had.

Determined to make someone else feel as bad as he did, James Daveggio and a friend, John Huffstetler, picked up a woman in a bar and offered her a lift home. Once in the vehicle, the men attacked her and Daveggio made her fellate him. Afterwards Huffstetler fired his pistol, the bullet just missing the traumatised woman's ear. Thankfully a nearby police car heard the shot and pulled over the abduction vehicle. Both men were arrested, and Daveggio was bailed the following day. It was also the date that he turned twenty-five.

Surprisingly, he was only sentenced to one year in prison for this offence – and within four months was on a work release programme and going to church. His time would perhaps have been better spent pursuing educational opportunities as his application for early release was almost illiterate, with 'welfare' spelt 'welfear' and 'allowed' spelt 'aloud'.

His second wife now divorced him, so by the time he left jail in July 1986, he was young, free and single again.

A third marriage

That year – his twenty-sixth – he briefly studied mechanics at college and met his third wife there. But, as usual, he didn't stay the course and was unemployed by the time he moved to Sacramento with her and her eight-year-old daughter from a previous relationship. The couple married in April 1988 and within four months were expecting a baby. James blotted out this latest problem with drink and drugs. His third wife produced a son in 1989, but it would be 1993 before he had the sense to get a vasectomy.

Biker gang

In the Nineties he joined a biker gang – The Devil's Horsemen – and was in his element. For the first time he had a complete 'family', albeit a somewhat anti-social one. He went out biking with them and hung out at their HQ, drinking and playing cards. He also cheated on his third wife during this period with a woman who beat him up as often as he beat her up. She soon found that he could only sustain an erection if she allowed him to take a sadistic role.

By 1995 Daveggio's world was increasingly unstable. He was caught driving whilst drunk and continued to cheat on the woman he lived with. He dated increasingly young girls as they were more biddable and less likely to leave the relationship when he slapped them around. He began to experiment with methamphetamine which can lead to violent behaviour, something to which he was already prone.

By now James Daveggio was in such a state that he couldn't even hold down bar-tending jobs. His girlfriend threw him out but he immediately found another to give him accommodation. It was only a matter of time before he alienated her, as he had with numerous girlfriends and three long-suffering wives.

But in October 1996, whilst at a friend's house, he met someone as potentially dangerous as he was. She was a vivacious redhead, a month short of her thirty-eighth birthday, who would soon help him torture, rape and kill.

Michelle Lyn Michaud

Michelle was born on 7th November 1958 in Casablanca, Morocco, the first child of an army father whose work ensured that the family constantly moved around. By the time that Michelle was four, the Michauds had relocated to the USA. There, the couple had two sons, the growing family still moving from military base to military base.

It must have been painful for Michelle to make friends only to lose them again, so after a while she withdrew into herself. She had a high IQ and was a good scholar but clearly unhappy – photographs show her as a pretty girl with long red hair, big eyes and a tensely smiling mouth. She would later allege that her father put her and her mother down constantly, that no matter how hard she tried she couldn't please him. She would also later allege that she was sexually molested by an unnamed offender at age ten.

It's possible that by her teens Michelle was already a fledgling psychopath. She lied constantly and over-dramatised every situation. Acquaintances noticed that she always had to be the centre of attention. One of her sister's boyfriends would later suggest that she had multiple personalities.

When Michelle was fourteen the Michauds settled in Sacramento and had a fourth child, another daughter. Curtailed by her authoritarian father, Michelle remained unhappy. A visitor at the house saw him criticise her for putting two slices of meat on a sandwich rather than one. The teenager would misbehave in order to get her father's attention, then would become very apologetic and submissive, a stance that she would repeat with various men throughout her adult life.

By fifteen the situation had become so volatile that she was made a ward of court. She would later allege that these teenage years included sexual abuse by a close male relative. He was subsequently mentioned on the internet, but as the abuse hasn't been substantiated, he will not be named here.

Michelle also alleged that this relative put her to work as a prostitute at age sixteen – but she later said that she daren't tell him of her prostitution, so her statements are inconsistent. Everyone who knew her would allege that she often tried to shock in order to get attention. But on other occasions she showed that she was desperate to be liked and, to achieve this, would tell people what they wanted to hear.

At seventeen she dropped out of high school and did casual work for a time, but by nineteen she was clearly considering sexual services as a career, writing a fantasy entitled *My Escapades In A Massage Parlour* which includes the words 'It sounds exciting and very dangerous, going into a room with a stranger, having sex and getting paid for it.'

By twenty she turned her massage parlour fantasies into reality, working legally from a Nevada whorehouse. Well-spoken and with a great figure, she was popular with punters who wanted a high class callgirl – and her popularity increased when she was happy to talk dirty and offer a wide range of sexual services. She prospered at the ranch for several years.

At twenty-three she gave birth to a son and moved in with the baby's father. They also invited another woman to live with them in a *ménage à trois*. Two years later Michelle had a daughter by the same man. But the relationship became increasingly violent and she left.

For the next few years she alternately lived off welfare and prostituted herself. Meanwhile her son was suffering from increasingly acute emotional problems so she paid for him to have specialist education. Her daughter, like many female children from dysfunctional families, withdrew into herself. Michelle continued to find work in massage parlours, though the sex work may have led to gynaecological problems, as at age thirty-one she had to have a hysterectomy.

Arrest for prostitution

In January 1991 she was offering erotic relief in a massage parlour as usual when a man came in and asked for sex. In a sane world, she'd have complied and been paid and both parties would have gotten what they wanted. But the man turned out to be an undercover police officer who arrested her as soon as she slipped a condom on him. She was fined, told to keep clear of areas frequented by prostitutes and put on probation for three years. By now she was beginning to look increasingly hard-faced and hostile and had begun to beat up her boyfriends and punters. She rented a house close to her parents but mainly visited their house when her father was out.

The dutiful daughter

Michelle now lived an increasingly schizoid life. By day she went clothes shopping with her mother and at night she prostituted herself to a succession of sugar daddies. One septuagenarian punter paid her rent and another took her on expensive vacations. They also paid for classy furniture, jewellery and restaurant meals. But she didn't appreciate their generosity and had wild mood-swings, taking hormone medication to help keep her symptoms under control. Battling to survive in this difficult environment, her daughter remained insular and her son became so distraught that she had to get him a psychiatrist.

Michelle became involved in religion, going to the local Catholic church and helping run the Altar Society. She regularly had the priest to her house and even got a religious team to bless the building. They said that her daughter's Wizard Of Oz witch statue and her son's Darth Vader poster were satanic, so she obediently got rid of them.

She turned to lesbianism for sexual kicks, telling anyone who would listen that she didn't like men, that they were merely a source of income. But then she met up with James Daveggio and changed her mind...

A lethal combination

Michelle and James went to bed together the first night they met and she noticed that he couldn't sustain his erection. This happened on subsequent encounters but the couple simply used more alcohol and drugs to fill in the time. She took him to meet her family and he demanded that they respect her. Michelle fell in love for the first time in many years.

Separately, Daveggio and Michaud were bad news – a psychopathic sex offender and a man-beating prostitute, both of whom were unpredictable heavy drinkers. But together they were lethal. Daveggio wanted to dominate women and Michaud now helped him in this by going to bed with him and one of her prostitute friends. Within weeks they'd upped the ante by persuading non-prostitute women to sleep with them. This became the norm as Daveggio couldn't maintain an erection unless there were two women in the bed.

But, outside bed, Michelle Michaud could be desperately

conventional, making him say grace before they ate their meals and telling him that he was the 'man of the house.' They had some of James's children to stay and Michelle started calling James 'Daddy'. She sent him off to work with a packed lunch every day. For a few months she was able to maintain her fantasy of this man as the head of her new family, but he soon became hypercritical and increasingly abusive towards her. The police became concerned that Daveggio, a registered sex offender, was living with young children and he decided to move back in with a former girlfriend.

This relationship lasted for a few weeks and then he beat up the girlfriend incredibly badly and she threw him out. He promptly phoned Michelle to come and get him. He said that he'd start a new life with her and she was moved to tears.

Superstition

Religion hadn't made her happy so she now turned to another belief system, witchcraft, and began to form 'spells'. But the spells didn't work either and she took to using methamphetamines to feel better about herself. In the short term, they blotted out the pointlessness of her existence. But in the long term she needed more and more meth, and alternated between depression and paranoia.

The meth quickly stole her looks, making her lose several stone in weight so that her face looked gaunt and clapped out. One of her sugar daddies left and the other only gave her money when she contacted him, whereas before he was always showering her with gifts. She had to go on welfare and sell her furniture, eventually being evicted for non-payment of rent.

James Daveggio now moved back in with one of his previous girlfriends but Michelle had to sleep in her van or over at her sister's house, where she left her children. This arrangement lasted for a month, then James moved into Michelle's van. Unemployed and increasingly unemployable, they spent their time getting high and feeling increasingly enraged at a world they believed had failed them. As such, they identified with serial killing couple Charlene & Gerald Gallego. Charlene had lured young girls to her van, then both she and Gerald had sexually assaulted them.

Outlawed by the outlaws

In the same time period, someone stole The Devil's Horsemen's safe. They blamed the meth-addicted James, though he was adamant that he didn't do it. In part settlement, they took his beloved bike.

The media often describes such killers as loners, and the word has become a negative one. But, as Anneli Rufus points out in her landmark book *Party Of One*, serial killers do not wish to be alone. She notes that James Daveggio was popular in school and during his twenties, and only became a violent criminal when his biker gang rejected him because of his excessive drug use. Rufus notes that 'No one wanted him around except the ex-prostitute who was his accomplice.' He'd take her with him on the final ride of his life...

Sexual assault and rape

Daveggio and Michaud now embarked on a four month crime spree during which they would assault seventeen girls and women, torture-killing one of them. Many were girls that they already knew, who felt safe with Michelle around.

One girl was a teenage friend of Michelle's daughter so she had no cause to be alarmed when Michelle showed up and took her to another friend's house. There the middle-aged woman shared drugs with the teenager, making her feel grown up. But after the drug-taking, Michelle produced a gun and took the girl into the bathroom where she made her strip and ordered the teenager to fondle her – Michelle's – breasts. The girl said no, whereupon Michaud dragged her into the bedroom and watched as James Daveggio raped her. Whilst the underage girl was being raped, Michelle pleasured herself.

Later she brandished the gun at the child again and warned that she'd kill her if she ever told anyone. The girl complied, scared that she'd get into trouble with her family for taking drugs.

Coerced sex

Later that week they picked up a pregnant hitchhiker and James Daveggio began to make increasingly heavy passes at her. She said no several times but eventually gave in and the three of them had sex. They gave her their phone number and dropped her off in Sacramento then drove on, looking for another victim to humiliate.

Rape

On 25th September 1997 they reached Reno in their increasingly untidy van. Michelle booked them into a hotel paid for by her sugar daddy's credit card, and the couple took voluminous amounts of drugs and watched pay-TV. When the credit card reached its limit, Michelle turned a few tricks, money which James quickly lost through gambling.

The vacation was becoming dull – but rather than look inwards and identify what was lacking in their lives, Daveggio & Michaud now went cruising for another victim. They spotted a lovely young woman, Juanita Rodriguez, waiting for her boyfriend, and Michaud parked the van and Daveggio jumped out and forced her into the back.

There, as Michelle drove around, he forced the girl to fellate him, ejaculating on her face in an obvious bid to humiliate her. He also fingered her anus and made her do the same to him. Desperate to survive, Juanita lied and told the couple that she was the mother of a newborn baby. At this stage, Michelle became very interested and asked her various questions about the child. James then suggested shooting her dead – but Michelle saved her life, saying that it was too dark for the victim to identify him. She warned Juanita not to look back at the van when she was released.

The torture van

They let her go, but Daveggio kept fantasising about how much better it could have been if the victim was *tied* down rather than simply *held* down. He now purchased rope and a ceiling mirror and Michelle let him turn her van into the type of mobile torture chamber that Charlene Gallego had owned.

James Daveggio removed the backseats, only leaving the long bench which ran along the very back of the vehicle. They then put pillows on the floor. The couple also put together a torture kit of handcuffs, gags, a whip and customised curling irons. Still retaining her religious beliefs, Michelle left her rosary hanging from the van's rearview mirror. From now on they would copy their heroes, the Gallegos, with Michelle luring young women into a quiet location after which the couple pounced and sexually assaulted them.

Mother-Daughter incest

The couple returned to Sacramento – and when the Juanita Rodriguez assault was featured on television, Michelle proudly told her daughter and friend 'we did that.' The following month they again set off in the van. Wanting to stay close to her mum, Michelle's thirteen-year-old daughter begged to come with them. It was a decision she would regret as James Daveggio soon began to touch her intimately. When she asked her mother to make him stop, Michelle said to let him, that the sex would do her good.

The following week they took the same daughter and her twelve-year-old friend (the one whom the couple had previously molested) on a journey to Oregon where they sexually assaulted both underage girls. Michelle told her daughter that she'd often fantasised about having sex with her. Afterwards the couple gave the girls drugs to dull the pain.

Shortly afterwards Michelle's daughter went into foster care and her son went to live with her parents. She would never parent either of them again.

Anal and oral abuse

Michelle now lured another of her friends to a hotel room where James Daveggio jumped on her. Michelle handcuffed and gagged the screaming woman, then James sodomised her. They left the woman sobbing and bleeding from the mouth as one of James's punches had cut her lip.

Another abuse victim

In early November they asked one of James's daughter's friends to use drugs with them. She willingly got into the back of the van whereupon Michelle battered her from behind and James punched her. The couple handcuffed the teenager and Michelle jumped in the front seat and started the van.

James Daveggio then made the girl fellate him – but he lost his erection when she said that the act reminded her of being sexually abused by her stepfather. Daveggio wanted to see himself as the virile young lover, not a deviant father figure. This is ironic as Michelle had tried to force him into the mould of a loving dad. Michelle now parked the vehicle and performed oral sex on the victim whilst James masturbated to orgasm.

Fearing for her life, the girl promised that if they freed her she would tell the police that she was abducted by a teenage gang. They let her go and she initially kept her word.

The net closes in

The couple now moved in with Michelle's sister and enjoyed a few days of normality – but their father had heard that James Daveggio was a sex offender and he demanded the couple leave. They drove to a hotel in Lake Tahoe where Michelle passed several bad cheques and was arrested for fraud. She spent the night of 9th November 1997 in jail.

Just over a week later, a teenage girl told her father that

Michelle and James had sexually assaulted her. He promptly called the police. They interviewed the girl and also interviewed Michelle's daughter. Both tearfully admitted being raped and terrorised with a gun. They also told the officers that Michelle had said she and her boyfriend had raped Juanita Rodriguez in Reno. A quick check on the couples backgrounds showed that James was a registered sex offender and Michelle was a sex worker with a criminal record. The authorities had her van registration number – but they had no idea where she and Daveggio were.

Further incest

Meanwhile James took one of his daughters and Michelle Michaud to a hotel, whereupon James went to take a shower and Michelle said 'Your dad is going to have sex with you.' James Daveggio then performed sex on his teenage daughter for forty-five minutes, after which Michelle joined in by fellating Daveggio. The desperately unhappy child would later tell police that her father had first sexually assaulted her when she was only ten years old.

That night she wrote in her journal 'I have never felt so unprotected in my life' and admitted that she wanted to kill her father and her stepfather, who had beaten her. Like so many children who are casually conceived, she was completely failed by the adults in her life.

The couple dropped off the traumatised girl then went to a sex shop and bought a ball gag. It was early evening on 1st December and they'd alienated everyone they'd ever known and had no worthwhile plans for the future. This time they were going to torture and kill.

A torture murder

On the morning of 2nd December 1997 they were driving along when they spotted beautiful twenty-two-year-old Vanessa Lei Samson walking to work in Pleasanton. Michelle parked the van and James grabbed the girl and forced her into the back. Two men working on a roof heard Vanessa scream – but when one of them glimpsed Michelle behind the wheel he decided that it was just a mother forcing her teenage daughter to go to school. Because it's legal for parents to act roughly towards their children, he didn't react. The man would later feel terrible when he realised that he'd overheard an abduction which led to a horrible death.

As Michelle drove off slowly to portray the illusion of normality, her boyfriend tied up and gagged his shocked victim. He undressed himself, preparing to transfer all of his hatred to this innocent girl.

Vanessa Samson was everything that Daveggio and Michaud were not. She had a degree in business studies and a good job in insurance. She was popular at her work, with her family and at her church.

Whilst Vanessa was captive in the van, Michelle parked outside a welfare office and collected her cheque. If she'd really been an unwilling accomplice of James Daveggio, she now had ample opportunity to alert the authorities. But she waited patiently, collected her money and left. She was also alone with the trussed-up and crying victim when Daveggio went to the restroom, but she didn't let the young woman leave.

Michelle Michaud now drove north whilst James Daveggio repeatedly raped Vanessa Samson. He also sodomised her with Michelle's curling irons – they had cut off the cord when adding it to their torture kit.

Eventually the couple booked into a cheap motel, parking the van next to their room door so that no one could see them carrying the bound and gagged twenty-two-year-old. They untied her and Daveggio went out for burgers but Vanessa only managed one bite before she vomited.

When she was trussed up on the bed again, Michaud joined in the torture – her fingerprints would be found on a second pair of customised curling irons, showing that one sadist pressed one side of the tongs against the girl's buttocks whilst the other inserted the second tong rectally. By afternoon, Michaud would later note, the victim was 'half dead.'

They now smuggled her back into the van and drove for a while, then got into the back where Daveggio looped a rope around Vanessa's neck. Michelle then took one end of the rope and James took the other as they'd agreed to kill in tandem. They pulled until their victim stopped breathing, then drove on and dumped her body in an isolated snowbank.

Captured

That morning, Michaud made a court appearance for passing bad cheques so law enforcement knew she was back in the area. That afternoon they arrested her and her boyfriend at their motel. A search of the room revealed crack cocaine and a loaded pistol, as well as paraphernalia which showed the couple were dealing in drugs.

The van yielded further evidence of the couple's crimes. Rape victim Juanita Rodriguez's hairs were found, as were curling irons stained with blood. There was also a saliva-soaked ball gag and recreational drugs.

Autopsy

Outwardly, Michelle Michaud was co-operative, agreeing that the police could search her hotel room and van. She answered all of their questions but remained exceedingly vague. At this stage the authorities only knew about the various incestuous assaults and the rape of Juanita Rodriguez, and she hoped that they wouldn't link her to Vanessa Samson who was still officially a missing person, though everyone suspected she was dead.

But two days later Vanessa's frozen corpse was found – and meantime the police had forensically tested the curling irons and found traces of Vanessa's blood and faeces. The subsequent autopsy showed bruising on the girl's buttocks which matched the pattern of the curling irons. Michelle's fingerprints were found on duct tape wrapped around the handle of the curling irons, showing that she was the one who'd turned them into a torture implement.

Confession

Michelle Michaud now decided to co-operate fully with the authorities, albeit seriously playing down her part in the rapes and murder. She said that Daveggio had molested her daughter, that *he* was the one who'd become fascinated by the Gallegos. Even more disingenuously, he'd put her hand on the rope which was tied around Vanessa Samson's neck and had told her to pull. She'd done so because the girl wasn't moving and she thought she was already dead. She said that she prayed for the girl every day and found it difficult to sleep.

On 15th December 1997 she pleaded not guilty to the Juanita Rodriguez rape. For the next eleven months she remained in jail, and by the end of that period she'd decided that she hated James Daveggio. By now she was aware that Juanita Rodriguez's hairs had been found in her van and that the FBI were suggesting she'd played as big a part as Daveggio in the murder so she decided to plead guilty to aiding and abetting the abduction of the girl.

Chameleons

By the time she entered her plea in court, Michelle Michaud looked nothing like the gaunt-faced drug addict who had tortured Vanessa Samson. Now her hair was short and curly and she wore glasses. Denied her beloved crystal meth, she had put on weight and resembled a suburban housewife, looking like court-taken photographs of British serial killer Rose West. Daveggio would also completely change his appearance for his trial, cutting his long hair and donning glasses so that he resembled a professor rather than the barely literate outlaw he actually was.

Fighting for her life

Michelle had helped snuff out Vanessa Sampson's life for a quick thrill – but she held her own life in higher regard and was determined to save it. As such, she suggested to the authorities that she should infiltrate the prostitution ring she used to work for and pass on their secrets. When this was turned down she told them about witnessing the murder of a bail bondsman by a biker – she could infiltrate the biker gang if the authorities set her free. When they refused to make a deal, she decided to become a prosecution witness at James Daveggio's trial – the man she had promised to love forever had now become her sworn enemy.

Sentencing

Her ex-boyfriend's trial for Juanita Rodriguez's abduction
and rape lasted for seven days – but it took the jury only
two hours of deliberation to find him guilty. He was
subsequently sentenced to twenty-four years.

On 12th August 1999 Michelle Michaud was sentenced
to twelve years in prison for the Rodriguez crime, namely
for aiding in the kidnap and rape of the Reno college
student. She wept during her pre-sentence statement and
said she wished she'd done more to stop her boyfriend
abducting and terrorising the girl. 'There is no way to
make you understand, because I still don't understand...I
don't know how it got where it got,' she said inarticulately.
Later she added 'I'm so, so sorry for not being stronger,
for not being able to stop things he has done.'

But realists pointed out that she'd had her own income
from a sugar daddy during the time of the rape, and was
not financially dependent on Daveggio. And she had
become very aggressive when other women showed an
interest in him. Moreover, James Daveggio's defence
produced witnesses who said that Michelle Michaud was a
strong woman who gave as good as she got.

She remained religious, telling a reporter that she
especially enjoyed reading Romans from the Bible, which
apparently concentrates on love.

Murder trial

In April 2002 the couple were moved to Almeda County
and tried together for Vanessa Samson's horrific torture
murder. A doctor for Michelle's defence said that the
abuse from her boyfriends and clients had left her with
post-traumatic stress disorder, with a propensity for

subservience. The prosecution countered that she often shared power with Daveggio and at other times was in charge.

Daveggio's lawyers argued that the couple had killed Vanessa Samson for thrills, not because she was a witness to her own sexual assault. Reaching new levels of legal madness, they suggested that the crime therefore lacked the 'special circumstances' that would qualify for punishment by execution. Daveggio's representatives later said 'you have to look at the defendant as a person...look at childhood, family illnesses.' And it was true that Daveggio had had a difficult childhood – but he'd *chosen* to pass on his pain to someone else.

The murder verdict
The jury, consisting of seven men and five women, spent two days of deliberations, then returned to find the couple guilty of kidnap, rape by an instrument and first degree murder. Daveggio reddened at the verdict and Michaud's hand flew to her mouth. The couple were subsequently sentenced to death for the horrific crime.

Other victims?
Carlton Smith, who wrote a book, *Hunting Evil*, about the case, has become convinced that James Daveggio murdered his former girlfriend Cassie Riley in 1974 in Union City. Another man called Marvin Mutch was convicted of the murder and has been in San Quentin ever since. Carlton Smith has informed the Union City police and the Alameda County district attorney of his findings, but they have refused to act.

Robert Scott, who wrote a later book, *Rope Burns*, about

Daveggio and Michaud notes that Daveggio's friend Michael Ihde spent four years in jail for assaulting and intending to murder a woman. Both Daveggio and Ihde were age twenty at the time. Ihde later went to prison for another murder and the authorities suspect that both men could be linked to other violent deaths.

Update

James Daveggio is currently on San Quentin's Death Row. In January 2003 he began advertising on the internet for penpals, writing 'I have never been out of the USA. Nor will I ever will be now. It may not be like coming to your country, but it will be as close as I'll get. I'll be looking forward to hearing from you.' Doubtless there will be females – convinced that all he needs to straighten him out is the love of a good woman – reaching for their writing pads and pens.

Michelle Michaud is on Death Row in California, one of only fourteen women there. The appeals process moves so slowly that she may remain there for the rest of her natural life.

11   SECRETS AND LIES
AMY GROSSBERG & BRIAN PETERSON

Couples who kill babies are understandably seen as especially reprehensible. Most such deaths occur when violent parents try to 'discipline' a crying or defecating infant (who is far too young to control such automatic reflexes) and go too far. And chapter fourteen, British Couples Who Kill Children, looks at another form of deliberate cruelty where adults let babies starve to death for monetary gain. But occasionally a couple murder a baby and it's possible to feel a modicum of sympathy for them, as in the following case.

Amy Suzanne Grossberg
Amy was born on 10th July 1978, the second child of Sonye and Alan Grossberg. Amy, her parents and her three-year-old brother lived in an attractive four-bedroomed house in New Jersey. Her mother, a former teacher, stayed at home until Amy went to school then she joined her husband as a furniture sales representative. The couple were very successful in their careers so Sonye was able to take her daughter on frequent shopping trips. Amy was intelligent and artistic and expected to excel academically. Throughout her junior school years, she was a model child.

When Amy was twelve, the family moved to a much larger house and hired a maid. Amy continued to do well in school and also made great strides in her religious studies, the family being Jewish. But at thirteen she developed irritable bowel syndrome which can be brought on by – and later exacerbated by – stress. Like most IBS sufferers she tended to worry excessively about everything and was terrified of letting her family down. It was vital to Amy's mother that she got good grades and once, when she got a B, Mrs Grossberg phoned the school and persuaded them to increase it to an A.

Fortunately the slightly shy girl had a few close friends to take her mind off these academic expectations and her IBS symptoms. And her happiness increased at age fourteen when she met Brian Peterson. The slender blonde boy was popular and athletic, only one month her senior. He was impressed by her cuteness, sweet disposition and artistic talent and they soon fell in love.

Brian Carl Peterson

Like Amy, Brian was an intelligent and sensitive teenager. He was born on 10th June 1978 to Barbara and Brian Peterson who lived in Long Island. His mother was a maths teacher who also had an evening job and his father was a computer programmer. The couple worked long hours so he came home to a babysitter every night. He was somewhat lonely but filled his time as best he could, attending classes in Catholicism, walking his dog and playing with friends.

Gradually his parents saw less and less of each other and when he was ten they separated and his mother moved to New Jersey. The couple agreed that Brian should remain in his childhood home with his father so that he could keep the same friends and attend the same school.

When he was fourteen he went to live with his mother and her second husband who ran a video distribution service with seven million dollars worth of sales per annum. Home was a large mock-Tudor house.

For the next three years Brian and Amy attended school dances, went to the cinema and had frequent meals with Amy's family. By seventeen they were ready to become lovers but they'd had very little sex education at school and the subject had never been raised in Amy's home. Amy's mother always took her to the doctor and she was too embarrassed to go there on her own and ask for the contraceptive pill. Similarly, Brian was worried about being seen buying condoms so they didn't always use them. Like many teenagers, they were playing Russian roulette with pregnancy.

A terrifying nine months

Eventually nature took its course and in March 1996 seventeen-year-old Amy didn't have a period. She didn't have one in April either and wrote to Brian suggesting she might be pregnant. By May the couple were discussing the topic regularly, still unsure if Amy was really expecting or if the worry about getting into the 'right' college was making her menstrual cycle irregular.

In June they graduated from high school and took summer jobs. Both of them turned eighteen that summer but emotionally they were still children, out of their depth.

They talked about getting an abortion and even drove past a clinic – but Amy lost her nerve and Brian was determined to support her in whatever decision she made, rationalising that it was her body. The following month Mrs Grossberg took her to the doctor for her pre-college medical and, though he palpated her stomach, he didn't detect the pregnancy. He asked her if she was pregnant as he wanted to give her an immunisation that can harm a growing foetus. But her mother was standing beside her so Amy said that she was menstruating and accepted the dangerous shot.

The couple now booked an abortion at a clinic and Brian withdrew the money from his savings account but again Amy was unable to go through with it, fearing that if she developed a post-termination infection, her mother would find out. By now her mother had noticed that she was gaining weight and hiding her figure inside baggy clothes, but she still saw Amy as her little girl rather than the sexually active – if immature – young woman that she actually was.

In August they left home for their respective colleges, Brian going to Gettysburg whilst Amy travelled to Delaware, a hundred miles away. Almost immediately another student asked Amy when her baby was due. Suspecting that she was the subject of campus gossip, she wrote to Brian 'I'm going insane.' Equally distraught, Brian began to speak to her on the phone several times every day. His new friends noticed that he was withdrawn and was finding it hard to concentrate. Small wonder as Amy was writing to him 'this is killing me, mentally, physically and emotionally.' She even hinted that she was considering suicide.

As the season turned into autumn, her condition worsened. By now, unknown to her, she'd developed toxaemia of pregnancy, which is potentially fatal. Her ankles swelled, her body ached all over and she lost her appetite.

Amy had been brought up to believe that there was a god and that he answered prayers, but though she prayed and prayed for her pregnancy to go away, it continued. By mid-October she was reduced to writing a letter which said

'Dear God, why does it seem like I just do everything wrong... Please help me. My life is ruined... I'm sorry that I did what I did but don't hurt me anymore.' She pleaded again and again for forgiveness, for the pregnancy 'not to go any further.'

But the pregnancy continued. Her parents visited her that month and noticed that she looked unwell and was still swathed in baggy clothes. She admitted that she wasn't feeling too good and was tired. Maybe if they'd asked her outright she'd have burst into tears and told the truth. But her well-meaning parents put her condition down to the stress of being away from home for the first time.

Incredibly, the too-good Amy was still studying hard, dragging her seriously ill body to all of her classes. By now she had terrible headaches and was constantly fighting back nausea. Worse, she could feel the baby kicking and her stomach was hurting constantly.

Birth and death

On 12th November her waters broke and she called Brian who immediately drove the hundred miles to be with her. The couple then drove to a motel, reaching it in the early hours. Brian had a fake ID in his wallet but booked into the motel under his own name. This suggests he didn't anticipate exactly what would happen next.

Shortly afterwards Amy went into labour and an equally terrified Brian started to hyperventilate. The young couple had been so intent on hiding the pregnancy from Amy's parents that they hadn't given much thought to the actual birth. Now the exhausted eighteen-year-old was giving birth for the first time without any medical intervention or pain-killing drugs.

Brian begged Amy to let him drive her to hospital, but she was still petrified of disappointing her mother. So they stayed in the sweat-drenched confines of the motel bedroom and he pressed on her stomach a couple of times to try and ease the baby's passage. Neither teenager knew what they should be doing medically, but soon Amy gave birth to a six pound son.

Exactly what happened next will probably never be publicly known. Amy had a cloth over her eyes (the pre-eclampsia she was suffering from ensured she had to shield her eyes from the light) so claimed she didn't see the baby. Brian said that it looked blue and didn't appear to be breathing. The umbilical cord allegedly tore when he picked the infant up. Amy begged him to 'get rid of it' (the baby) so he went out to the car to get bin bags to enclose the infant's body and the blood-soaked towels. Journalists would later wonder if Amy kicked her newborn son with her heel at this point – or if Brian came back and tied a bin bag around the little boy, suffocating him. What's definite is that they made no attempt to get medical help for the sickly infant. Weeping, Brian took the bag containing the tiny body to a nearby Dumpster and tossed it in.

Aftermath

Two hours later, Amy and Brian left the bloodstained motel bed and drove back to her college – and two hours after that she tried to get up for her first class of the morning. Brian persuaded her to rest but she still went to her midday class. By now she was getting terrible abdominal pains as her condition had worsened into full blown eclampsia.

Back in her room she collapsed and began to have

seizures. When she regained consciousness she pleaded with her room-mate not to phone an ambulance, but thankfully the teenager called one. At the hospital she had another seizure and became too ill to talk.

Later she revived slightly and the medics asked her about her recent pregnancy but she continued to deny it. She went into a third round of seizures, her blood pressure dangerously elevated. They removed the placenta from her womb and gave her anti-epileptic medication plus Valium. She had every one of the symptoms caused by post-eclampsia – including tongue and eye swelling – and was at high risk of lapsing into a coma leading to death.

Meanwhile the hospital had contacted Amy's parents and told them that she was very ill, phoning them again to confirm that she'd recently given birth. The couple were devastated. But they rallied and phoned Brian who eventually admitted that Amy had been pregnant and that they'd gotten rid of the child.

Admission
The police soon brought Brian in for questioning and the exhausted young man admitted that Amy had given birth in the motel room. The police asked if the infant could still be alive and he said no, that it was dead. His first concern was still for his critically-ill girlfriend and he told police 'I felt so bad for her.' He wept, terrified that his brief attempt to help deliver the baby had made Amy ill. The police asked 'Was the baby born alive?' and the trembling teenager replied 'I'm not sure.' He was charged with concealing the death of a child.

A police dog found the male infant and the autopsy found air in the lungs and bowels, suggesting that he had been born alive. There were also injuries to the skull but it was debatable whether these had occurred before or after he was thrown into the Dumpster. The skull injuries were probably the cause of death. Later examination also showed that the baby had been born with schizencephaly which can cause retardation and paralysis.

Amy was taken in handcuffs from the hospital to the police station then taken to a correctional facility to await trial. Brian was also kept in custody and refused bail.

Culpability

The next few weeks saw a frenzied media and judicial system trying to lay blame. Pro-choice groups argued that there was a clear need for better sex education and abortion facilities so that teenagers no longer had to endure such trauma whilst anti-abortionists argued the reverse.

Doug Most, an award-winning journalist who wrote a detailed book about the case, interviewed numerous youth representatives. Most noted that affluent teenagers like Amy and Brian were well-educated but emotionally immature, having never made any important decisions for themselves. The parents of such children tended to have very high expectations for their offspring and had never given them the message that it was okay to fail occasionally, that it was better to seek help than try to hide a pregnancy.

Sadly, there was still a lot of denial going on, for Amy's parents said that Amy had done nothing wrong, a stance which unfairly suggested that Brian alone was culpable. The defence said that the baby had been born dead and that the skull injuries had occurred in the Dumpster post-mortem. But the prosecution contended that the injuries were pre-mortem and said they would seek the death penalty.

For the first few weeks of awaiting trial, Amy and Brian still wrote to and phoned each other, their love as strong as ever. But Amy's mother was afraid that Brian would give information about her daughter's legal case to his lawyers so gradually the phone-calls stopped.

The rift between the lovers was complete when one of Amy's lawyers said that Amy hadn't even known she was pregnant, that Brian was wholly responsible. It was a cruel attack on the young man – and an outright lie. Brian's defence could prove that he'd withdrawn money from his savings account to pay for an abortion, which meant that Amy had to have known about her pregnancy. And the numerous letters she'd written to him begging for the pregnancy to 'go away' were found in his room.

Brian pleaded guilty to manslaughter and agreed to testify against Amy if she went to trial. Amy eventually followed his lead and plea bargained her charge down to manslaughter. She would be given a slightly heavier sentence than her boyfriend because he pleaded guilty from the start.

On 9th July 1998, the day before Amy's twentieth birthday, the couple were sentenced. Amy was given eight years but most of it was suspended. She would spend two and a half years in jail and serve three hundred hours of community service, counselling pregnant teenagers.

Brian was sentenced to two years. Both he and Amy were initially put into isolation for their own protection. Later Brian was given work in the prison laundry and Amy taught handicrafts to her cellmates. The youngsters lost weight in prison and aged visibly.

Update

Amy and Brian are now free and remain close to their respective parents. They have not seen each other since the trial. Their unwanted baby was buried beneath a headstone which bears the dubious message *Always In Our Hearts*.

12   THE AWAKENING
MYRA HINDLEY & IAN BRADY

Myra Hindley was an ill-educated teenager until Ian Brady awakened her interest in books and philosophy. Unfortunately his philosophy was one of moral relativism and he eventually convinced her that 'laws and externally enforced moral and ethical norms are put into their proper secondary perspective in affairs of emotion when it makes one feel good to break the law.' Put simply, this translated into the couple luring three children and two teenagers to their deaths.

Myra Hindley

Myra was born on 23rd July 1942 to Hettie and Bob Hindley in Crumpsall, Manchester. Her father – a hard-drinking aircraft fitter – didn't like her and her mother was too busy working as a machinist to spend much time with her, so by age four she was sent to live with her gran. That same year the Hindleys had a second daughter, Maureen, whom Myra adored.

Unfortunately the Hindley household remained deeply divided. Bob frequently hit his wife, and Myra saw some of that violence. She also received it. And she saw that the relationship between her mother and grandmother was very poor.

With no good role model in her life, she grew up to be an awkward child, old beyond her years yet emotionally vulnerable. But this made her an excellent babysitter as she was desperate to be liked. She'd spend hours caring for the neighbourhood infants and toddlers, basking in their approval and in the appreciation of their parents.

Myra had been brought up to believe that education didn't matter for girls, so left school at fifteen and drifted from one unskilled job to the next, her life increasingly dreary. But when she was eighteen she started her fourth office job and immediately noticed Ian Brady, the handsome clerk. He ignored her completely – just as her father had done when he wasn't hitting her – but soon she was writing in her diary that she was in love.

Ian Stewart Brady

Ian was born on 2nd January 1938 to Margaret Stewart, an unmarried waitress. (Years later she married and became Peggy Brady.) She lived in the Gorbals, a slum area in Glasgow, Scotland, and had to work nights to support herself and newborn baby Ian, so he was frequently left alone. Babies who aren't cared for in their first few months of life often become psychopaths as the neural pathways which ensure that they bond with other people remain unstimulated. Brady would later show classic psychopathic traits.

At three months he was unofficially fostered out to a couple who already had four children. But as he matured he felt different to them and remained withdrawn. Peggy visited him every weekend, but he was merely told that she was a family friend. At eleven, desperate for stimulus, he broke into a house but didn't steal anything. The following year Peggy moved to Manchester and he felt increasingly adrift.

He began to play truant from school and wandered the streets for hours on his own. He committed further burglaries and ended up, at age thirteen, before the juvenile court. At fourteen he faced the juvenile court again and was bound over for nine months, but he continued to steal.

At sixteen he was put on probation and sent to live with Peggy in Manchester. She'd now married a meat porter named Patrick Brady and Ian was given his surname. It was an awkward reunion as he'd hardly seen his mother for the past four years and his stepfather was soon threatening him with violence if he didn't shape up. The man found him a labouring job (which was beneath him as he had a high IQ) where the Mancunians laughed at his Scottish accent. Increasingly alienated, he retreated into his room.

Mocked and underestimated by the world, he found reassurance in books which were about gaining power – books about the occult, about extreme sexual sadism, about Hitler. He even eventually taught himself German in order to read Mein Kampf.

When he helped to dispose of some stolen lead and was caught, he was given the harsh sentence of two years in Borstal, a type of detention unit for criminal and usually violent young men. There, he may well have been sexually assaulted. He was definitely badly treated and his resentment against society grew.

By the time he took a clerical job at a Manchester chemical firm called Millwalls, he was a lonely young man who hated conventional society.

The lovers

Initially, Ian saw Millwall's typist Myra as being part of this mindless society. After all, she was a desperately conventional girl who wanted marriage and babies, who went to church and lived for weekend dances. But after a year of ignoring her, he realised that she would make an excellent disciple and began to try out his philosophy that it was the natural order for the strong to overcome the weak.

Myra bought into this from the start – she'd probably have agreed to anything to please the man she was in love with. Though originally against sex before marriage, she gave him her virginity on their second date. And she swiftly agreed to anal sex, despite the fact that she found it painful. She also let her new lover beat her with a whip and revealed the marks for his camera.

The dynamics
The violence and lack of positive parental attention in Myra Hindley's childhood had left her with a histrionic personality, and people with this personality disorder are very susceptible to suggestion. Ian wanted a lover with an anti-social approach to life so the previously friendly and conventional Myra became determinedly anti-social. He wanted to be dominant so she became sexually submissive. She expressed her enjoyment of the murder books he lent her and pretended to enjoy the brutality of the war films which they saw.

Not that Myra Hindley was completely without her own needs and desires – the treatment she'd received from her father had left her with unexpressed hostility and Ian brought this out.

He began to talk of rape, suggesting that sexual fulfilment and the satisfaction of other bodily appetites were society's only real values. Again, Myra wasn't shocked (or pretended not to be shocked) as his fantasies edged increasingly closer to reality.

Pauline's murder

On the evening of 12th July 1963 Ian asked twenty-one-year-old Myra to procure him a child to rape. Myra saw a girl she knew, sixteen-year-old Pauline Reade, en route to a dance and told her she'd lost an expensive glove on Saddleworth Moor. Pauline obligingly got into Myra's car and was driven to the sunlit moorland. The friendly teenager had no idea that Ian Brady planned to follow them on his motorbike.

Myra would later allege that she went back to the car after Ian appeared, leaving him with the terrified teenager. (But Ian would eventually say that Myra helped him sexually assault the girl.) Whatever the exact nature of events, a struggle ensued in which he raped Pauline and cut her throat. He showed Myra the still-gurgling body then they buried Pauline's warm corpse in a hastily dug grave.

The couple were shaken by the reality of this first murder. Brady had found it very difficult to overpower a struggling sixteen-year-old whilst Hindley had been horrified when she saw the dying girl. She'd later say that she considered leaving him but that he threatened to hurt her family. In truth, it's more likely that she stayed because she remained in love with him – he'd literally become her life. Her father hated her, her mother was too busy working to spend much time with her and her grandmother, who she still lived with, was increasingly infirm. Myra had also sided with Brady at work so was regarded by her more balanced colleagues as increasingly secretive and aloof. And she'd given up on her friends because Brady proclaimed they were worthless. He'd also moved in with her and her gran, which meant that she lived with him and worked with him. They were together twenty-four hours a day.

John's murder

So Myra stayed with Ian because she believed that she couldn't face life without him. And four months later – on 23rd November 1963 – they targeted their next victim, twelve-year-old John Kilbride, by offering him a lift home. Myra knew what was going to happen this time as she'd bought the knife. The couple took the boy to the moor and Myra remained in the van as look out. Meanwhile Ian raped, spanked and strangled the unfortunate boy.

The knife was too blunt to cut the child's throat, so he strangled him with string and buried him on the desolate moors. Later, he took photographs of Myra posing on the child's grave.

Keith's murder

Another seven months elapsed then, on 16th June 1964, the couple offered twelve-year-old Keith Bennett a lift to his gran's house. He too was driven to the moors where Brady raped and strangled him. Strangling is considered to be an especially sadistic crime, and Brady kept books about torture in a locker at the local railway station. Being in control meant everything to Brady, whose childhood themes had been those of humiliation and abandonment. Afterwards, Brady buried Keith Bennett's body on the moorland. Despite frequent searches by the police and by members of the devastated Bennett family, his remains have never been found.

Lesley's murder

Six months later – on Boxing Day 1964 – the couple lured ten-year-old Lesley Ann Downey away from a funfair. They took her to Myra's gran's house (her gran was away visiting relatives) and ordered her to strip.

They bound and gagged the increasingly distraught little girl and took lurid naked photographs which Ian Brady planned to sell. He also tape-recorded the child pleading 'Please God, help me.' Later she begged Myra to help her but Myra callously threatened to hit her and told her to put the handkerchief-gag back in her mouth. The tape, which lasted for seventeen minutes, also recorded Lesley crying for her mum.

At some stage Ian raped the little girl. Myra said she was in the bathroom whilst this crime was taking place, and that when she returned the child was dead. Ian backed up this version of events for many years but, after the couple became estranged, he said that Myra had strangled Lesley with a silken cord. The following day they buried the little girl's body on their beloved moors. It was ten months before her corpse was found.

Greater stimulus

By now Ian Brady had murdered a teenage girl, a prepubescent girl and two prepubescent boys. But he had the psychopath's typical low boredom threshold and wanted to increase his excitement by bringing in a third party. He chose a youth he was already friendly with, Myra's seventeen-year-old brother-in-law David Smith. The teenager was married to Myra's younger sister, Maureen, and was unemployed, broke and bored.

Myra was against involving David – she'd aged visibly

since the murders and had frequent nightmares. She also begged her relatives and neighbours not to make conventional statements around her lover, as this always increased his wrath. The insecure young woman wanted to have Ian Brady's full attention, and being his sole disciple in the murders was the ultimate way of maintaining this. But he'd already decided to bring the innocent David Smith in on their fifth kill...

Edward's murder

On 6th October 1965, the couple went to a bar and Myra chatted up a seventeen-year-old boy, Edward Evans. She told him that Ian Brady was her brother. The threesome left the pub together and returned to Myra's gran's house where they probably all had sex whilst her gran slept upstairs. Afterwards, Ian ordered Myra to fetch David Smith – and David arrived at the house to find Ian battering a hatchet into the screaming Edward Evans' head. The petrified youth continued to fight for his life, so Brady partially suffocated him with a cushion then strangled him to death.

Afterwards Myra retched and David went home and was violently sick. He told Maureen what he'd witnessed and, at first light, the terrified teenagers went to a phone box and called the police.

Meanwhile, the killer couple had gone to bed. Ian slept well, convinced that David Smith would prove to be as obedient an acolyte as Myra Hindley. She, for her part, slept fitfully and arose early next morning, aware that Edward Evans' body was still locked in a trunk in the spare room. The police came to the door and arrested Ian Brady for the murder and she denied knowing where the key to the trunk was. She tried to act tough to please Ian – but it's telling that the first detective who spoke to her thought that she was at least twelve years older than her actual twenty-three.

Arrest and trial

Myra believed that Ian would get bail so she virtually camped at the police station. Eventually they had to tell her mother to take her home.

Meanwhile the police found the key to the railway locker which held the photographs and tape-recording of the missing Lesley Ann Downey. Myra and Ian's aggressive voices were on the tape, placing them both at the scene.

When Myra was arrested she said that she had been where Ian had been, that she had done what he had done. But when they were tried for the murders of John Kilbride, Lesley Ann Downey and Edward Evans, both put forward a Not Guilty plea. It wasn't yet known that they'd murdered Pauline Reade and Keith Bennett, though police strongly suspected they had.

The trial began at Chester Assizes on 27th April 1966 amid tight security, as the general public wanted to lynch the killers. The prosecution alleged that the couple were equally responsible for the three sex murders, and the defence countered that Ian Brady had been the leader and Myra Hindley the follower. (The latter viewpoint is true – but Ian would have had difficulty luring his victims to remote locations without Myra. The children had been told not to go off with strange men but they understandably believed that a woman posed no threat.) She remained enamoured of her lover and stared at him devotedly throughout the trial.

The couple's guilt was a foregone conclusion – the tape and photographs linked them to Lesley Ann Downey, though Ian Brady claimed they'd merely photographed her then let her leave the house with two male pornographers. John Kilbride's death was also closely linked to the couple, as his body was located when the police found a photo of Myra posing on top of his makeshift grave. And David Smith had watched Brady murder Edward Evans whilst Myra urged him to help.

On 6th May 1966, the fifteenth day of the trial, the jury returned their verdict. The couple were jointly found guilty of the murder of Edward Evans and Lesley Ann Downey. Brady was also convicted of murdering John Kilbride, whilst Myra was convicted of being an accessory to the killing, (because she'd driven the boy to the moor then driven home without him, so clearly knew that something bad had happened). She looked close to collapse as she was jailed for life plus seven years for her part in John Kilbride's abduction. Meanwhile her beloved Ian was given three life sentences.

Judge Sparrow, who attended the case in his capacity as a journalist, recognised that she was redeemable and would later write that she 'could be made the subject of successful psychotherapy.' And two days later the judge who had sentenced her said that she could be salvaged, but that Brady could not.

An enduring love

Ian Brady was sent to Durham Prison and Myra Hindley to Holloway, where they remained devoted to each other for the next six years, writing frequently. He even went on hunger strike in an abortive attempt to be allowed visiting rights. But as she approached thirty, she at last began to form close relationships with other female prisoners and realised that he'd helped ruin, rather than positively define, her life. She told him to stop writing to her and she began to have lesbian relationships, though other prisoners have noted that these were more emotional than physical.

Admitting the early murders

Myra's life remained relatively static for the next twenty years as she worked in the prison sewing room, had visits from her mother and crushes on various other female prisoners. Meanwhile Ian Brady's mental health deteriorated and in 1985 he was diagnosed as a psychopath and moved to Ashworth Hospital, a psychiatric prison. His emotional wellbeing remained incredibly changeable, with some visitors finding him alert and normal whilst others noted that he was close to collapse. He suggested to various journalists and detectives that he'd committed other murders whilst acting alone, but they checked back and found that his stories were either mental confusion or outright lies.

Myra, too, had lied to her fellow prisoners for almost twenty years, telling them that she had no part in the murders of Pauline Reade and Keith Bennett. Then – in 1985 and 1986 – she received counselling from the Reverend Peter Timms and decided to confess. (Peter Timms is interviewed in *Women Who Kill*.)

Both killers were taken separately onto the moors to locate the graves and the information Myra gave helped the police to locate Pauline's body. But Ian became much more confused so Keith Bennett's skeleton remains undiscovered to this day.

Nothing to live for

The numerous boring days spent in prison – and the nights sleeping with the lights on to escape her demons – took their toll and in 1999 Myra Hindley collapsed during an angina attack and was rushed to hospital. The medics warned her that she had to stop smoking and start exercising, but she remained depressed and chose not to heed their advice. She had technically met all of the criteria for parole but had never been granted this, and was losing the will to live.

The following year, five lawlords upheld the Home Secretary's decision that Myra Hindley should die in prison. Meanwhile Ian Brady wanted to die as soon as possible in prison. He attempted to starve himself to death for the next three years, but the authorities force fed him through a tube.

Ian Brady hadn't changed much in prison – but Myra Hindley had, earning a degree in humanities and reverting to her previous working class conformity. She got religion again and made various influential religious friends. She was never going to attain Brady's superior IQ or elevated vocabulary, but at the same time she was no longer a danger to anyone else.

But as far as the tabloids were concerned, Myra Hindley wasn't allowed to change. When she cuddled her friends' babies in jail they suggested a sinister motive – but she had genuinely loved children before meeting Ian Brady and was a trusted babysitter. Similarly, they suggested that she acted fawningly around animals whereas she genuinely loved them too. Much was made of the fact that she had lesbian lovers in prison, but the reality was that these affairs were based on writing impassioned poetry and having someone to dream about.

Diana Athill, an editor for Andre Deutsch, was given some of Myra Hindley's prison writings and began to understand how a nineteen-year-old from an unambitious family could have become besotted with a well-read man whose philosophy was 'above the petty considerations which governed most people's despicable little lives.'

Diana describes her impressions of Myra Hindley in her intriguing portrait of the publishing world, *Stet*. 'She was intelligent, responsive, humorous, dignified.' Diana came to the conclusion that Hindley only managed to live with her murderous actions by blurring the part that she'd played in her mind and by exaggerating her fear of Brady. The editor decided that making Myra confront the true gravity of her actions might result in a nervous breakdown so she decided not to commission the book.

Many newspapers continued to give the impression that Myra Hindley was a cold, heartless prisoner but in truth she was a timid woman who was too frightened to go into the television lounge with the other prisoners for fear of censure – and when she was violently attacked and had her nose broken she refused to strike back.

In contrast, Ian Brady, the mastermind and instigator of the murders, has remained wedded to violence. He wrote in his book *The Gates of Janus*, published in 2001, that serial killers (presumably including himself) have chosen to spend one day as a lion rather than decades as a sheep. Yet many of us choose not to live as sheep – and we still don't resort to killing children. He also suggests that most serial killers choose victims who have had much nicer lives than they themselves. But – given that many serial killers select girls who have been in care and then become prostitutes – this simply isn't true. Brady himself was earning a reasonable salary as a clerk and had enough money for wine, cigarettes and a motorbike when he selected impoverished working class children to kill.

He also says, rightfully, that latent homosexual men often turn their aggression towards the object of their desire – yet he has never dared examine his own victim choice. Only the first victim, sixteen-year-old Pauline Reade, had a developed female body – and Myra Hindley chose her for him. He demanded that she procure smaller victims in future. Three of the other victims were male and Lesley Ann Downey was only ten so she had a boyish frame.

It's clear that Ian Brady had some confusion in his head about his own sexuality. He liked to have a candle inserted into his anus during sex play and we know that he raped Keith Bennett and John Kilbride prior to their deaths. The bar where he met his final victim, Edward Evans, was frequented by gay men and he explained this to Myra Hindley by telling her that 'he was going to rob a queer.' He denied at the trial that he'd had sex with the youth – but someone had, for hairs from Myra's dog were found around the boy's anus. And Brady had sent Myra from the house, leaving him alone with the teenage boy.

Whilst bringing the axe down on the terrified Edward Evans, Brady shouted again and again 'you dirty bastard.' It was the most violent of the five deaths and he said himself that it was 'the messiest yet.'

So what drove Myra's normally quiet lover to such paroxysms of rage? Was he raped at Borstal by older inmates? Did he feel a need to both repeat such rape and also take murderous revenge? He was clearly ashamed when the prosecution said that he'd frequented gay bars and stammered that he liked to mock the homosexuals there.

The Gates Of Janus makes it clear that, even today after over thirty years in a special hospital, he sees murder as the supreme pleasure and believes that people should do exactly as they wish regardless of who they hurt. He believes that none of us are capable of genuine charity, suggesting that we only make charitable gestures in order to feel good about ourselves, making it an essentially selfish act. In short, he apparently has no feelings for other people, the benchmark of the psychopath.

But the situation may be slightly more complex than that. He voluntarily transcribes books for the blind, has allegedly offered to donate one of his kidneys to anyone who requires it, and has told journalists that he can't bear to think of the murders because he feels ashamed.

So why the disparity between his actions and his written word? It's possible that Ian Brady had mellowed slightly in old age but that recent events in prison led to this outpouring of anger. He alleges that hospital staff broke his wrist when forcibly moving him to the Personality Disorders Unit in 1999. (An errata slip to *The Gates Of Janus* issued on behalf of Ashworth Hospital states that his wrist wasn't broken in the move, but that medical evidence showed 'an undisplaced crack fracture of his right arm.') He also alleges that guards have talked loudly outside his door all night to keep him from sleeping, something which the hospital disputes. Ian Brady notes that he was unable to edit *The Gates Of Janus* because he was kept 'in conditions of captivity, where all items of interest are sold to the tabloids by officials.' The book, then, may be his final way of saying 'up yours' to what he perceives as a hypocritical and corrupt world.

Unfortunately he doesn't mention Myra Hindley in the book so we don't get to know what he thought of her in 2001. Most sources believe that he hated her for distancing herself from their shared crimes, but one visitor noted that he sometimes slipped up and called her 'my girl.' Myra was probably the first girl he ever had sex with – and the last.

Death

At the start of November 2002, Myra Hindley collapsed in her cell at Highpoint Prison in Suffolk and was rushed to hospital suffering from a suspected heart attack. She stabilised and was returned to prison but was readmitted a fortnight later suffering from a severe chest infection which was leading to respiratory arrest.

At lunchtime on the day that she died – Tuesday 15th November 2002 – my phone started to ring and literally didn't stop until 11pm that night, starting again at 7am the next day. Because I'd profiled her in *Women Who Kill*, numerous radio, television and print journalists wanted me to make a statement. When they wanted to know how I felt about the prospect of her dying (by early afternoon she'd been given the last rites) and, hours later, about her death at 5pm, I said it was the inevitable sad end to a blighted life.

I was interviewed by dozens of broadcasters that day, but none of them wanted to know the truth. Instead, they'd already decided that she'd been born evil, remained evil and died evil. When I suggested that she'd originally been comparatively normal (albeit with unresolved issues resulting from her upbringing) they changed the subject.

When I said that she hadn't been a risk to children for decades the interview would swiftly come to an end. Several other writers – notably esteemed psychologist Oliver James and distinguished crime writer Brian Masters – said the exact same thing but they got very little airplay compared with journalists who said that she was a hundred percent bad.

Over the years, the nation had largely divided into two camps, those who thought that she was still a cold-hearted manipulator who should die in jail and those who thought that thirty-five years in prison was excessive given that she probably didn't kill any of the victims. I was indifferent as to whether or not she was released, merely pointing out that technically it had been years since she met the conditions for parole. She'd shown remorse and had improved herself by studying several languages. She hadn't shown any sign of violence since leaving Brady's thrall yet she died with the press still suggesting she was a monster, rather than an inadequate person who had once done monstrous things.

Update

Ian Brady remains in Ashworth Hospital near Liverpool. Colin Wilson, who wrote the introduction to Brady's deeply depressing but often insightful The Gates Of Janus says that 'it is the only work in world literature in which a criminal right man argues his case that society is really to blame for his crimes.' He also describes it as 'paranoid, obsessive and wrong headed.' Brady, who is sixty-seven, still expresses the wish to die. He often refuses food and is sometimes skeletally thin. His birth mother Peggy is now dead.

David Smith, Myra's brother-in-law, who had the courage to testify against the couple, eventually moved to Ireland where he married, found employment and a much-deserved tranquillity.

Myra Hindley was cremated at a Cambridgeshire crematorium, the service attended by a dozen close friends. Her father and her sister Maureen are long dead but she is survived by her mother, who has commendably refused to sell her story to the newspapers and who lives in relative penury.

Rose and Fred West were born into violent, incestuous families and, like many abuse survivors, they longed for children and domestic bliss. But their shared love of cruelty and need for control ensured that they physically and sexually abused their offspring then graduated to abducting girls whom they eventually buried under their beloved home...

Rosemary Pauline Letts

Rose was born on 29th November 1953 in Northam, Devon, to Bill and Daisy Letts. Bill, an electrical engineer who'd spent years in the Navy, was a paranoid schizophrenic who viciously abused his wife and all seven of his children. Daisy, a housewife, eventually had a breakdown and was given electric shock treatment whilst pregnant with Rose. She received six of these controversial treatments, the sixth one taking place just days before Rose was born.

By the time she was a toddler, Rose had picked up on the violence and tension in the household and she'd rock herself back and forth for hours in an attempt to self-comfort. Like many children from chaotic backgrounds, she also frequently lapsed into a fugue state.

Rose was somewhat withdrawn by the time she started school and couldn't relate to children her own age, so she was mocked and bullied. But by twelve she'd learned to hit back. Some criminologists believe that her father took her virginity at twelve, but all that's certain is that by age thirteen she'd begun to masturbate her ten-year-old brother. At fourteen she was allegedly raped on two separate occasions by strangers (she didn't report either incident) and at fifteen she found comfort in casual sex. Her deeply religious mother now disowned her and left her father. Rose was at his mercy and he liked young girls...

Her vulnerability remained apparent, especially to sexual predators. So it's no surprise that a sexually-insatiable labourer called Fred West approached her at a bus stop and began chatting. Though she was only fifteen and he was twenty-eight, he soon asked her out.

Frederick Walter Stephen West

Fred was born on 29th September 1941, the first son of Daisy and Walter West. The couple had him baptised, his christening card reading 'He that believeth and is baptised will be saved.'

Daisy was still a teenager when she gave birth to Fred but Walter was twenty-seven years old. The couple lived in a tied cottage in the tiny Herefordshire village of Much Marcle, where Walter worked as a farm hand. They had lost their first baby, a girl, after which the already introverted Walter turned to drink.

During the next few years, the household became increasingly crowded as Daisy gave birth to John, David, Daisy, Douglas, Kathleen and Gwendoline. (David died when he was a month old.) She put on weight with each child and became seriously obese.

But Fred was her favourite and she beat him less than her other children. As a result his siblings teased him for being a mummy's boy. He was even bullied by his younger brother but refused to fight back.

Fred went to school at five years old, and it was soon apparent that he had a low IQ. He had great difficulty with reading and writing. In fairness, he had to work incredibly long hours on the farm to help his parents, so possibly had little energy left to concentrate in class. He had to milk the cows, chop wood, pick berries and bring in the harvest. He learned to drive a tractor when he was nine years old.

Walter West had begun sexually abusing his daughters when they were young – and when Fred was twelve his mother took his virginity. Fred saw this as entirely normal and went on to sexually assault other young female relatives and their friends. Walter may also have sexually abused Fred. He also practiced bestiality, telling the boy how to disable a sheep by trapping its back legs in his wellington boots in order to have sex with it.

The house also remained casually violent. Fred was playing with a plastic sword one day and inadvertently pushed it into his mother's stomach. She promptly battered him with the coal shovel that she had in her hand.

Fred finished his schooling at fourteen, a sub-literate but apparently docile incest survivor. He left home the following year without telling his parents and found work in the city. But when he eventually returned, his mother took off her belt and beat him black and blue.

He took off sporadically thereafter, but otherwise lived and work on the farm with his parents, an apparently mild-mannered youth and a hard worker. But there were still family problems, his mother becoming enraged when he bought himself a motorbike. She wanted to keep him close to her and also banned his girlfriends from the house.

At seventeen Fred accidentally drove into a wall, hit his head and was unconscious for a week. After the accident, in which he fractured his skull, broke his nose and his leg, he became withdrawn and irritable for a time.

Two years later he suffered a further head injury when he sexually assaulted a girl he'd been chatting up at a disco, and she pushed him away. He hit his head on a metal fire escape and was knocked out for twenty-four hours. It's possible that he incurred damage to the left side of his brain, the side which controls our impulses. Without this control, a person is liable to explode into violence.

That same year – his nineteenth – Fred West impregnated his thirteen-year-old sister. The case was scheduled for court but she dropped the charges. Fred's parents were angry that an act of family incest had been made public and they insisted he move out.

Fred took a labouring job and began to date Rena Costello, who was pregnant by an Asian bus driver. They married and moved to a town near Glasgow, Scotland, where she'd grown up.

But it was a difficult marriage from the start. Fred liked bondage and anal sex and thought only of his own pleasure. They briefly split up and she began to prostitute herself to earn a living, something which she'd done sporadically before. Even when she gave birth to a daughter – who she named Charmaine – she continued to solicit men for money, a practice which excited Fred. After all, he'd grown up watching his father having sex with his sisters – and other family members may have watched him having sex with his mother and his father. Voyeurism had dominated his sexuality from the time he was a boy.

Now he began to drive an ice cream van for a living, a job which brought him into close contact with young girls. He often had sex with – and sometimes impregnated – them.

He also impregnated his wife and she gave birth to their daughter, Anne Marie, in July 1964.

Sadly, Fred increasingly parented as he'd been parented. His life had been severely controlled when he lived at home, with endless tasks to perform from first light till bedtime. Now he expected to control his little children, and put chicken wire around their bunk beds so that they were caged in for the day. Rena would let them out, but if he came home and found them playing he'd beat her and terrorise the kids.

When he accidentally killed a small boy with his ice cream van and received death threats he realised it was time to leave Glasgow. He returned to his parents' cottage in Much Marcle, bringing his daughter Anne Marie and his stepdaughter Charmaine with him. Two months later, Rena joined them and they moved into a caravan. Chillingly – in light of the way that he would later carve up his victim's corpses – Fred found work in an abattoir. Not that killing animals was new to him: as a teenager his parents had ordered him to slaughter the family pig. These annual slaughterings had brought tears as he'd become fond of the animal – but now he began to enjoy carving up blood-red flesh.

Soon Rena left the increasingly violent Fred, and to punish her he insisted on keeping the children. He would put them naked on his lap and rub them against his penis. He also took a girlfriend eight years his junior, Anne McFall. Soon she was pregnant with his child and declared that she was in love with him. Fred claimed that he loved her too – but when she was eight months pregnant he took her life.

The session may have started as bondage sex, as he

definitely tied a dressing gown cord around her wrists. It may be that this led to a flagellation session (he owned several whips) and that he beat her so hard that she went into cardiac arrest. Or he could have suffocated her by accident during one of his erotic breath control games.

Fred took her body to his lockable garage, where he cut off the fingers, toes and kneecaps, using the skills he'd learned in the abattoir. He also cut the foetus from her body then buried both mother and baby in a field near his childhood home. (It would be discovered sixteen years later in 1994.) It seems that this murder, planned or unplanned, was enormously exciting to Fred, as shortly afterwards he murdered Mary Bastholm, a waitress who disappeared on her way to meet her boyfriend. Her body has never been found but Fred – who frequented the café where she worked – hinted to various people that he'd buried her in a field.

Rena now moved back in with Fred and the couple relocated to another caravan site. But she soon left again to escape his violence, and Fred met Rose...

Fred dates Rose

At first sight, Fred and Rose were an unlikely couple – he a small, glib man in his late twenties, she a slow-talking fifteen-year-old. But they actually had a lot in common: both had been sexually abused by a parent and had sexual contact with a sibling. Both had watched their siblings being repeatedly beaten and had themselves occasionally suffered parental violence. They were from households where education wasn't seen as important, and where life revolved around basic animalistic needs. Both also had mothers called Daisy who had been household servants before marrying and repeatedly giving birth.

Fred wasn't big on formal dates, so soon took Rosie (as he called her) to his caravan to meet Anne Marie, aged five, and Charmaine, aged six. Fred had them in and out of foster care and on one occasion social services had taken them to an orphanage after finding them in a 'deplorable condition.' But the thinking of the day said that a child should be with its parents so when Fred and Rena got a caravan they were given the children back. Since then Rena had abandoned Fred again and he left Charmaine and Anne Marie alone for hours on end, so they were desperate for attention. And at first the superficially-maternal Rose provided this. She quit her job at the bread shop and became Fred's nanny but was afraid to tell the Letts, who had reconciled again.

But eventually Rose took Fred home, only for Bill Letts to let loose his explosive temper. He was violently jealous of his daughter's relationship and his supposed solution was to put Rose into care. But the teenager had at last found a semblance of love, and she sneaked out to the caravan park every day to see Fred. And when she left the orphanage at sixteen she went to live with – and soon became pregnant by – him. Her father tried to beat the foetus out of her, but it survived.

The foursome moved to various run-down accommodations in Cheltenham then to a flat at 25 Midland Road, Gloucester. In October 1970 Rose gave birth to Heather, their first daughter, in hospital and returned home to find Fred in a neighbour's flat having sex, and Charmaine and Anne Marie alone in the house, unfed and unkempt.

Deluded as ever, the couple told themselves that they

now had an enduring love and a perfect family – but in reality, Rose soon started to batter Charmaine and Anne Marie, just as she'd watched her father batter her siblings. And Heather's crying drove her to distraction, so that she eventually fled back to her mum's house. But her religious parents told her that marriage was for life and she reluctantly returned to Fred.

She now took to tying the children to the bed and beating them, whilst Fred looked on without showing any apparent emotion. Outwardly Rose appeared to be the perfect mother, forever boiling nappies and buying groceries – but behind closed doors she became the tyrant that her father had been.

Charmaine West's murder

Fred had been a kleptomaniac since his head injury at age nineteen, but now he was caught stealing tires and was sentenced to ten months' imprisonment from October 1970 until the summer of 1971. Rose now had complete power over the family unit, and she beat the older girls with an increasing intensity. Like most unhappy children, they began to wet the bed and she beat them for this too. Charmaine was treated at the local casualty department for an ankle injury which may have been a knife wound (Rose would later run at Fred with a knife during an argument) and Anne Marie had to have stitches in her head after Rose cracked it open with a cereal bowl because she didn't wash up her breakfast crockery quickly enough.

In May or June 1971 she murdered Charmaine, possibly during an act of so-called legitimate punishment which went wrong. She then told anyone who asked that the child had returned to her birth mother, Rena. Meanwhile her father began to visit the house, and it's possible that she began having sex with him again.

When Fred was released from prison, he fetched Charmaine's corpse from the cellar and dismembered it, then buried it in the backyard. It's likely that by now he'd told her about murdering Anne McFall – leastways, Rose told her mother that Fred was capable of murder.

Prostitution

Fred had been happy to have his wife Rena prostitute herself (she was now living in Glasgow and presumably still soliciting) and he now suggested the same thing to Rose. He told her that he favoured coloured men because they were allegedly better endowed. He also believed that their sperm had special powers which would help him avoid premature ejaculation. So he'd listen behind the door as Rose had sex with a Jamaican man, then would have sex with her after her lover went home.

Wedding bells

Anyone with self-esteem would have walked away – but Rose had been told by her parents all of her life that she was useless. Now she asked Fred to marry her. He was still married to Rena – but a pathological liar like Fred didn't let a little detail like that prevent him from taking Rose as his wife.

On 29th January 1972 Rose Letts became Mrs Rose West at the local Registrars. As usual, there was an enormous difference between the fantasy and reality, for the couple swore they were devoted to each other, but Fred didn't even want to change out of his greasy work clothes or take a bath before the ceremony.

On 1st June, Rose gave birth to their daughter, Mae. She'd been due in May so was going to be called after the month of her birth. The Wests kept the name but Mae later changed the spelling of it. As a result, Fred always remembered her birthday, but he didn't remember previous or future children's birthdays. They weren't unique individuals to him, simply small people he could alternately be sentimental about or abuse.

Cromwell Street

In the same timeframe, Fred's boss lent him the money to buy a bigger house at 25 Cromwell Street, a few streets away from their existing Gloucester apartment. The house had previously been divided up into bedsits, something which suited the impoverished Wests. They took in male students who Rose enthusiastically slept with. She also slept with Fred's boss and some of Fred's workmates whilst an approving Fred watched or listened outside the door.

Doubtless worn out by having so many men – and by the oversized dildos which Fred liked to use on her – she turned increasingly to other women for sexual pleasure, seducing acquaintances and neighbours then becoming violently dominant towards them. Once again, the voyeuristic Fred West was thrilled.

Rena West's murder

But his happiness ebbed in the late summer of 1972 when he heard that Rena, his legal wife, had turned up at his parents' house and was demanding to see Charmaine. If she found the child missing, she'd contact the authorities and Rose would go to prison for murder. He himself would face jail for concealing such a horrific crime.

He'd already murdered Anne McFall and possibly Mary Bastholm by now, so killing Rena was the obvious solution. He consequently took her to the pub and plied her with drink. When she was semi-conscious he probably took her to a farmhouse outbuilding and bound her tightly before restricting her breathing for his erotic pleasure. He probably wound tape around her face, putting a pipe in one nostril to allow in a little air. Then he could have partially removed and reintroduced the pipe, relishing her terror and experiencing the ultimate control. Leastways a slim pipe was found with her remains when Fred eventually confessed his crimes.

Incest

Fred West had behaved inappropriately towards his daughter Anne Marie from the time she was an infant, rubbing her naked body against his. But when she was eight years old, Rose and Fred decided together that it was time to 'break her in.'

The perverted couple took her to the cellar where Rose made her undress and held her down on a mattress. She scratched the little girl's chest until she drew blood.

Fred tied Anne Marie up and raped her, whilst Rose watched. The little girl suffered internal bleeding but Rose's only response was to keep her off school for several days, telling her 'It's something everybody does but nobody talks about.' Rose also warned her to keep quiet about the abuse and denied her medical care. A few weeks later she bound Anne Marie to a metal frame and flogged her then violated her with a vibrator. She was having consensual powerplay sex with various partners but preferred the complete power she could have over a helpless child.

Anne Marie would later accurately describe Rose as an evil torturer – but her life briefly improved when the couple took in a nanny, Caroline Owens.

Interview with a survivor

In April 2004 I travelled to the Forest Of Dean to interview Caroline, who is now in her late forties. (Her name is now Caroline Roberts.) She first met the Wests in early September 1972 when they saw her walking home alone and offered her a lift.

'I was wary at first in case there were two men in the car – then I saw Rose sitting in the passenger seat and I relaxed,' says Caroline who was almost seventeen at the time. She had no reason to fear the friendly couple, and got into their Ford Popular. They were soon asking her all about her life.

So what were her first impressions of Rose & Fred West? 'She was pretty young so I thought that he might be her dad,' Caroline recalls, 'I suppose in my subconscious I tended to see older men as father figures. But they soon told me that they were married and there was so much banter between them that it was obvious they were very happy together.'

Caroline admitted to the caring couple that she wasn't getting on well with her stepfather, whereupon they told her that they were looking for a live-in nanny. They had identified someone who might be vulnerable enough to take part in their sex games and wanted her to move in right away. But Caroline did the sensible thing and insisted they meet her parents before she moved into the Wests' three-storey house in Gloucester.

When she moved into the couple's Cromwell Street home, she noticed that they were very demonstrative. 'Fred was always grabbing her bum and he'd kiss her goodbye in the morning then grab at her breasts.' But, these displays of love and lust aside, it was a very domesticated household. 'Rose taught me how to cook a Sunday roast and how to make pastry and cakes. We'd prepare the vegetables together. The children came home to cooked meals at set times.'

The Wests later cruelty to their children has become legendary, but Caroline noted that – whilst the babies were small – the violence was restrained. 'Rose did the slapping and shoving. Fred often smiled and winked at the kids when she wasn't looking. Anne Marie, who was the oldest at age eight, got the worst of it.'

Feminists would later suggest that Rose was completely dominated by her older husband, so did she ever appear afraid of him? 'No, she had sex as a weapon in her favour,' says Caroline, who is now a Substance Misuse Project Worker, 'He was clearly in her sexual thrall.'

Caroline loved the Wests' children and worked hard to keep them out of Rose's way when she was in one of her darker moods. After a while she also had to avoid Fred's sexually outrageous comments. One day he suggested that his eight-year-old daughter Anne Marie wasn't a virgin – but when Caroline looked horrified he backtracked and said that she'd broken her hymen whilst playing with her bike.

For the first few weeks that she lived with them, Fred would make dirty jokes and Rose would eventually tell him to leave Caroline alone. But one night she and Fred both asked the teenager to join their 'sex circle' which they said comprised themselves and a few men. When Caroline demurred and said she wanted to go home, Fred threatened to tell her stepfather that she'd had sex with two of her boyfriends during her stay at Cromwell Street.

The following day, one of the Wests' friends saw that the seventeen-year-old was still upset. She told him what had happened and he volunteered to drive her to her parents house in the Forest Of Dean.

Caroline fled the West household without telling them that she was leaving, but deep down she felt guilty – Rose had been a good friend to her and she'd loved the Wests' children and felt protective towards Anne Marie. Moreover, like many teenagers raised in a difficult environment, Caroline had been brought up to feel that everything which went wrong was somehow her fault.

A month later she was hitch-hiking home after seeing her boyfriend when the Wests drove up and apologised profusely for asking her to join their sex circle. Rose said that she missed her friendship and Fred added that the kids missed her too. Caroline's gut instinct told her not to get into the car but she ignored it and accepted a lift home.

The couple chatted to her till she relaxed, then Rose's mood turned ugly and she made a pass at her. When Caroline objected, Fred punched her hard in the head. They stopped the car and bound her, drove her to their house and subjected her to a prolonged and sadistic sexual assault.

Caroline recalls the attack. 'It was obvious that I was there for her pleasure rather than his, a dummy run for her to see if she could take over the control, if she could be the dominant party. They wanted to see how far she could go on her own.'

Rose forced herself upon Caroline both digitally and orally then Fred beat her with his belt. This obviously turned the couple on and they had sex on the bed in front of the teenager. Rose – who had often walked around naked in front of her brothers – didn't appear embarrassed by this public display. 'It's as if she was in a porn movie,' Caroline recollects.

They left her tied up overnight but when she heard someone at the door the following morning she screamed for help. Rose then started to suffocate her with a pillow. Caroline believed she was about to die – then Fred pulled the pillow away. He told her that they were going to keep her in the cellar and let her be used by the sex circle and that when they'd tired of her they'd bury her under the paving stones of Gloucester.

The couple gagged her and left the room but Fred returned and quickly raped her before bursting into tears. He begged her not to tell Rose, saying that Caroline was only there for her pleasure. Caroline nodded frantically, agreeing with him in a desperate bid to save her life.

'After Rose half-suffocated me, I wondered if they already had another girl chained up in the cellar,' Caroline remembers. When the couple untied her she tremblingly promised to rejoin their household, to become their nanny again. Fred and Rose had both been raised in incestuous families so they apparently believed her – they were used to sexual assaults punctuating periods of domestic harmony.

They cut Caroline's hair free of the sticky tape that they'd wound around her head and she got dressed, her clothing covering the rope burns and weals. They had a cup of tea together, then they all got into Fred's car with the children and he dropped them off at the nearest launderette. 'I felt stronger after Fred had gone,' Caroline admits, 'And the atmosphere changed. Rose was much more nervous now that we were alone and she busied herself putting washing into the machines. I told her that I was going to the local shop for cigarettes and she looked very worried as I hurried out.' The seventeen-year-old was terrified that Fred West would return but he was on his way to work and 'luckily there were no mobiles in those days.'

So why does Caroline think that the Wests let her live when, within months, they'd go on to murder another female lodger? 'They really thought they had me completely under their control, that I'd rather be with them than face the repercussions of my stepdad finding out what I'd been up to. They could spot a victim a mile away.'

They were partly right, as Caroline's stepfather refused to call the police – but her mother saw her bruised face and obvious distress and contacted them regardless. Caroline was worried that Anne Marie might be an incest victim and mentioned this to a detective. 'If she'd been examined and found to be sexually abused, the Wests' sexual assaults could have been stopped immediately.' Sadly, no one investigated further. 'Everything else Fred said was so far-fetched that it was generally believed he'd made the story up.' (One of Rose West's lovers would later phone social services and tell them that he thought Anne Marie was being sexually abused, but this too wasn't followed up.)

Seventeen-year-old Caroline gave a statement about her

horrific experiences, but understandably couldn't bring herself to go to court to testify about the rape. As a result the couple were charged with assault in January 1973 and only fined a total of a hundred pounds. A married couple with three children, the Wests didn't superficially fit the judiciary's image of sex criminals so they assumed that it was a consensual threesome which had gotten out of hand.

The sex circle
The legal system genuinely didn't realise the extent of the Wests' depravity at this point – but later authorities may have turned a blind eye to the fact that Rose went on to prostitute Anne Marie. Fred West had become a police informer, telling them when male lodgers were doing cannabis deals and, as a result, the police frequently raided the lodgers rooms in the Seventies but kept away from Rose and Fred's floors of the house. By now Rose was taking paedophiliac photographs of Anne Marie. She'd go on to take such photos of all of her other children when they were about the same age, obviously the age that Rose was sexually fixated on.

There have subsequently been suggestions that some police officers attended the Wests' sex parties. This would explain why calls to the authorities from Rose's clients suggesting that Anne Marie was being sexually abused weren't followed up.

Linda Gough's murder
It's likely that the couple made a conscious decision after going to court that they would kill future sex slaves to evade justice. Leastways, in the spring of 1973 – a mere three months after abducting Caroline Owens – they

murdered one of their lodgers, nineteen-year-old Linda Gough.

Linda had dated two of the Wests' male lodgers in the past and had also done some babysitting for Rose, so she fled to Cromwell Street after having a difference in opinion with her parents. At first the arrangement worked out perfectly as Linda again babysat for Heather, Mae and Anne Marie.

Rose was now five months pregnant with Stephen – and Fred told everyone that her lesbian urges were at their strongest during pregnancy. Whatever the motivation, someone took Linda into the cellar and wound brown tape around her face. They probably also suspended her from holes which had been drilled into the ceiling at the appropriate height.

It's believed that the Wests flogged their victims and penetrated them vaginally and anally with extra-large dildos. They did this with initially-consenting partners, some of whom later testified that the consensual sadomasochism quickly descended into outright abuse.

After Linda died, she was extensively dismembered, despite the fact that the dirt floor of the shed where he buried her was big enough to take an intact corpse. But someone – presumably Fred with his love of operations and bodies found in car crashes – severed the thighbones at the hip and decapitated her. Later he built a bathroom extension over her makeshift burial site, a site which remained untouched for the next twenty-one years.

But Linda wasn't one of the many forgotten girls who the Wests killed. Her anxious parents went to Cromwell Street but Rose claimed she'd never heard of Linda, despite the fact that she had Linda's slippers on her feet. This surely points to Rose's guilt in the murder – if Fred had murdered the girl without Rose's knowledge, Rose would simply have told the Goughs that their daughter had moved on. Later Rose told the Goughs that she now remembered Linda and that the teenager had gone to Weston-Super-Mare. (Years later she would also suggest that her daughter Heather – in reality buried under the patio – had also gone to the seaside town.)

When the other lodgers queried Linda's sudden disappearance, Rose told them that the teenager had started to hit nine-year-old Anne Marie so Rose had thrown her out. In reality, Rose remained the hardest hitter of the household, striking Anne Marie with a belt, knife, household implements and her fists.

There's a common misperception that an angry act always gets the rage out of a person's system. Unfortunately this isn't true of pathologically dangerous men and women like Fred & Rose West. Neither had dealt with the sexual and physical abuse suffered during their childhoods, so violence now suffused their childrearing and their lust.

Carol Anne Cooper's murder

That August, Rose gave birth to Stephen and for a few months she was busy nursing him, but by November the Wests were ready to kill again. They saw fifteen-year-old Carol Anne Cooper waiting for a bus and probably offered her a lift.

Carol's mother had died when she was eight and she'd been unhappy living with her father and his second wife, so had ended up in a children's home. She was a tall, healthy girl but would have been no match for Fred and Rose. It's possible that they stabbed her through the head during the initial struggle because a deep indentation was found in her skull. Or the injury might have taken place post-mortem as Fred attempted dismemberment. She, too, was gagged with surgical tape which covered her mouth, jaw and the back of her head. Further tape was wound around her upper head and fabric was bound around her arms. A clothesline was also involved in the abuse.

After the torture, her naked body was decapitated and the bones were chopped up, with several of the smaller ones being taken away. She too was buried under the cellar floor and would remain there for over twenty years, finally being unearthed – the gag and bondage still intact – on 8th March 1994.

Lucy Partington's murder

A month later they abducted their most high profile victim, Lucy Partington, a cousin of the novelist Martin Amis. It was evening on the 27th December 1973 and Lucy, a medieval studies student, was visiting a friend. She walked to a quiet country bus stop to catch the bus home – but by the time it arrived ten minutes later than scheduled, she was gone.

Lucy would never have voluntarily accompanied the couple, so its likely that they physically forced her into the car. Fred later suggested, obscenely, that he and she had been lovers but the academic Lucy would have had nothing in common with the illiterate labourer, and she wouldn't have had casual sex with anyone, having converted to Roman Catholicism three months before.

The twenty-one-year-old was taken to the cellar in Cromwell Street where she was doubtless bound and gagged: leastways her makeshift grave included a long length of plastic rope and the type of masking tape which the Wests liked to wrap around their victim's faces. She may have been abused for several days, as a week after her disappearance Fred West visited the local casualty department at midnight with a lacerated right hand, presumably injured whilst cutting up her flesh.

Lucy's corpse was decapitated and extensively dismembered: three of her ribs were removed as were her left kneecap, right shoulderblade and seventy-two of her bones, including her fingers and toes.

Twenty years later her body was found in the Wests' cellar, buried alongside the knife used to dismember her. The gag and bondage materials also remained in the grave alongside two hair pins.

Rose the paedophile

Lucy's family were devastated by her disappearance and began to distribute posters throughout the area. Perhaps for this reason, for the next few months the Wests kept a lower profile. They didn't murder any more young women, instead contenting themselves by having sex with children from the nearby girls home. Fred would park outside the orphanage and offer the young girls cigarettes then tell them that his wife could help them with their female problems. Many of the girls, anxious for a mother figure in their lives, accepted an invite back to Cromwell Street.

At first Rose was suitably maternal, offering them juice and cakes and listening to their problems. But after a few visits she'd begin to stroke their hair, then progress to touching their thighs. Most of the children were too embarrassed to protest – and two, used to such sexual abuse, allowed themselves to be led up to the bedroom. There the sex immediately became terrifying as they were tied down and sodomised with large vibrators until they bled.

Rose also forced Anne Marie to take part in these sex sessions, some of which involved her clients, and others including Rose's father Bill Letts.

Theresa Siegenthaler's murder

By April 1974 the Wests felt sure that they weren't going to be implicated in Lucy Partington's disappearance so they picked up another twenty-one-year-old, sociology student Therese Siegenthaler. She felt safe hitchhiking during the Easter holidays, as she was trained in self-defence.

But Theresa was overpowered by the Wests on her way to see a priest friend and was taken to Cromwell Street where her hands and feet were bound and a silk gag or mask was wound around her face. Her head was also bound with a knotted loop of nylon cloth. After the abuse and murder, her naked corpse was dismembered and many of her finger, wrist, toe and ankle bones taken away. Her longer bones where chopped up in order that she could fit into a three feet hole in the cellar, near to the children's playroom. Not that the children were allowed to play normal noisy childhood games – if they made any noise they were beaten by Rose, the hymns from the adjoining church drowning out their cries of pain.

Shirley Hubbard's murder

Seven months later – in November 1974 – the couple offered fifteen-year-old Shirley Hubbard a lift home. The attractive teenager had been in and out of foster care, though she'd recently started a work experience course as a beautician and seemed more settled than she had for some time.

It's likely that dumpy twenty-one-year-old Rose took an instant dislike to slender, groomed Shirley Hubbard. Leastways, she suffered the most appalling treatment, having a mask wound around her face which completely obliterated her features, leaving only her eyes uncovered. Someone then inserted a slender straw three inches into each nostril through which she had to breath. One of the tubes later fell out or was deliberately removed during the torture and would later be found loose in the grave.

Again, her naked body was eventually decapitated and her legs were cut from her body before she was buried under the cellar. Many of the toes and fingers were taken away.

Juanita Mott's murder

Another five months elapsed, then the couple abducted another of their former lodgers, eighteen-year-old Juanita Mott. She was hitchhiking to a friend's house when one or both of the Wests picked her up. In their cellar, she was gagged with her own tights and socks and was tied hand and foot with seventeen feet of plastic rope. The amount of rope used suggests that the Wests might have been trying out a particularly complex or severe form of bondage on the teenager.

At some stage her skull was caved in by a hammer blow – and after death her body was dismembered and the kneecaps and many of the smaller bones taken away before she was buried in the infamous cellar.

Shirley Robinson's murder

Juanita was murdered in April 1975, after which Fred renovated Cromwell Street and built a garden extension. His energy was phenomenal as he'd do his regular manual job all day, come home and work on his house late into the night. He'd always had difficulty sleeping and preferred to work himself into an exhausted state.

Rose also worked hard at what she did, prostituting herself for her regular clients and deliberately becoming pregnant by one of them. In the same timeframe, the couple got to know another prostitute called Shirley Robinson and invited her to move into Cromwell Street as a babysitter. The pretty, animated young woman was bisexual, so probably formed a *ménage à trois* with Fred and Rose.

But by the autumn of 1977, Shirley had become pregnant with Fred's baby and began to tell the other lodgers that she loved him. Rose was jealous and made it clear that Shirley had better watch out. Unfortunately the teenager had nowhere to go, so contented herself with sleeping in another lodger's room in Cromwell Street in the hope that Rose wouldn't assault her in front of witnesses.

Sadly, her attempts to protect herself failed and in May 1978 she disappeared, probably taken to the cellar and strangled. She wasn't tied up or gagged like the other victims, but her body was dismembered and the eight-and-a-half-month-old foetus was cut from her womb. Her kneecaps were also cut out, as were her fingers and toes, before she was buried in the garden near the back door.

Rose threw out Shirley's clothes then told the other lodgers that the teenager was visiting relatives in Germany and that she'd gone for good. The other lodgers noticed that both Wests looked particularly happy that day.

Further children

Rose now gave birth to her first mixed race child, a little girl. The following year she had another mixed-race daughter. (She would eventually have four mixed-race children, and her mother Daisy disowned her because adultery went against her moral code.) Fred was especially proud of these children and invited his workmates round to admire them. He saw black men as genetically superior and believed that they were more fertile than white men like himself.

But Rose and Fred continued to fight for power in their own relationship. By now she was in charge of the family finances – rent from the lodgers, cash from her prostitution and Fred's wages. However Fred continued to determine who she slept with, and when. He still liked to look and listen, recording the noises that his wife and her sexual partners made. He also continued to measure the amount of semen that her lovers left in condoms, and generally took a quasi-scientific interest in her sexual life.

Sometimes she was tired and wanted a break from the sex, whereupon he occasionally hit her. At other times she hit him, once stabbing him accidentally with a knife.

Alison Chambers' murder

Shortly after Rose gave birth for the sixth time, the couple asked seventeen-year-old Alison Chambers to become their nanny. Alison had previously run away from an orphanage in Wales and had been relocated to Jordan's Brook, a home for troubled adolescent females. She was bullied there as she was more ladylike than most of the other girls, wearing a skirt suit and carrying a briefcase to school.

Alison wrote to family members telling them that she was starting a new life with a loving family in the countryside, and enclosing a photo of her supposed rural home. In truth, the photo was taken from an estate agents details and she was really living in the cramped confines of Cromwell Street and helping Rose with the kids.

But in September 1979 she became their latest victim, as they gagged her with a belt, stripped her and tied her up. After the sexual abuse, she was murdered and decapitated. Her body was dismembered and several of the fingers and toes were taken away. She was buried in the garden beneath the bathroom window, on the site where the Wests' children had previously had a paddling pool.

That year, Fred West got his daughter Anne Marie pregnant. Not quite fifteen, she was taken into hospital to have the ectopic pregnancy aborted, though the couple gave her the impression that she was simply having a gynaecological operation. Shortly afterwards, following yet another beating from Rose, she ran away and slept rough for several days.

In May 1979, Rose's father Bill Letts died of lung cancer. After this, no further bodies were buried under their Cromwell Street premises for eight years. But the sexual abuse continued within the house, with Fred constantly grabbing at his daughters. And Stephen, Heather's brother, would later say that Fred raped Heather for years.

Heather West's murder

Heather left school in May 1987 and applied for a job cleaning holiday chalets in Torquay. When she was turned down, she cried for hours. Fred and Rose West were alarmed, knowing that if she left the house she might tell about what went on there – the constant beatings and sexual abuse.

On 19th June 1987 she was strangled by either Rose or Fred. Rose had previously almost strangled Stephen and Anne Marie into unconsciousness during arguments so may have done the same thing to Heather, only going further. Her remains were naked when found, suggesting sexual abuse, but she hadn't been gagged.

Both parents told the children that Heather had gone off with another lesbian. (In truth, the years of abuse had left the teenager determinedly asexual.) Later they pretended to receive a phone-call from her. Both were tearful after her supposed desertion, but later Rose told her relatives never to mention Heather's name again. Yet she seemed genuinely shocked when the detectives eventually informed her that Heather's remains had been found in the Cromwell Street garden.

In turn, Fred would eventually explain the murder to detectives by saying that he'd ordered Heather to stay in the house, but that she'd tried to defy him. He'd caught her around the neck with his hands, only realising how strongly he'd been holding her when she turned blue. He'd then tied a pair of tights around her neck to make sure that she was dead before cutting her up, twisting her head off and burying her beneath the patio.

The power differential changes

After Heather's disappearance, Rose continued to have sex with both men and women – and Fred continued to listen or to watch them. He made home movies of these marathon sex sessions, some of which he rented out to friends. He remained obsessed with sex and with car crashes, describing seeing bodies smashed into bits, lying by the roadside.

But as Rose moved into her thirties she tired of this home-based life and Fred's increasingly bizarre conversations. She wanted to go out in the evenings but fifty-year-old Fred remained wedded to his work and to Cromwell Street, so after numerous violent arguments, Rose started going out to a country and western bar on her own. She was soon having an enthusiastic affair with one of the barmen, and would disappear upstairs with him for hours at a time.

She also rented a flat to take her clients to, and didn't tell Fred. Unable to control his environment for the first time since childhood, he promptly went to pieces. He worked even more obsessively on the house and would pace back and forward whenever he was between DIY tasks. He spent even less time than usual on his grooming, often wearing the same clothes for days and neglecting to take a bath.

Further paedophilia

Fred wanted to take control of another female, and eventually decided to have sex with one of Rose's younger daughters. He took the fourteen-year-old to an upstairs room where he raped and sodomised her. In typical West fashion, he also videoed the abuse. The child screamed so loudly that her half brothers and sisters tried to come to her aid, but Fred had locked the door and Rose was out at the shops. When Rose did hear of the incident, she simply told the teenager 'You were asking for it.'

The girl remained deeply shocked after the rape and eventually confided in a schoolfriend whose father was a policeman. The police now visited Cromwell Street.

Rose answered the door and the police told her they wanted to search the house for the video of Fred raping his stepdaughter. Rose's typically violent response was to assault one of the two officers. After arresting her, they took the five youngest children into care. Later they spoke to Anne Marie and she reluctantly admitted the years of abuse then tried to retract her statement, afraid of what Rose and Fred might do. Meanwhile Fred was arrested for sodomy and rape and was remanded in custody.

Lonely on her own, Rose adopted two dogs from the local pound. But she beat them as brutally as she'd beaten her children. Ironically, the children were given the option of going back to her after the rape victim refused to testify and the case against Fred collapsed. But the five youngsters asked to remain in foster care – and began to tell their foster parents that Fred had joked about Heather being buried under the patio.

The foster parents told a social worker and the social worker went to the police. They investigated and found that Heather West, Charmaine West and her mother Rena West were missing. It was time to search Cromwell Street...

The bodies are discovered

Mae West opened the door on 24th February 1994 to a police team with a search warrant. Rose told them that they were wasting their time, but when they started to dig up the patio she screamed at her son Stephen to phone Fred and get him home. When Stephen eventually tracked Fred down, he promised to return in a few minutes – but he didn't arrive back for several hours. It's likely that he went to an outhouse where he was keeping body parts from previous victims and destroyed the evidence.

The following day, the search team found Heather West's dismembered body – and a third thighbone. Alerted to the fact that there was a second body, they charged Fred West with Heather's murder and continued to dig up the garden.

Rose was also taken in for questioning, though Fred told them that Rose knew nothing about Heather's murder and dismemberment. Rose alternately cried and shouted at the police, telling them that Heather had been a lesbian and that she was glad she'd left the house. She made up various other stories to explain her eldest daughter's disappearance, but appeared to go into shock when the police told her that Heather was dead.

After forty-eight hours of questioning she was moved to a safe house, pending further enquiries. She promptly swallowed a bottle of aspirin and was taken to hospital to have her stomach pumped out. Afterwards she was given medication for depression and began to overeat due to boredom and stress. Questioned further over her abuse of Caroline Owens, Rose answered 'No Comment'. She was also questioned about a video, apparently taken in the Cromwell Street cellar, which showed a woman being hung from the ceiling and abused by two men. She answered 'No Comment' to that too, a reply she would give again and again.

During the last days of February and throughout March, the bones of further victims were disinterred from the garden at 25 Cromwell Street. They were eventually identified as the remains of Heather West, Shirley Robinson and her foetus, Shirley Hubbard, Alison

Chambers, Lucy Partington, Theresa Siegenthaler, Juanita Mott, Carol Anne Cooper and Linda Gough.

By April the authorities were digging up the Wests' previous flat at Midland Street, and it yielded Charmaine's remains. That same month they also found Rena West, Charmaine's mother, in Letterbox Field, Much Marcle, in the vicinity of Fred's childhood home. Two months later they found Anne McFall's skeleton – and the tiny skeleton of her unborn child – in the nearby Fingerpost Field.

Rose wasn't charged with Rena West's and Anne McFall's murders as the bodies were found miles away from Cromwell Street and the murder of Anne McFall had taken place before Rose knew Fred. But she was charged with the murders of little Charmaine plus the nine girls found buried in her garden and under her cellar. On each of the charges she said 'I'm innocent.'

Fred was charged with all twelve homicides. He at first denied involvement in most of the murders, but gradually admitted killing one he called Scar Hand (one of the teenage victims had a bandaged hand at the time of her abduction) and 'a Dutch girl', actually the Swiss student Therese Siegenthaler. He said that he'd strangled Heather after an accident and added insult to injury by suggesting that he'd killed Lucy Partington because she wanted to marry him. He remained vague about the reason for Anne McFall's death, writing of her as his 'angle' (he meant angel) and suggesting that they shared a perfect love.

Suicide

On 30th June 1994 Rose and Fred were charged together. He reached out to her as they stood in the dock but she flinched away, and when he tried again a policewoman knocked his hand aside. By now Rose was telling everyone that he was 'wrong in the head' and that she wanted nothing more to do with him.

Meanwhile Fred desperately rewrote history, starting a journal in which he suggested that he'd been the perfect father. Both Wests had physically, emotionally and sexually abused their children but he'd somehow convinced himself that he'd given them a perfect life. He wrote of the garden he'd made for them and of idyllic caravan holidays, sometimes taken with Rose's incestuous dad.

Incarcerated in Winson Green prison whilst awaiting trial, Fred kept begging his son Stephen to persuade Rose to write to him but she was adamant that the marriage was over. This contributed to the depression he already felt at having Cromwell Street torn apart in the search for bodies. Everything he held dear – his house and his ownership of Rose – had gone. Like most serial killers, Fred also feared being on the receiving end of violence and he was constantly on guard lest someone in the Birmingham prison beat him up. He wept when his son Stephen visited, admitting that he constantly had to watch his back. In his last telephone call to Anne Marie he murmured 'Goodbye my angel.' The call took place ten days before he died.

As the winter began, Fred realised that he had nothing left to live for. He began to collect laundry ties from his prison job, weaving them through strips of his bedsheet and fashioning them into a long, strong noose. Then he waited till New Year's Day, knowing that the prison would have a skeleton staff.

When his prison wing was quiet, he wrote Rose a letter that said 'All I have is my life. I will give it to you, my darling.' Then he threaded the noose through the bars of his window, stood on the laundry basket to knot it into place, and kicked the basket away.

When Rose was given the news of her husband's death, she was put on suicide watch, but she remained emotionless. Her supporters now believed that she'd be freed. But the prosecution realised that her surviving victims could prove that she was a sadistic sexual predator in her own right, rather than the innocent wife of a murderer. Several of them agreed to testify so the trial went ahead.

The trial

The trial opened on 3rd October 1995 at Winchester Crown Court. Several of Rose's female sexual partners took the stand and described how the initially-consensual sadomasochistic sex had soon become increasingly frightening. One woman had been shown breath-restricting rubber masks which had clearly been worn. A teenage girl told of being led upstairs by Rose then terrorised by her and Fred together. The abuse had included being sodomised with a candle or a dildo, something which had made her bleed.

Caroline Owens described her kidnapping to the jury, recalling how Rose had held her still in the car whilst Fred gagged her with sticky tape. Rose had then pushed her onto the floor of the car. Later Rose kissed her, becoming angry when she pulled away. Fred had then told Rose to fetch the cotton wool – and Rose had stuffed it into Caroline's mouth.

When the teenager was undressed and tied up on the bed, Rose had fondled her all over, pinched her nipples and digitally penetrated her. Rose had also heard Fred threaten to keep Caroline in the cellar – and she hadn't looked shocked. The following day Rose was the one who began to suffocate Caroline with a pillow when she screamed for help.

Anne Marie also took the stand, recalling the numerous times that Rose had beaten her. Rose had also helped her own father, Bill Letts, Fred's brother John and several of her clients sexually assault the helpless child.

A voluntary prison worker testified that Fred had told her Rose was involved in several of the murders and that she'd killed Shirley Robinson and her unborn child.

Rose then testified on her own behalf, suggesting that she was completely dominated by Fred – but her behaviour with her own children suggested otherwise. She had often tied them up and beaten them during the day when Fred was at work, then joined in his laughter when he came home and saw how cowed they were. And she could have remained in her lounge with the various teenage girls who saw her as a mother substitute – but instead she'd taken them upstairs to Fred and had non-consensual sadomasochistic sex with them. Rose now tried to reinvent herself as a shy, softly-spoken woman, but the jury were allowed to hear tapes of her shouting and cursing at the police.

After a six-week trial, the jury retired to consider its verdict. Within two days they found her guilty of all ten counts of murder. She was sentenced to life imprisonment, a sentence she received without emotion, though she apparently wept afterwards downstairs.

Obliterated

In October 1996 Gloucester City Council demolished 25 Cromwell Street and landscaped the ground to create a path leading to the city centre. To prevent the public taking away parts of the house as ghoulish trophies, the debris was removed, crushed and incinerated.

Para suicides

Unsurprisingly, given their violent childhoods, Rose's children have continued to suffer from depression and low self-esteem. Anne Marie took an overdose of pills during Rose's trial and had to have her stomach pumped out. And in 1999 she jumped into a freezing river and tried to drown herself. One of her children has subsequently spent time in foster care.

Stephen also became suicidal when his marriage broke up. He attempted to hang himself but the noose broke. His uncle John – one of Fred's brothers – successfully hanged himself whilst awaiting the court's verdict on whether he had sexually molested Anne Marie.

Stephen continues to indulge in self-destructive behaviour and, on Friday 3rd December 2004, he was jailed for nine months at Worcester Crown Court after admitting several counts of underage sex with a fourteen-year-old girl.

A return to religion

After her imprisonment, Rose West returned to her childhood religion. Hearing of this, Caroline Roberts wrote and asked if she'd now consider confessing for the sake of the other victims' families, but Rose didn't reply.

It's taken many years, but Caroline has come to terms with her ordeal and is a lively, caring and strong woman who looks ten years younger than her actual age. She's suffered numerous stresses (her hair fell out as Rose West's trial approached) but has steadfastly rebuilt her life.

She complements her work as a substance abuse worker with Reiki healing and is also a trained acupuncturist.

As I prepared to leave her friendly home in April 2004, I asked her if she had any final thoughts about the Wests' case. 'Yes, what happened to the rest of the sex circle?' she asks. It's a telling point which remains uninvestigated.

Rumours

It's not just the fate of the Wests' sex circle which has continued to cause controversy. In January 2003 a Sunday newspaper claimed that Rose West was about to wed the bass player of a Seventies rock group, but both parties – who admitted to being good friends – denied that nuptial bliss was on the cards. (Some newspaper stories are pure invention: one newspaper headline trumpeted that singer Jonathan King had been badly beaten up in prison and now had two black eyes. But King, who had a music column in prison magazine Insider, was able to report that he hadn't been attacked.)

In 2004 an expert in witches' covens said that the Wests' murders were about human sacrifice and that they were probably supplying a powerful local cult with victims. He cited the fact that the bar in the Wests' lounge was called The Black Magic Bar. But Rose preferred black lovers to white, which probably explained the reason for the moniker.

The expert noted that all of the victims had fingers and toes missing and said that this linked in with an occult spell known as 'the magic hand'. But another expert said that the spell involved cutting off the *entire* hand, not just individual digits, though such digits could be ground into powder and used in other spells.

The reality is that we may never know what the Wests did with the missing digits, ribs and kneecaps. They may have eaten some of them – Dennis Neilson, Jeffrey Dahmer, Arthur Shawcross and Ed Gein are just a few of the world's most notorious male cannibal killers. Female cannibals are more unusual, but there have been cases reported in Germany and Australia. Fred even ran a café for a while with Rose West's father, so he could have cooked human flesh there.

Satanic experts have also suggested that the Wests were working for powerful professional people – but would professionals have employed a nonstop talker like Fred West who endlessly drew attention to himself by offering to perform home abortions? People who are into such religions tend to read widely about their chosen craft, but Rose West admitted to her daughter Mae that she was enjoying reading romantic sagas in prison as she'd never had time before.

Fred West was even more poorly read than his wife. He struggled with writing, spelling, punctuation and grammar, as an extract from his prison diary shows. (He was writing about finding his child Anne Marie being sexually abused by Rose West's father.) 'I Wint up stair to him and said What going on anna Was With Me Bill said Rose said anna could sleep With Me, but anna playing up.'

A life sentence

Rose West is currently incarcerated in the high-security Durham Prison, but as it's facing closure she will be recategorised and moved to another women's prison. She still has supporters who – ignoring the fact that she sexually abused Anne Marie, beat all of her children, abducted Caroline Owens and brutalised teenage girls from the nearby orphanage – believe that she is not a sadistic sexual predator. The Home Secretary has said that she will never be released.

It's comparatively rare for a couple to be found guilty of murdering children. The Moors Murderers and the Wests were, but they also murdered young adults so are profiled separately.

At least one child a week dies in Britain at a parent's hands: for example, over eighty children were murdered in 2001, most by a family member. But, though both parents may have offered violence to the child throughout its unhappy lifetime, it's invariably only one parent who deals the fatal blow. So records show that it was a mother *or* father who killed.

These cases attract minimal publicity. At best, a paragraph appears in the local paper along the lines of 'a Birmingham man was arrested today for the suspicious death of an eighteen month girl.' The public rarely hears of the catalogue of cruelty this father inflicted on his firstborn, so they can continue to believe in the sanctity of the family and convince themselves that the main risk is from stranger danger, which is actually comparatively rare. The mother's part in her child's death – everything from looking the other way to helping demonize the infant as the source of all of the couple's problems – is likely to be minimised by a feminist interpretation which assumes that she's suffering from postnatal depression or is afraid of the man.

When it's the mother who kills, a significant percentage of the public simply refuses to believe she's guilty, and if she has a partner he's often criticised for being insufficiently supportive. Modern society tends to scapegoat one of the couple for blame.

But historically couples have occasionally killed children for profit and out of sadism, though sometimes one of the couple was not found guilty despite grossly failing to protect the children in their care.

Margaret Waters & Sarah Ellis

Margaret Waters, an educated middle class woman, became a widow at age twenty-nine, at which stage she opened a lodging house in Brixton. She took in her sister Sarah Ellis, seven years younger, who was separated from her husband. Together, as the 1860s progressed, they began to advertise for babies to adopt, usually asking for five pounds per child.

The two women treated these infants abominably, leaving them lying in their own excrement for days at a time. They also gave them sleeping draughts. Police eventually raided the house and found it completely unsanitary. The seven babies in the house were so drugged and undernourished that they did not move or make a sound. Five older children were found locked in the yard, also in a poor state of health.

Taken into the workhouse, the babies were found to have numerous health complaints. Some were so weak that they could not feed and one by one they began to die. Ironically it turned out that they were the favoured children as they were boarders whose parents might visit them – other adopted infants had simply disappeared.

At the trial, it transpired that the infants would be brought down from the upstairs bedroom in the morning and left lying on the settee until the evening. Meanwhile Margaret Waters continued to advertise for more babies to adopt and admitted taking in at least forty in the past four years.

As is often the case, she was tried for only one murder, where a father had handed his baby over to her and paid the required sum, only for Mrs Waters to disappear. When he tracked down his son he was desperately dehydrated, drugged, filthy and suffering from thrush and diarrhoea. He took his child from the household but the shrivelled infant couldn't feed properly and soon died.

When she took the stand, Margaret said that she took full responsibility for the children (though she denied that they'd been ill-treated) so her younger sister Sarah was acquitted of the murder. But Sarah was charged with obtaining money by deception though she was allowed to keep her own child.

There was speculation as to how many children had been murdered. Forty had been taken in by the sisters, of whom five had died. The women claimed these deaths were natural causes. Another five had died in the workhouse. And the sisters' maid said that another six had disappeared with nineteen others remaining unaccounted for. Incredibly, Margaret Waters blamed the parents, saying that if women didn't have children out of wedlock then there would have been no need for baby farmers like herself.

She continued to show no remorse for her incredible cruelty to her helpless charges and was executed at Horsemonger Jail on 11th October 1870.

Anne Barry & Edwin Bailey

Edwin Bailey allegedly had a relationship in the 1870s with an eighteen-year-old servant called Susan Jenkins. She duly gave birth to an illegitimate baby and obtained a court order requiring him to maintain the little girl. The baby was left with Susan's mother as Susan had to work.

Edwin, who owned a shop in Bristol, bitterly resented the five shillings a week he had to pay. He constantly complained about the situation to his housekeeper, a thirty-one-year-old charwoman called Anne Barry. He sent her to Susan's house incognito to find out the real father of the child. Anne kept visiting the baby, saying that it reminded her of her own dead daughter. She seemed to grow fond of the infant and recommended special teething powders when the little girl was in pain. The grandmother replied that they couldn't afford such powders, so naturally they were pleased when three packets arrived in the post, allegedly from a charity to whom they'd applied for aid.

The next day Anne arrived at the baby's house and it was clear that she had been crying. She explained that this would be her last visit as she was moving away. She urged the grandmother to give the infant one of the powders and the grandmother duly mixed a powder with water, breadcrumbs and sugar and fed it to the child.

Susan then carried her baby out into the garden and immediately the infant began to scream. Her body went rigid and even her jaw locked. Ten minutes later she was dead.

Poison wasn't found in the infant's corpse but rat poison was found in the two remaining powders. They hadn't been sent by the charity.

Edwin Bailey and Anne Barry were tried on 22nd and 23rd December 1873. The letter from the charity was found to be in Edwin Bailey's handwriting. Anne claimed to know nothing about the murder, claiming she only visited the baby on her employer's instructions to find out who the father was.

Both were found guilty and executed together in Bristol on 12th January 1874.

Jessie King & Thomas Pearson

Jessie and her lover Thomas Pearson lived in an Edinburgh lodging house. Both used the surname of Macpherson and various other aliases. She was in her early twenties, had a low IQ and lied frequently. He was an overweight, bald labourer at least thirty years her senior, a stronger character than she, though equally shiftless. They were poor and often turned to drink.

When their landlady was away on holiday they brought a baby to the house and the landlady's daughter saw them with it. But when the landlady returned from her vacation, the infant had disappeared. Jessie said that she'd been given twenty-five pounds to adopt the child but had farmed it out to someone else for eighteen pounds in order to make a profit. She then added that if a young woman should call at the house, the landlady should say that Jessie wasn't there. Worryingly, there were baby clothes in the house but Jessie explained this by saying that she was planning a pregnancy.

On 28th October 1888, children opened an oilskin-wrapped parcel they found lying in an Edinburgh street and found it contained the corpse of a tiny baby. A cord around its neck suggested strangling was the cause of death. When the discovery was made public, Jessie King's landlady went to the police.

The police searched the lodgings and found another corpse in the basement, also wrapped in an oilskin. This baby was female and approximately six weeks old. She had been strangled and a cloth had been tied tightly over her mouth.

It soon came to light that a third baby had died after being handed over to Jessie King. Someone had seen her giving the infant whisky. She now claimed that the baby had choked on the whisky and accidentally died.

Jessie, now age twenty-seven, and her lover were tried at the Edinburgh High Court on 18th February 1889. It became clear that she'd looked after two of the babies for several weeks, perhaps only killing them when the adoption money ran out or when she tired of their crying. She said that she'd strangled one of the babies whilst Macpherson was out because she couldn't afford its upkeep any more. She added unconvincingly that he knew nothing of the murder. She'd allegedly killed the second by accident whilst he was out working and she refused to make any statement about the third.

He, in turn, said that he'd been told by Jessie that she'd sent the babies to orphanages and that he believed her. He denied any prior knowledge of the corpses in the basement. He was let go by the court as they simply could not prove his guilt, but they believed him to be as culpable as she.

It took the jury only four minutes to find Jessie King guilty and she was carried, crying and then half fainting, from the dock. Over the next few days she tried to commit suicide several times, tearing strips of cloth from her skirt and winding it tightly around her neck. She was a Roman Catholic, so the authorities found her a priest and two nuns to talk to, and after that she appeared to settle down. She was hanged on 11th March 1889 clutching a crucifix.

Ada & William Chard-Williams

William Chard-Williams was a respectable schoolteacher age forty-six who worked in a private school. He married the dark-eyed, small-framed Ada who was only half his age. She persuaded him to adopt two children but treated them abysmally, often hitting and neglecting them. Neighbours heard her husband pleading with her to stop hurting the children – but she merely threatened to hit him too. He often fed and changed the half-starved youngsters and was horrified by the weals he found on their backs. But for some unfathomable reason he didn't take the children from the house and he remained deeply in love with his young wife.

Given that she clearly despised children, it's unclear why she decided to adopt more, taking in an illegitimate baby girl for a small amount of money. One day she picked the infant up by its feet and swung it against the wall, smashing its head before strangling it.

In September 1899 a brown paper parcel containing the infant's body was recovered from the Thames. The knots tied in the blind cord used to bind the parcel were unusual and would help link her to the crime.

When a description of the body was published, the baby's mother went to the police and explained that she'd answered an advert from a couple asking to adopt a baby. She'd given the woman – who was using the pseudonym Mrs Hewerson – three pounds and promised to pay her the two pounds balance later. But when she went to the woman's home she found that it was merely a shop used as an accommodation address.

Strangely, Ada – still posing as Mrs Hewerson – now wrote to the police explaining that she'd given the baby to someone else and had played no part in its demise. Police went to her last known address but she and her husband had fled, leaving the rent unpaid. However, they found pieces of blind cord tied with the exact same knots that they'd found around the parcel containing the dead child.

The Chard-Williams had by now left the area (Barnet) but they were found that December working in a coffee shop in Hackney. Their little foster son was still with them and neighbours admitted they'd often heard him screaming. Mr Chard-Williams looked equally overwhelmed by life.

The couple were arrested but it soon became clear that William Chard-Williams had played no active part in the baby girl's death. (Though, like all adults who do nothing whilst their spouse hits the children, he was culpable by remaining silent. Worse, it was admitted that two other foster children had died whilst his wife was ostensibly caring for them and he hadn't informed the authorities.) The judge reluctantly ordered the jury to acquit him. That same jury soon determined that Mrs Ada Chard-Williams should hang.

On hearing the death sentence she lashed out at the wardens and screamed abuse at them. She was the last women to be executed at Newgate, going to the gallows on 6th March 1900.

It's likely that Ada Chard-Williams took a sadistic pleasure in hurting her foster children. Perhaps she also derived excitement from their deaths – after all, she killed three of them. She had married a man almost twice her age so perhaps he was impotent or, at best, an infrequent lover, and she took her pleasure from inflicting pain on her helpless brood.

Annie Walters & Amelia Sach

Amelia Sach trained as a midwife, married and had children whom she appeared devoted to. Whilst still in her twenties, she set up a nursing home in East Finchley. She later hired a woman called Annie Walters.

Annie was in her fifties, poorly educated and much more worn-down by life than the attractive and intelligent Amelia. But they had one thing in common – a desire to make money and a callous indifference to the babies entrusted to their care.

Amelia placed adverts in local newspapers offering birthing facilities and adding 'baby can remain.' As this was the start of the twentieth century, when illegitimacy was still frowned upon, she had many requests for such long-term baby care. Amelia took a minimum of fifteen pounds from each mother or father and told them that their baby had been adopted by wealthy families. But no one ever traced these families and the babies simply disappeared…

We don't know where Annie was living when she first began working for Amelia Sach but by 1902 she'd become the lodger of a policeman and his wife. They were concerned when the middle-aged woman brought a baby to the house, only for the child to quickly disappear. A few days later she brought another child to the house, saying it was a little girl who was to be adopted. But the policeman's wife checked on the infant and found that it was actually a little boy. Later she heard the boy give a strange cry so she asked after his health and Annie said that she'd given him a strong sleeping medicine and that he must not be disturbed.

The couple reported these events to the authorities and

Annie was intercepted carrying a brown paper parcel which held the corpse of the baby boy. She immediately said 'I didn't poison it' and added that she'd planned to commit suicide that very night, having been jilted by a man.

The police found documents in her handbag which led them to her partner in crime, Amelia Sach. She refused to give a statement. Both women were tried at the Old Bailey on 15th and 16th January 1903. Annie Walters was charged with murdering the baby whilst Amelia Sach was charged as an accessory after the fact. But it was clear that Amelia was the mastermind and Annie the pawn, albeit a ruthless pawn.

At the trial, one unmarried woman testified that she'd given Amelia Sach thirty pounds to care for her baby. Annie Walters had taken the child away. Later she was seen in a café holding a baby completely swathed in a shawl. But when the shawl slipped a waitress saw a face so waxen that she thought it was a doll. Annie said that she'd given the baby sleeping medicine as it had been ill – but the unfortunate child was never seen again.

A doctor testified that he'd helped out at some of the births and had afterwards asked Amelia Sach where the babies were, only to be told that they'd been taken away by various relatives. These relatives were traced but they hadn't been given the children. The baby boy found in the brown paper parcel had by now been autopsied and death was due to asphyxia, possibly provoked by the sleeping draught which Annie Walters said she'd administered.

Amelia Sach remained silent to the end, but the amount of money in her savings account – and the fact that she had stored away over three hundred baby clothes – spoke volumes. Witnesses spoke of giving her thirty pounds per child.

Both women were found guilty and hanged at Holloway on 3rd February 1903. They were also buried there.

Ask the general public about couples who kill and they'll invariably name the Moors Murderers who killed five victims. But some of the British couples in the case studies which follow were responsible for several murders yet haven't remained as firmly in the public consciousness.

Archibald Thompson Hall (aka Roy Fontaine) & Michael Anthony Kitto

Acting alone, Archibald Hall was responsible for one murder, that of his male lover. Then he teamed up with Michael Kitto and killed two women and two men...

Archibald was born on 17th July 1924 to Marian and Archibald Thompson Hall. The family lived in an impoverished part of Glasgow, Scotland, though they were considered better off than many of their neighbours. His father was a post office clerk who sorted the mail.

Young Archibald's father was very religious, a lay preacher and member of the Scottish Presbyterian Church, who had a difficult relationship with his wife, Marian. She'd been brought up by a domineering mother and was now equally imperious. She was subject to terrible fits of depression and black moods which must have affected her little son though he would later say that he loved her dearly and that they were always close.

But visitors to the house witnessed terrible rows between herself and young Archie (and later with her other children), rows that his father tried to keep out of. There were also arguments between husband and wife because Marian spent money freely. After an argument she'd sulk for hours.

Crime writers would later describe the household as law-abiding but, in truth, Marion received stolen goods and her younger son Donald would do prison time for burglary.

Archie did well at school but he hated his forename and by ten was telling friends to call him Roy, the name that's used for him in this case study from now on.

In his tenth year Roy didn't just acquire a new forename – he acquired a new sister, as his parents adopted a baby girl. Roy adored her. But he loved the expensive jewellery and clothes he saw in high street shops even more and already knew that he wanted a less ordinary life.

By thirteen he was sent before the local justice of the peace on a charge of malicious mischief. Presumably seeing the incident as a boyhood prank, the JP admonished him. But seven months later he was back in court on a theft charge, where he was admonished again. Perhaps believing that he was invincible, he started going around the richer parts of Glasgow with a charity box, keeping a percentage of the proceeds for himself.

Early sex

With his dark hair, full lips and large dark eyes, Roy was a good-looking youth who was having regular sex by his mid-teens. At sixteen his sex education increased markedly when he was seduced by a female shopkeeper in her early thirties. He did casual work at her shop but she was soon taking him out for expensive meals, after which he shared her bed.

Most young men would have fallen in love with her – but Roy was already more interested in her worldly goods. He started to steal regularly from the shop till, using the money to buy tailored clothes which allowed him to patronise upmarket restaurants and mingle with the rich.

She gave him an expensive jacket, a gesture which angered his father. The man shouted in the youth's face, demanding that he return the gift. Sixteen-year-old Roy produced a knife to counter this verbal violence. His father backed off, never threatening him again.

A life of crime

Roy Hall left school at the earliest opportunity and started to steal for a living, taking cash or jewellery from shops and houses. When the family moved to Catterick Army Camp in Yorkshire during the war, he stole from the soldiers there too. His mother began an affair with a major and was soon pregnant, giving birth to a son, Donald, upon the family's return to Glasgow. Roy would never like this half-brother and would eventually murder him.

Bisexuality

The Halls now took in a Polish Freedom Fighter as a lodger, and when he made a pass at Roy, the teenager enjoyed the experience. The young captain fellated him and they formed a close friendship which involved visiting museums and classy restaurants. From now on, Roy would be bisexual, enjoying what he called the best of both worlds – though he was the first to admit that he preferred men to women, that only a man could give him what he truly desired. He was equally enamoured of stealing, and would later write that 'just holding jewels made my cock hard.'

He eventually took a post as a trainee receptionist in a

four-star hotel in Rothesay, using his time there to study the rich patrons. Sexually voracious, he also slept with several of the guests. After giving up the hotel job he ran a second-hand shop and made good, legitimate profits. But he was bored and soon returned to crime.

Eventually these crimes caught up with him and he was sent to prison, released and soon recaught and resentenced, doing time in Barlinnie, Wandsworth and Pentonville. His combined prison sentences would eventually add up to over forty years. He would later say that 'prison hardens a man, providing justification for the crimes he is going to commit.' But that didn't explain how he could steal from his shopkeeper lover who had shown him nothing but kindness when he was sixteen.

Whilst still in his teens he was diagnosed by a psychiatrist as being 'maladjusted...an exhibitionist, always anxious to be the centre of attention.' He was possibly mirroring his mother's histrionic behaviour. By age twenty-two his psychiatric assessment had worsened and he was certified as insane. Sent to a Glasgow mental hospital, he soon escaped and headed for London. But in December 1944 he was detained indefinitely at Perth Criminal Lunatic Asylum, being released in February 1946. No further information is available on his early diagnosis – but given his subsequent failure to learn from his mistakes and his ability to ill-treat people who were good to him, he probably had psychopathic traits.

He was clearly a compulsive liar, sometimes telling friends that he'd landed an exclusive butlering job when he was really working in a school kitchen. One of his girlfriends would later say that he lived in a fantasy world and that he'd sometimes leave her bed in the middle of the night and drive hundreds of miles, having had a premonition that he was in danger. His magnetic personality helped him get away with those frequent lies and sudden absences, most of which glamorised every aspect of his life.

He continued to reinvent himself, even using the surname Fontaine as an act of homage to his favourite film star, Joan Fontaine. He spent the proceeds of his many thefts on living in the finest hotels, dressed and spoke like a gentleman and educated himself about etiquette and antiques. No one meeting the handsome cultured man in a London or Edinburgh hotel lounge would have believed he came from one of the poorest areas of Glasgow, that he was the son of a post-office clerk.

Separated

By now, Roy's mother had left Roy's father, running away with Roy's best friend John Wootton. Archibald Hall senior refused to give her a divorce so the couple lived together until his death. (Prior to which, he hadn't seen Roy for years.) Thereafter they married so that Roy's friend became his stepfather. All three would remain close, though Marian's moods remained and she once walked out on her second husband for two weeks. She also ordered her adopted daughter (by then an adult) out of her house one night at midnight, knowing that the girl would have to spend hours on a freezing coach to get home.

The love object

The former son of a post office clerk continued to seduce both men and women, sometimes being paid by famous gay men to attend parties where he was openly admired and fondled. But at the end of the Sixties, during one of his many prison sentences, he fell in love for the first time. His lover was called Dave Barnard and he was doing eighteen years for shooting a policeman and for armed robbery. He was in his twenties whilst Roy was forty-six.

By 1970, Roy had been released on parole and Dave still had years to serve. Determined to have a go-between, Roy seduced a barmaid and single-mother-of-eight called Mary Coggle. Thereafter she cheerfully smuggled letters and gifts to Dave Barnard when she visited him in jail.

Roy had been staying in a prison-approved hostel, but when he got to know a shopowner called Hazel, he moved in to her apartment. She adored him but he merely saw her as a means of support and only slept with her because he believed she expected it. During this period he also slept with a young male chef and with his half-brother's girlfriend.

Surprisingly – given that he still professed to love Dave Barnard – he now married a woman he met at a party, Ruth Holmes. He'd later tell a reporter that he merely liked her and had fun with her – but years later he'd write that he loved her for her independent streak and her intellect and that she was incredibly special to him.

Unfortunately, during sex with her one night he called out Dave's name and had to admit to his continuing bisexuality. Ruth tried to come to terms with this but when he was sent back to prison the marriage floundered, with Roy admitting that he preferred men. Ironically, the love of his life, Dave Barnard, was at last out of prison – but, of course, it was now Roy who was in jail.

The forty-nine-year-old arranged for his lover to have a Jaguar but Dave Barnard lost control of the car and was killed outright. Roy would later try to excuse his homicides by writing that the killing of innocent people would never have happened if the car had reached its destination – in other words, he only killed because he no longer loved life, his reason for caring having died in the car wreck. He also said 'I had waited all my life for love, only to have it shown to me and then be snatched away.' But this simply isn't true – many of his girlfriends and his wife loved him but he stole their life savings or was repeatedly unfaithful to them.

The first murder

Roy continued to kick his heels in prison, taking various lovers including a beautiful young bisexual convict called David Wright. The meeting took place in 1973 and continued after Roy was released. By 1977 Roy was working as a butler for a Lady Peggy Hudson and suggested that she hire David Wright as a live-in handyman. Unfortunately Wright (who was on the run after killing a man in a public toilet) soon stole an expensive ring from the lady of the house. Angered, Roy Fontaine told his lover to give it back but David Wright refused and threatened to tell Roy's employer that Roy was a lifelong professional thief.

Wright stormed out of the house and Fontaine eventually went to bed, only to be woken in the early hours when a bullet whistled past him and lodged in the headboard. The two men struggled with the rifle which the drunken Wright was wielding and it battered into Roy's face, splitting open his cheek. The younger man eventually broke down in tears and helped bandage his lover's wound so Roy Fontaine pretended to forgive him, but he'd already decided to kill him the following day.

The morning of the proposed murder dawned, and Roy took David Wright up on the moors, ostensibly to shoot rabbits. When Wright had used up all of his bullets, Fontaine raised his gun. He'd tell a reporter that he fired into the back of the youth's head – but by the time he wrote his autobiography he'd embellished the tale and said that he told David Wright exactly what he thought of him before shooting him in the head. What's certain is that the youth crumpled after the first bullet struck him whereupon his lover shot him again in the chest, firing a total of four shots.

That night he returned to the moors and stripped the body before weighing it down with boulders at the side of a stream. For the ensuing week he returned to the murder scene every day, planting heather and ferns around the body. 'Killing' he would later write, 'is very stressful, very tiring.'

He realised that by murdering someone he had crossed a line, that there was no way back, and said that he could feel himself changing. Years later he would write in his autobiography 'I would say to someone who is thinking of killing: "Don't. Whatever it is that's released, you don't want set free".'

After the murder, the fifty-four-year-old Fontaine went to France for a few weeks, then to London, but he felt restless and lonely. By late 1977 he'd found himself a new butlering post, living with a former Labour MP Walter Scott-Elliot and his wife Dorothy.

Dorothy Scott-Elliot used to slap some of her staff on the legs if they displeased her, but she liked Roy Fontaine from the start and introduced him as her friend rather than as her butler. She and her husband had no idea that he was collecting their bank account numbers and learning how to forge their signatures. They were extremely wealthy – a wealth which Roy Fontaine intended to make his own.

Roy told his lover Mary Coggle about the opulent household he was living in, and she introduced him to one of her other lovers, Michael Kitto. The two men's actions following that meeting would result in another death.

Michael Kitto

Michael's early life had been even less stable than Roy's. He was born on 11th August 1938 to an unmarried mother who worked in a chemists. She couldn't keep him so he went into an orphanage, being fostered within a few weeks. At ten he was sent to a boy's home in Buckinghamshire where he remained until age thirteen when his foster parents took him back. Unfortunately details of his childhood remain obscure but given his later sexual confusion it's likely that he was abused by older boys whilst in care.

In 1953 he joined the Royal Navy's boys' service but was soon discharged as unsuitable. Thereafter he had several casual jobs in Battersea, supplementing his wages by robbing gas meters and similar petty crimes. At eighteen he joined the army, going into the Rifle Brigade in 1956 and serving in Malaya. But within four years he was court martialled for robbery with assault.

Kitto liked the *idea* of being a big-time crook but he simply didn't have the knack for it. A detective would later say that the man had probably committed a hundred burglaries but that most of them only netted him a few pounds.

Michael married and had a daughter but soon lost them as a result of his ongoing bisexuality. A second marriage also ended in divorce and he led an increasingly rootless existence, relying on drink.

Moving to London, he hung out at various strip clubs hoping that he would meet big-time crooks such as the Kray brothers – but he only succeeded in committing more and more petty crimes. He would steal and receive a fine or, more rarely, a short jail sentence. On his release, he'd work as a bouncer or a porter for a while then steal again. He'd repeat this small-time-crook pattern until meeting Roy Fontaine in November 1977. By then Kitto was on the run, having stolen a hundred pounds from his employer whilst working as a barman. He was sleeping with Mary Coggle (who by now was working as an early morning cleaner) but was aware that she slept with other men, sometimes for cash.

Kitto and Fontaine established a working relationship in which Fontaine identified wealthy properties and Kitto climbed through their windows to rob them. (By now, Roy Fontaine was fifty-four and overweight, whereas Michael Kitto was thirty-nine and slender.) The suave, big-time conman Fontaine and the small-time thief Kitto had little in common, but Roy was happy to boast of his prowess and Michael was easily impressed by tales of the older man's exploits and was eager for money-making tips.

The exact nature of their relationship remains unclear. Roy swore that the sandy-haired, balding and moustached Kitto simply didn't appeal to him sexually, that they merely had a professional relationship. Kitto at first said the same thing, but later told his barrister that he'd been sexually dominated by the butler, had played the passive role.

Roy offered to show Michael the Scott-Elliots' fabulous antiques and jewellery and the two men made their way to the impressive house. His employer, Mr Scott-Elliot, would be safely tucked up in bed and would know nothing of the late night visitor, and his wife was supposed to be spending a few days in a private clinic as her health was poor.

The second murder

Believing that they had the run of the house, Fontaine and Kitto approached Dorothy Scott-Elliot's room. To their horror, her door swung open and she stammered 'Roy, what's this man doing in my house at this time of night?' In answer, Michael Kitto (according to Roy Fontaine) sprang at her, covering her mouth and nose with his powerful hand until they started bleeding. She collapsed and when Fontaine took her pulse he found that she was dead.

The next day they put her corpse in the boot of a friend's car. Bizarrely, Roy then got Mary Coggle to dress in Dorothy Scott-Elliot's clothes. The trio gave Mr Scott-Elliot a large doze of sleeping tablets and settled him beside Mary in the back seat of the car, explaining that they were taking him to join his wife in Scotland. Roy added that Mary was a friend of his and the old man stared at her in drugged confusion, probably recognising his wife's fur coat. Having Mary dress as Dorothy Scott-Elliot was important to Roy Fontaine and Michael Kitto, because it meant that the casual observer thought that the woman was still alive. It also helped them to cash Mrs Scott-Elliot's cheques in various hotels and shops.

Kitto, Fontaine and Coggle booked into a Blair Atholl

hotel and spent the night eating and drinking the finest fare whilst Mr Scott-Elliot dined alone in his hotel bedroom. They'd enjoyed his money and now wanted to return unseen to rob his house. It was time for him to die.

The third murder

The trio set off the following morning and drove to the Highlands, their unsuspecting victim dozing in the back. When the old man woke up and wanted to urinate, Roy Fontaine helped him out of the car. He nodded to Kitto and they crept up behind the eighty-two-year-old.

Fontaine started to strangle him with a scarf, but the former MP managed to get his fingers beneath the garment. Struggling, the two men fell to the ground. Kitto took over the strangling whilst Fontaine kicked the old man in the chest. They thought that he was dead but suddenly he groaned and the butler screamed at his accomplice to get a spade from the boot and batter Walter Scott-Elliot about the head. Michael Kitto did just that and eventually their victim succumbed to the crushing blows. Fontaine and Kitto then buried Mr Scott-Elliot and drove on with Mary Coggle to Aviemore.

The fourth murder

By the time they booked into an Aviemore hotel, the camaraderie between Roy Fontaine and Mary Coggle was breaking down. Drunk, she phoned several of her prostitute friends, telling them of the high life that she was living. Roy, who knew that the trio would face a life sentence for murder if they were caught, was appalled.

After enjoying Aviemore's hospitality for a few days, Kitto and Fontaine returned to the Scott-Elliot's home and cleared it of all its expensive property. Meanwhile, Mary took off around the village in Mrs Scott-Elliot's mink coat. The two men discussed her inappropriate behaviour and eventually agreed that they should kill her – but both first had sex with her multiple times.

The killing was a joint operation with Kitto pinning Mary to a chair by her arms whilst Fontaine battered her with a poker. As she lost consciousness, the former butler fetched a plastic bag and put it over her head and the two men sipped brandy as they watched her suffocate.

Roy Fontaine's attitude to the murder, as with everything else, would change over time. He initially told writer James Copeland that Mary was a stupid and greedy little woman, but years later he'd decided that she had a heart of gold.

Afterwards they dressed the corpse in male clothing, hoping to make it look like a lesbian murder. The following morning they drove to Dumfries and put her body in a stream.

The men now lived in the Scott-Elliot's home for several days, enjoying the wealth of their victims. Then Roy received a phone-call from his stepfather to say that his half-brother, Donald, had arrived and wanted to live with him.

The fifth murder

Donald Hall, like his half-brother, Roy, was no stranger to prison and had just been released from a three-year sentence for burglary. But, unlike the clean and well-dressed butler, he was dirty and unkempt. Roy would also say that he was a paedophile but the evidence for this is almost non-existent – Roy's ex-wife Ruth had said she 'thought' she saw him touching a schoolgirl once.

What's certain is that Donald Hall was violent and had beaten his wife so badly that she left him. He also drank heavily and couldn't hold down a job.

It's clear that Roy Fontaine had to psych himself up to commit each of his first four murders – calling David Wright a blackmailer, blaming Dorothy Scott-Elliot's death on Kitto, telling himself that Walter Scott-Elliot had to die if he himself was to survive. Similarly, he'd reminded himself over and over again of how stupid Mary Coggle was being, told Kitto that she deserved to lose her life. Now he persuaded himself that children were at risk from Donald Hall, thinking of him as 'lowlife, nonce, ponce, scum.'

Having no idea what his half-brother was thinking, Donald Hall went all out to impress when he arrived. He demonstrated various tying-up manoeuvres that he'd been shown in prison – but as soon as he tied his own thumbs together, the killers struck. Kitto grabbed the middle-aged man and held him tightly whilst Fontaine forced a chloroformed pad to his nose and mouth.

But his half-brother fought ferociously for his life, managing to break free of his bonds and scratch Kitto's face. Determined to kill him, Roy kept the chloroformed pad over his face.

Eventually Donald Hall appeared to be dead (and the subsequent autopsy would show that he did indeed die at this point) but to play safe they put him in a water-filled bath and held him under for five minutes. Then they drove to Berwick with his body in the boot.

When they stopped for the night at the Blenheim Arms Hotel, the manager thought that they looked like car thieves. He phoned the police who found that the number plate on their car didn't match the road-tax disc. The men were taken into custody for questioning but Roy escaped through a bathroom window. When recaptured, he took the barbiturates he habitually carried, his overdose kit, but was found unconscious and had his stomach pumped out.

Confession and another suicide attempt

By now the police had found Donald Hall's corpse in the back of Fontaine's car. The two men were questioned endlessly and eventually Kitto said that there were two more bodies. Realising that the game was up, the butler then told them about the first solo murder, that of David Wright. He admitted 'I can't feel anything for killing these five people – not even remorse' and added the criminal's usual passive statement of 'why did this have to happen?' rather than 'why did I make this happen?'

Alone in his cell, he tried to commit suicide again, taking Librium tablets that he'd concealed in his rectum. For the second time he had his stomach pumped out.

In January 1978 he directed the police to the burial sites. In the Highlands they found Walter Scott-Elliot's disembodied head whilst Lady Hudson's estate offered up one of David Wright's feet. Dorothy Scott-Elliot was also decomposed. Mary Coggle's corpse was in better condition as it had been found by a shepherd on Christmas day.

Sentencing

That summer, at Edinburgh Crown Court, Roy Fontaine was found guilty of murdering David Wright and Walter Scott-Elliot. He pleaded not guilty to murdering Dorothy Scott-Elliot, who had collapsed after being grabbed by

Michael Kitto. Fontaine and Kitto both got two life sentences for their respective parts in the Scott-Elliots' untimely deaths. As he was taken from the dock, Kitto grinned at the reporters and said 'Life begins at forty' but he was later to change his mind as he had no friends in the Scottish prison system and only had one visitor. At this stage Roy still liked Michael and made out a will leaving Michael's daughter one hundred pounds.

That October the men were transported to the Old Bailey to stand trial for the murders of Mary Coggle and Donald Hall, as they'd both been killed in England. By now Kitto was trying to implicate Roy's stepfather in the murders so Roy turned completely against him. He'd later allege that he tried to have Michael Kitto killed by putting pure nicotine in his food. Kitto suspected poison and didn't eat the meal but other cons – who hated the fact that he was a grass – apparently poured boiling cocoa over his head.

Kitto's defence during the murder trial was that he was afraid of Fontaine, but in truth he'd had numerous opportunities to leave the older man's company. Nevertheless, he was seen as the lesser of the two evils and found guilty of manslaughter, with a recommendation that he serve at least fifteen years. The butler was given another two life sentences with a recommendation that he never be given parole unless seriously infirm.

Hunger strike

As a five-times killer in Hull Prison, Roy Fontaine now found himself unpopular with the prison staff. They would put him in a filthy cell, wait until he'd cleaned it thoroughly then move him to another dirty cell.

Eventually he went on hunger strike and starved himself for eighty-four days until his weight dropped from thirteen stone eight to five stone four. But he decided that he didn't want to die, for as the son of a religious man he believed in an afterlife and later wrote 'Who knows what judgement I will receive, when I finally depart this world. I dread to think my torment will continue.'

He failed to add that his torment was all of his own making – he had been loved and had robbed or rejected his many devoted lovers. He'd had legitimate business opportunities but had spurned them in favour of a life of theft.

The rationale

So what kind of man robs employers, partners and friends then goes on to kill two lovers, two employers and a half-brother? Roy himself wrote 'I am not a man prone to introspection,' qualifying this later by adding 'I have killed for money or for self-preservation.' But those who knew him recognised that he also killed out of revenge. David Wright had once used some of Roy's expert knowledge to pull off a very lucrative burglary, but hadn't given the butler any of the promised proceeds so Roy was determined to get his own back – and did just that when he fired his rifle into the young man's head.

Similarly, he believed that his half-brother had once grassed him to the police, and this may have been the real reason behind chloroforming him until he stopped breathing. Only three of the murders – the Scott-Elliots and Mary Coggle – came about because they stood between Roy Fontaine and immense wealth.

Yet he wasn't all bad, showing kindness to one of the

girls he lived with, Margaret. He admitted that her vulnerability touched him and that he identified with her loneliness. He also maintained a loyal friendship with his mother's second husband, though he tended to phone the poor man at all hours of the day and night asking for a lift to a safer city than the one he was in.

He also loved animals, doting on a little cat, Whisky, who he befriended in prison. He wrote that keeping an animal allows a con to 'reveal his gentler side.' During another prison stretch he cared for various pet birds, including a canary and a cockatiel.

Reading about his life, one gets the feeling that he used crime as more than just a way to make money, that it gave him an excitement that was missing in his daily life. Many young men find that excitement in sex, but Roy Fontaine wasn't quite satisfied with his abundant sex life. The sex he had with other men was somewhat aggressive and he was always the active partner during sex.

But again there are contradictions in his sex life. He was asked to beat one man with a birch and afterwards decided that sado-masochistic sex did nothing for him. It was a statement he had to reverse somewhat after a dominant female employer took him into her bed. She talked him down, slapped his buttocks as they had intercourse and squeezed his testes, and he later admitted 'I was unable to separate what I was enjoying and what was just pure pain...if ordered, I would probably have gone down on my knees in compliance...being controlled and humiliated while you orgasm does strange things to you.' Despite this experience he decided that he preferred to be master of his own destiny and never slept with her again.

Planning a complicated scam or actively stealing jewels

and antiques was always his greatest aphrodisiac. He was the first to admit that he was addicted to the adrenalin rush he got during a theft.

In contrast, Michael Kitto does not appear to have been an adrenalin junkie. Indeed, he insisted on driving hundreds of miles during the couple's exploits, refusing to let Roy take the wheel as he was such a poor driver. Rather, Kitto craved oblivion and often drank heavily – on the night of Dorothy Scott-Elliot's murder he claimed to have had twenty vodkas, an amount which would have floored a normal man.

Michael Kitto had a minor record for violence before meeting Roy Fontaine, but he might not have committed murder if he hadn't entered the Scott-Elliots' lavish home and suddenly found his drunken self being confronted by the lady of the house. He probably wanted to impress his new friend with his ability to control the situation, grabbed the woman too firmly – and the rest is history.

It seems that Kitto was less keen to kill than Fontaine was. He promised to kill Mary Coggle but didn't follow through, so the butler took over planning her homicide. Similarly, Fontaine signalled to Kitto when it was time for Mr Scott-Elliot and Donald Hall to die. The younger man would later say that he feared the butler would take his life, but it's clear that the mistrust was mutual. The men had a rifle but made sure that one of them kept the bullets whilst the other kept the gun.

Michael Kitto was a weak man with a criminal record who was initially impressed by the well-spoken and comparatively wealthy Roy Fontaine. He wanted similar treasures and for a short time he had them whilst both men lived illegally in the Scott-Elliots' palatial home. Roy seemed to offer travel opportunities and a salubrious hotel-based lifestyle. Kitto followed willingly, a path which took him all the way to a life sentence in jail.

Death

Roy had hoped at the start of his murder sentence that he might eventually be released, telling friends that they'd have a celebration dinner at The Savoy. But he ultimately accepted that he was going to die in prison and urged other potential prisoners not to follow the path he'd taken, writing 'Think again. In the final analysis my life is an impoverished nightmare.' His best friend in his final years was a cockatoo.

On 16th September 2002 he suffered a stroke in his cell at Portsmouth's Kingston Prison. The inquest ruled that he had died of natural causes, his death far less frightening than the suffocation, strangling and bludgeoning deaths he forced his victims to endure.

Trevor Joseph Hardy & Sheilagh Farrow

Sheilagh Farrow (like Myra Hindley) didn't actually murder her lover's victims. But by covering up two of the three brutal murders that her common law husband committed, she ensured that he was free to kill again. If she had gone to the authorities after he bludgeoned and mutilated his second Manchester victim, the third murder would not have occurred. Sheilagh Farrow does not fit into the 'couples where one is exonerated' chapter as she was given immunity.

Trevor Hardy's family life was unstable so he was familiar with violence from an early age. By eight he'd become a bully and eventually ended up in the approved school system. He regularly ran away from its brutal regimes, only to be sentenced to further punishment. He took to hanging about with much younger children as this made him feel important, the leader of an undemanding pack.

Early crimes

Whilst still in his teens, Hardy took to burglary. He was caught and, age fifteen, sent to an adult prison. Doubtless this showed him an even less palatable side of the world. He liked to dress up in women's clothes – and men who have come from cold, unloving backgrounds are more likely than others to have this particular fetish. But others described his relationship with his mother as abnormally close. His relationship with his siblings wasn't close, for they feared his temper. He was habitually drunk and full of rage.

In November 1974, he left prison after serving a two year sentence for wounding a man during a drunken altercation. He'd soon kill for the first time.

The first murder

In the early hours of 1st January 1975, Trevor Hardy saw a young girl getting out of a taxi. She was a stranger called Lesley Stewart, but he'd later tell prosecutors that he believed she was a girl who'd rebuffed him years before.

Hardy approached the fifteen-year-old and she warily asked him 'What do you want?' In answer, he punched her to the ground, kicked her, then knelt by her side with his knife and cut a major blood vessel in her throat. He watched as she clutched impotently at the wound, as she lost consciousness. He'd later say that 'I didn't give a damn after what I'd been through.'

Trevor Hardy went home to mother, but left the house

again in the early hours of the morning and returned to the body to bury it. Later, he dug it up, allegedly to remove the hands, feet and head which might aid with the cadaver's identification. But psychologists have privately speculated that he also returned to the body out of lust or rage. As the body decomposed over the next few weeks, he sometimes put his knives aside and rent the limbs apart with his hands, taking away the right thighbone. He threw the decomposing head into a nearby lake.

A new girlfriend

Trevor hadn't been a hit with the ladies so far, but now found himself a girlfriend, Sheilagh Farrow. She was ten years older than him, a divorcee, who would later be described as a pitiful creature. She said nothing as her new beau went out at night – presumably she had no idea that he was returning to the putrid corpse of Lesley Stewart, whose remains still hadn't been found. Trevor even removed jewellery from Lesley's body, washed it and gave it to the morally-bankrupt Sheilagh as a gift. By now the couple were cohabiting in a flat in Newton Heath, but love had done nothing to quell Hardy's violence. In July 1975, six months after the first murder, he had a row with Sheilagh and stormed out in a rage, ready to kill again.

The second murder

This time Wanda Skala was in the wrong place at the wrong time. The innocent young woman was on her way home after a work night-out when Hardy pounced, battering her head in with a stone until she collapsed on the ground. He kicked her again and again in the vagina and tried to strangle her with her own socks, and when this failed he hit her in the face with a brick. This murder also involved mutilation as he bit her right nipple off.

The alibi

Hardy went home covered in blood, but Sheilagh Farrow's only response was to swiftly launder his clothes, and when the police came round (checking out all the usual suspects) she told them that he'd been with her all evening. They had no option but to let him go.

Thankfully, one of Hardy's younger brothers had more of a social conscience. He told the police that Trevor Hardy had privately admitted – indeed, boasted – that he was responsible for the murder, so the police arrested him again.

Farrow's duplicity

By now it had occurred to Trevor Hardy that his teethmarks had been left in Wanda's breast when he bit off her nipple – so he asked Sheilagh Farrow to smuggle a file into prison, explaining that he wanted to change the shape of his teeth. There could have been no doubt in her mind by now that he was the killer who the police and community so desperately sought. Nevertheless, she brought him in the file and, alone in his cell, he filed his teeth to points. Odontologist tests couldn't prove that he'd been the man who bit Wanda – so he was set free to kill again. The police were privately convinced that they'd had the right man in custody, but Sheilagh Farrow's actions ensured that they had to let him go.

Attempted murder

In March 1976 he attacked another girl in a pub toilet, strangling her so viciously that she bit through her own tongue. Thankfully others came to her aid before he could kill her, and he fled.

The third murder

Three days later he was trying to break into a factory when a seventeen-year-old girl walked past. Sandra Mosoph was on her way home from a party in the early hours of the morning when Hardly lunged at her. She fought desperately to escape, but he stabbed her in the stomach with a screwdriver and choked her, finishing her off by removing her tights and pulling them forcefully around her neck. He also bit her left nipple off.

The triple-murderer threw the body into the river, went home – then calmed down and realised that he'd again left his bite mark on a visible victim. Returning to the scene, he entered the river and used his knife to slash dozens of times at the girl's already mutilated breast.

Arrest

The mutilations to Sandra's body were so similar to Wanda's that the police arrested their prime suspect Trevor Hardy again. This time they leaned harder on Sheilagh Farrow and she admitted that her lover had committed both murders. And, once imprisoned awaiting trial, Hardy confessed to Lesley's murder as well as the other two. He also tried to implicate Sheilagh Farrow, saying that she'd been with him when he'd murdered Wanda. He claimed he'd only planned to mug the girl, but had thought she recognised Sheilagh so had panicked and killed her to prevent being identified.

Immunity

Caught between a rock and a hard place, Sheilagh Farrow now provided the police with evidence against her lover, given on the proviso that she herself earned immunity. The victim's relatives were understandably outraged, wanting her to be prosecuted for harbouring and aiding the murderer. But the authorities knew that her statement would help keep her partner behind bars.

Trial

In 1977, Hardy was tried for the three murders. At the last moment he changed his plea to guilty of manslaughter on the grounds of diminished responsibility. But the jury didn't buy his insanity defence and he was sentenced to life.

Interview with an expert

Dr Geoffrey Garrett was the home office pathologist who dealt with the first victim – Lesley Stewart's – remains, being shown various bones and ribs which eventually comprised half of the teenager's skeleton. The head, hands, feet and right thighbone were missing. I met Dr Garrett when we shared the stage at a crime conference in Manchester, and he still remembered the case vividly. It is overviewed in his fascinating book, *Cause Of Death*, which he co-authored with Andrew Nott.

In February 2004, whilst researching *Couples Who Kill*, I interviewed Andrew Nott about the three murders, asking him why they hadn't remained in the public consciousness the way that the Moors Murders had.

'The case didn't really grip the public imagination because it wasn't immediately a serial killer event,' Andrew – who is crime correspondent with the Manchester Evening News – explained. 'And with the Moors Murderers the victims were children and the evidence included the tape-recording of Lesley Ann Downey. With the Hardy case the victims were young women and Sheilagh Farrow played a lesser role.' He also notes that the later finding of two of Brady & Hindley's victims kept the case in the public consciousness whereas with Hardy & Farrow there was only one trial and she appeared as a witness rather than a defendant, even though she was guilty of helping him escape justice for a time.

The Moors case also had a witness to one of the murders in the form of the terrified David Smith, whereas 'Hardy's younger brother told the police that Hardy had admitted to one of the murders but this was just hearsay.' And the handsome Ian Brady and deliberately-scowling Myra Hindley had photogenic appeal whilst Trevor Hardy & Sheilagh Farrow were seen as lowlife and not particularly interesting in tabloid terms.

Hardy was originally seen as being guilty of two murders rather than three, as 'police didn't link one of the murders to Hardy's other two killings until he led them to the burial site.' Andrew Nott admits that no one knows why Hardy chose to belatedly admit this murder, that of his first victim Lesley Stewart.

But one possible motive is that the undistinguished killer wanted to be as infamous as possible. He'd even hinted after the second murder that he'd killed other victims, saying that he'd 'throated one of them. That usually works.' Yet he'd stabbed the first victim and bludgeoned the second after failing to strangle her, so throating hadn't been part of his successful modus operandi at that stage. Andrew Nott sees this as bravado, an attempt to appear like an even more heinous serial killer on Hardy's part. 'There are no missing persons from that era – and Trevor Hardy didn't travel far. He had his comfort zone of Northern Manchester.' He thinks it more likely that Hardy throated other victims into unconsciousness, stopping short of killing them.

Very little information has been made public about Hardy's childhood but Andrew says he was from a 'fairly problematic family.' He adds 'most violent drunks like Hardy have a violent past.' It's certainly true that all of his violence was drink-related – though alcohol only makes already-disturbed men become violent. 'He attacked his brother when drunk and murdered the victims whilst under the influence. It's a pretty safe bet that he hit Sheilagh Farrow when drunk – and she probably hit him as well at times when she had the psychological upper hand.'

So, given that she was ten years older, did Hardy see her as a mother figure? 'Yes – he'd cry on her shoulder every time that he thought the world was against him, and as he was an inadequate man he spent most of his life believing that the world was against him.' Not that she was some shining light in his life. 'She was pretty dim.'

She was also immoral enough to smuggle the file into prison, knowing that this would allow her killer boyfriend to change the pattern of his bite and be set free to kill again. As a result of her actions 'the relatives of the murdered girls desperately wanted to see her brought to justice, but she was given police protection and immunity.'

Andrew notes that Sheilagh Farrow disappeared from public life after the case. If she is still alive she will be in her sixties. Meanwhile Trevor Joseph Hardy is incarcerated in a maximum security prison, and, though now in his fifties, is still considered to be highly dangerous.

John Frances Duffy & David Mulcahy

This case is one of the most unusual in British criminal history. Two men committed a series of rapes, then one of the men began to rape alone. Eventually the violence culminated in three murders – known as the Railway Murders because of their locations – and John Francis Duffy was forensically linked to two of them and given life imprisonment in 1988. More than a decade later, he began to hint to his prison therapist that he'd committed the murders in conjunction with another man. When the police questioned him, he named his accomplice as David Mulcahy, his erstwhile best friend.

Early writers on the case wrote singularly of 'the railway rapist' and 'the railway murderer' though some knew that several of the rapes had been committed by two men, one of whom had never been identified. Later, when David Mulcahy was convicted, most journalists simply reiterated the John Duffy story and added David Mulcahy's name, despite the fact that only John Duffy's belated testimony links David Mulcahy to the three deaths. These press accounts also left out the pieces of the puzzle which didn't fit. Rather than do likewise, this case study tries to give every side of the story, even when some of the information is contradictory.

An unhealthy friendship

John Francis Duffy was born in Ireland on 29th November 1958 but his parents soon relocated the family – John and his five siblings – to London. Not only were his first and middle names that of saints, but he was persuaded to become an altar boy. He wasn't a popular pupil at Haverstock school and before long was being picked on by the bullies. At age eleven he made friends with another boy who was also being bullied, David Mulcahy.

John was small in stature with reddish hair. By his early teens he had particularly bad acne, which would leave him with a permanently pock-marked face. He also suffered from very low self-esteem. David was much more outgoing and confident than John, was of normal height, with dark hair and an easy smile. He was somewhat hyperactive and outwardly confident but needed to be liked. Like many bullied or abused children, the boys looked for smaller victims and were witnessed being cruel to animals.

The friends left school at sixteen and took various forms of employment, such as painting and plastering. At one stage David Mulcahy was a minicab driver and John Duffy trained as a carpenter with British Rail. He was to become so familiar with the railway network's more isolated locations that he eventually chose them as his murder sites.

The teenagers continued to socialise together, though they looked an unlikely duo, David being five foot eleven whilst John was five foot four. They bought air rifles and took them out on Hampstead Heath, shooting out windows. They eventually joined a martial arts school and became devotees of kung fu films.

Marriage

In June 1980 John Duffy married Margaret Byrne against her parents' wishes. The couple wanted to start a family but no child was forthcoming and eventual tests showed that the problem was John's as he had a low sperm count. Most people would have settled for a good, childfree life or perhaps adopted – but infertility was a bitter blow to a man who already had such low self-esteem.

Meanwhile, David Mulcahy also married and started a family. He and his wife Sandra would have six children together, two of which would eventually die of cancer and one which was stillborn. Perhaps needing a focal point in their own relationship, John and Margaret bought themselves an Alsatian puppy, but it somehow fell off the flat roof of their house and died, leaving Margaret deeply upset.

Duffy began to rent videos in which women were humiliated and raped, and he told his wife and her friends that rape was 'a natural male instinct' (whereas in truth many men's first instinct is to feel protective towards women) and generally talked and acted misogynistically. On another occasion he suggested that he'd raped a girl due to Margaret's supposed frigidity. During this period he tied his wife up – but these weren't harmless reciprocal bondage games. Instead, he terrorised her and only became aroused when she was genuinely afraid.

Within two years the marriage had become so unstable that Margaret left John. This coincided with a series of London rapes.

Multiple rapes by two men

The first rape took place in June 1982, when a twenty-three-year-old woman walking near Hampstead railway station was dragged into a derelict building by two men who bound and gagged her. After the rape, they escaped via the North London line.

There were another four rapes carried out by two men that year, and thirteen further rapes in the first six months of 1983. The men always ordered their victims not to look at them or they wore balaclavas which they partially removed during some of the sexual assaults. The women were sometimes threatened at knifepoint and ordered to remove their clothes. Some of the assaults stopped short of rape when the victims screamed or when the rapists heard other people nearby.

But if a rape *was* completed, the men would order the young women to wipe out their vaginas with tissues – tissues which the duo took away from the scene. This wasn't a fetishistic quirk, simply an attempt to destroy forensic evidence. At that time, however, the police weren't doing DNA testing in forensic work.

Meanwhile, John Duffy was sacked from British Rail for poor timekeeping and took to wandering around the neighbourhood for hours at a time. (Police would later speculate that he used these hours to suss out ideal locations at which to rape future victims.) Sexual fantasy and rape-planning was becoming more important to him than everyday life...

Au pairs raped

On Sunday 15th July 1984, two Danish au pairs were walking near Hampstead Heath at 2.30am, having become lost after a night out in the West End. Two men walked past them, one tall and one of average height. One of the au pairs thought that both men were black. Moments later the men donned dark blue woollen masks and walked alongside the girls before manoeuvring them up a grassy bank. The men separated the girls and the tall one told his victim 'Now you have to be real nice to me. Okay?' He moved the mask halfway up his face to kiss her and she noticed that he had thick lips.

He told her to take off all of her clothes and lie down, adding that he'd do the same. The man then raped her for a few seconds before requesting oral sex.

Meanwhile her friend was raped by the other man, after which their attackers robbed them of two pounds. The girls were found in a distressed state by a mini cab driver who took them to Hampstead police station.

Other rapes

This pattern was to be repeated, albeit more usually with one victim rather than two. The women sometimes found it difficult to give a detailed description as it was dark and they were often blindfolded. And terror made some of them overestimate both rapists' heights. But several of them described one attacker as being five foot four with reddish hair and piercing eyes and the other as being around five foot ten with a tanned complexion and dark hair. The dark haired man sometimes apologised to his victim before fleeing the crime and on one occasion he burst into tears. The victims noted that he often failed to get an erection and that when he did, he sometimes failed to ejaculate. The man later identified as Duffy often raped and sodomised the victims whilst the other man (who on at least one occasion was described as being shorter than the five foot four Duffy) performed oral sex or demanded fellatio.

As the men became more confident about their ability to control the situation, they spent longer with the victims, ordering them to commit specific sexual acts.

The rapes abruptly stopped for a time in the second half of 1983. In the same period, John and his wife Margaret briefly got back together and tried to have a baby – but, fearful of his brooding temper, she soon left him again. Other trial reconciliations would follow but fail and she saw her once quiet husband turn into a cold-hearted man with staring eyes.

By 1984 some women were being raped by two men and others by a solo rapist. One July evening, three separate women were sexually assaulted by a man, and their statements showed many similarities and included a description that could have been John Duffy. That November, acting alone, he raped a woman at knifepoint on Barnes Common.

In June 1985, Margaret left John for good. By now she had a lover (by whom she would have a child), something which incensed her estranged husband. That August he viciously attacked and raped her and also assaulted her lover with a knife. The police arrested him and noted that he lived in Kilburn, the area of many of the sexual attacks so they added him to their long list of possible rape suspects. He was only 1505 on a prioritised list of over 2000 suspects as in those days domestic violence wasn't taken seriously.

At the start of December 1985, John Duffy went to Hendon Magistrates Court to answer these domestic abuse charges. Whilst there, he recognised one of the women he had raped. She didn't recognise him, but it was a close call and Duffy knew that the next time he wouldn't be so lucky. He saw his options as ending the rapes – or killing the next victim. Twenty-seven days later, he murdered for the first time. (And twelve years later, in late 1997, he would suggest that he did so in tandem with David Mulcahy, his one-time friend.)

The first murder

During the rapes, Duffy and his co-rapist had trawled an area close to home – but Hackney Wick in East London was the locale for the first murder. Duffy would later say that this was a deliberate ploy to stop the police associating the murder with the rapes.

On 29th December 1985, a nineteen-year-old secretary called Alison Day was grabbed and subdued on a quiet railway path. She was dragged into a derelict garage where some of her clothes were cut off with a knife. These pieces of cloth were then used to gag her, though there were few people in earshot on that quiet Sunday night. Her arms were bound behind her back with coarse string and police would later note that the teenager's thumbs were tied together and her hands were bound in a praying position, forms of bondage that John Duffy had used on his wife.

The teenager was raped and battered unconscious with a brick. Thereafter, a strip of cloth torn from her blouse was made into a ligature with a piece of alderberry wood. Again, police would later note that Duffy was familiar with ligatures and had once tried to commit suicide by using one. This Spanish windlass was used to slowly strangle Alison Day to death.

Her corpse was weighed down and dumped it into the River Lea, where it wouldn't be discovered until the following month. The only remaining forensic evidence would be some fibres from a tracksuit – and Duffy often wore a tracksuit whilst stalking victims as it made him look like a jogger rather than a predator.

The second murder

The second murder – four months later in April 1986 – was even more fiendishly planned, taking place beside a lonely footpath near Horsley which was clearly used by cyclists. Someone stretched a piece of rope across the path, knowing that a cyclist would either run into it and be thrown from their bike, or else see it and have to dismount. Either way, the person who tied the rope would have access to a vulnerable female but could just remain hidden amongst the wild bluebells and bushes if a male cyclist came along.

Sadly, fifteen-year-old Maartje Tamboezer was in the wrong place at the wrong time. The schoolgirl cycled through the sunlit woods that lunchtime, straight into danger. She too was tied in an unusual way, stripped, raped, brutally beaten and strangled with a Spanish windlass. Burning paper tissues were stuffed into her vagina post-mortem to burn away any semen. Her body was found in the midst of hundreds of bluebells, so the police named the case The Bluebell Enquiry.

Another rape

John Duffy now went out trawling for another victim, finding a fourteen-year-old girl at a train station. He put his razor-sharp butterfly knife to her throat, dragged her to the nearby woods and raped her. But for some reason he let her live.

The third murder

A month after the second murder, the third sexual killing took place. The date was 18th May 1986, the place another quiet railway spot, Brookmans Park in North London. The victim was twenty-nine-year-old Anne Lock, a recently-married secretary who had caught the late train home. She entered the station bike shed to collect her bicycle but was pounced on and dragged to a remote part of the railway line. One of her socks was used to gag her and the other to blindfold her. She was raped and terrorised – many years later Duffy would suggest that she was made to walk along the outside of a bridge, so that, if she fell, she'd plummet into the freezing water to her death.

Anne Lock was eventually strangled and her genitals were burnt post-mortem in an attempt to destroy forensic evidence. It would be ten weeks till her decomposing body was found, weeks in which her completely innocent and grieving new husband was regarded with deep suspicion by the police.

A convenient amnesia

The police interviewed Duffy again as semen traces found on Maartje Tamboezer's body indicated that he was the right blood group – in those days the police couldn't actually match semen samples. He must have realised that the net was closing in so came up with a plan, persuading a martial arts friend, Ross Mockeridge, to beat him up and slash his chest. (Mr Mockeridge would later deeply regret this act.) Afterwards, John Duffy staggered into a police station claiming that he'd been mugged and had lost his memory. The police took him to hospital, where doctors believed he had amnesia and admitted him.

Later, when the police came round to interview him about the rapes, the medics turned them away, explaining that their patient mustn't be subjected to further stress. But Duffy recovered enough to be treated as a part-time patient – and whilst out for the day he raped a schoolgirl. Unfortunately she was too traumatised to give a clear description of him.

The memory loss man was let out on bail in September, and his release coincided with another rape, this time in Copthall Park near Barnet.

The profile

Meanwhile, the police had brought in a psychology professor, David Canter, to help them identify the solo rapist. After looking at where the rapes had occurred, Dr Canter drew up a profile which suggested the rapist would have an indepth knowledge of the railways and would live in Kilburn. John Duffy had been a British Rail worker and he lived in Kilburn. Canter noted that the rapist liked to talk to the victim before the sexual assault: this suggested to him that the man had previously been in a long-term relationship with a woman. As he combined sex with violence, that relationship had also probably been violent. Duffy, who had viciously sexually assaulted his ex-wife, again fitted the bill.

The professor said that the killer wouldn't have children, and indeed he did not. David Canter suggested he'd have two close friends, and this was indeed the case. In total, Canter suggested seventeen factors about the rapist, thirteen of which would apply to John Duffy. As a result, he became the first criminal to be identified from an offender profile.

Arrest and trial

On 7th November 1986 Duffy was arrested but he remained aloof when interrogated by the police. He stared at them unblinkingly, occasionally muttering 'What's the worst they could give me? Thirty years? I can do thirty years.' Five of his victims identified him in a line-up and he was charged and subsequently sent to trial.

Trying to find the identity of the second rapist, the police put John Duffy's friend David Mulcahy in several line-ups but none of the victims identified him so he remained a free man. The police also questioned him about the murders but there was nothing to link him to them and he was released without charge.

When Duffy went to trial in 1988, the jury heard that several rape victims had identified him – his short stature, reddish hair and staring eyes made him very distinctive. There was also forensic evidence: detectives had gone to his mother's home and found the unusual string he'd used to bind his victims. Fibres from Alison Day's sheepskin coat had been found on one of Duffy's sweaters and a man matching his description had been seen running from one of the rape scenes and catching a late night train.

Moreover, Ross Mockeridge had admitted that he'd beaten Duffy up and slashed him with a razor at Duffy's request so that he could fake amnesia and avoid being interviewed by the police. Duffy himself was a martial arts expert – and Maartje Tamboezer's corpse had been found with a bone in her neck broken by a martial arts blow. He'd also kept keys from each of the victims as a souvenir, and had thirty-seven of them. Rather than attempt to explain this, John Duffy claimed that he was still suffering from amnesia and this formed part of his defence during his trial.

In court he showed no emotion, not even when found guilty of the murders of Alison Day in East London and Maartje Tamboezer in Surrey. He was found not guilty of the murder of Anne Lock, as her body was so decomposed that it no longer bore his distinctive bondage signature. He was given seven life sentences with a recommendation that he serve at least forty years. The hunt to find the man known as the Railway Killer had cost three million pounds.

Prison sources now suggested that John Duffy wanted to be as infamous as possible, to go down in history like the Yorkshire Ripper. He was allegedly devastated when the Stockwell Strangler's trial started on the same day and the press devoted equal attention to it. (The Stockwell Strangler, Kenneth Erskine, had killed seven elderly victims as they lay in their beds.)

For the remainder of the Eighties and most of the Nineties, John Duffy served his sentence in various Category A prisons. Meanwhile his childhood friend David Mulcahy remained married to Sandra and raised their surviving children. He worked as a plasterer for Westminster Council and liked to go roller-skating with family and friends.

The police still believed that he was the second rapist, so they questioned him every time that another local rape was committed, but none of the victims identified him and, where forensic clues were available, his DNA did not match.

A new statement

The police occasionally interviewed John Duffy, hoping that they could tie him to other unsolved rapes or that he'd 'remember' the name of his co-rapist. (He was still claiming amnesia.) By 1998 he'd formed a good relationship with his prison therapist, Dr Jennie Cutler, and hinted that the killings had been committed in tandem and that he wanted to talk to the police again. Eventually he told them that his partner in crime for the rapes and killings had been David Mulcahy.

He talked about the joy of 'hunting...finding a victim and travelling to an area' and said that he and David used to drive around at night in David's car, playing a tape of Michael Jackson's album *Thriller* and fantasizing aloud about what they'd like to do to women. He said that these fantasies included a great deal of violence.

He told the police that he and David Mulcahy would target a victim, sometimes tossing a coin to decide who got to rape her first. One of them would then blindfold and gag the woman, threatening to mutilate her with a knife if she offered resistance. The other would walk a short distance away, keeping a lookout for witnesses, until his friend finished the sexual assault. Then they'd swap places. On other occasions, one man would rape the victim whilst his friend offered crude encouragement. The violence escalated with time.

He added that rape had become addictive, saying 'We would have balaclavas and knives...We did it as a bit of a joke, a bit of a game...It is very difficult to stop.' But the second man in the series of rapes appears to have eventually stopped – and there was no forensic evidence to suggest that the murders had been committed by two men.

Duffy's second trial

The forty-year-old was taken back to the Old Bailey where he admitted to seventeen more sex crimes, namely nine rapes, six conspiracies to rape and two burglaries with intent to rape. The assaults had taken place between 1975 and 1986 in London and Hertfordshire. The judge asked for psychiatric reports, explaining that he would pronounce sentence after Duffy gave evidence against another man in a forthcoming trial. (The man was David Mulcahy though he couldn't be named at this stage for legal reasons.)

David Mulcahy reinvestigated

According to the police, David Mulcahy's reinvestigation hadn't just come about because John Duffy decided to confess. They said that by coincidence they were investigating a new series of rapes committed in Hampstead and wondered if an earlier rapist had resurfaced. As a result, they looked at the forensic material they had kept from various old cases, including the Railway Rapes. By now advances had been made in DNA testing – and the police were able to rule David Mulcahy out of the new Hampstead rapes. But when they looked at the semen they'd retained from one of the 1984 rapes (found on one of the Danish au pair's panties and the crotch of her trousers) they found that they had a match.

In 1998, David Mulcahy was arrested. He was very relaxed at the police station because he'd often been accused of rapes which he hadn't committed. But when the police said that they'd forensically tied him to one of the 1984 rapes, he apparently paled and was violently sick.

David Mulcahy's trial

On 3rd October 2000, John Duffy went back to the Old Bailey to testify against his former best friend. He steadfastly refused to look at David Mulcahy as he gave his evidence.

Mr Mulcahy had said that his friendship with Mr Duffy had ended after Duffy went into hospital to avoid being questioned by the police – but prosecution witnesses, including John Duffy's relatives, stated that the friendship had continued. In contrast, Mr Mulcahy's friends noted that he didn't even mention John Duffy's name to them.

The prosecution said that the two men had formed an evil bond after being bullied at school, and that by their early twenties they'd started stepping out from behind trees in the nearby woods to shock both gay and heterosexual courting couples. The police would later describe the men's behaviour as immature.

The CPS suggested that 'both seemed able to disassociate themselves from the awful reality of what they were doing and treated their victims only as objects rather than people.' In contrast, the defence noted that David Mulcahy had never been identified by any of the victims and that his wife didn't recognise the prosecution's description of him as 'evil.' She was standing by him, as were his friends.

John Duffy now stated that David Mulcahy had become so violent that he, Duffy, feared for their victims' safety. Yet he alleged that he met up with Mr Mulcahy to attack Alison Day on 29th December 1985.

But the defence noted that Mr Mulcahy had been ill with bronchial pneumonia from the beginning of December 1985, and that he'd had a home visit from a doctor a few days before. His employer confirmed this. His wife Sandra was in India so he probably had a friend or relative helping look after his three sons, who were seven, five and just over a year old at the time.

Mr Duffy said that Mr Mulcahy had made Alison walk along the outside edge of the bridge that they used to cross the canal. He said that his friend raped her twice and that they both strangled her with a portion of her blouse and a piece of wood. He became tearful as he described her death.

Turning to the murder of Maartje Tamboezer, Duffy said he and David Mulcahy had attacked her as she returned from a sweet shop, and that they'd split the twenty pounds she had with her. But the defence noted that the day after the murder, Mr Duffy had paid twenty pounds off his TV arrears. He claimed that the money came from his own bank account, but this was disproved in court as his bank records didn't show a withdrawal for that period.

Mr Duffy also said that the string used to tie the victim's hands had come from Mr Mulcahy – but forensic tests proved that the string came from a ball found at John Duffy's parents home.

John Duffy said that he'd raped Maartje Tamboezer and that David Mulcahy hit her across the head with a heavy stone. Mulcahy had then allegedly wound the girl's belt around her neck and told John Duffy to 'do this one.' Duffy said he'd twisted a piece of wood into the belt to make a tourniquet and used it to kill the teenager. At one stage during Duffy's fourteen days of testimony, David Mulcahy shouted that it was 'all lies.'

The prosecution said that Ms Tamboezer was subjected to a long and terrifying walk through fields, and that one man couldn't have acted alone. But the defence noted that John Duffy had controlled various rape victims on his own – after all, he owned several knives and was skilled in martial arts.

Finally, turning to the murder of Anne Lock – which he'd initially been acquitted of due to lack of forensic evidence – John Duffy said that he had raped her but that David Mulcahy had strangled and suffocated her.

This murder had taken place on a Sunday (18th May 1986) but Sandra, David Mulcahy's wife, said that he always spent Sundays with her and the children. It was their regular family day out.

Most of the five month trial centred around John Duffy's testimony, and for several months the jury were subjected to photographs of the murder victims. Three of the rape survivors also attended the trial.

David Mulcahy was linked to six of the rapes by Duffy's testimony and purely circumstantial evidence – in other words, as a young man he'd been Duffy's best friend and they'd enjoyed scaring courting couples together. But he was linked to the rape of one of the Danish au pairs on scientific evidence as a forensics laboratory had found that semen stains on her briefs and trousers matched his DNA profile. (Confusingly, the au pair had thought that her attacker was black.) The prosecution stated that there was only a one in a billion chance that the DNA was not David Mulcahy's whilst the defence argued that the bag which contained the items of clothing had been opened at least four times since being stored away in 1984 and could therefore have become contaminated.

In February 2001 David Mulcahy was found guilty of raping and murdering Alison Day in December 1985,

Maartje Tamboezer in April 1986 and Anne Lock in May 1986. He was also found guilty of seven rapes and five conspiracies to rape, given three life sentences and incarcerated at a high security prison in York. The trial had cost more than two million pounds.

Since then the forty-three-year-old, who was in his twenties at the time of the murders, has continued to protest his innocence of all these crimes.

The controversy continues

David Canter, who produced the insightful profile which helped to identify John Duffy, has subsequently written of the case that 'There are still unanswered questions around these assertions, even though Mulcahy had now been convicted of the crimes.'

In March 2004 I wrote to David Mulcahy, noting that though John Duffy and the police's version of the Railway Murders had been widely reported, his own version had not. I asked to see his document *A Case For Innocence*, as its existence had been briefly referred to in the London press.

Mr Mulcahy wrote back and I spoke on the phone with one of his friends. I subsequently received *A Case For Innocence* and a second set of papers relating to the case.

David Mulcahy states that after John Duffy raped Margaret Duffy, he asked Mr Mulcahy to provide him with a false alibi, but that Mr Mulcahy refused. When the police approached David Mulcahy, he confirmed Duffy owned the weapons which were used during the rape on Duffy's wife. Subsequent to John Duffy being arrested for this rape, his blood was cross-referenced to various rapes and ultimately to the murder of Maartje Tamboezer. He believes that this gave John Duffy a reason to want revenge. (An obvious question is why Mr Duffy waited for twelve years to exact this revenge but when he was asked by his mother in 1999 why he hadn't told the police about his accomplice over a decade sooner, he simply replied 'the time wasn't right.')

Mr Mulcahy also pointed out something previously detailed in this profile – that the Danish au pair who was linked to his DNA described her rapist as being black. The *Ham & High* newspaper dated Friday 20th July 1984 describes both rapists as coloured.

A fragment of Afro-Caribbean hair was found on one of the Danish au pair's undergarments, which tied in with her assertion that her attacker was black but the forensic report held at the testing lab had been lost by the time of David Mulcahy's trial, so this evidence wasn't available for the defence to test. He notes that the bag which contained the other au pair's briefs had 'four incisions made into it, all of which had been resealed and signed' and states 'Due to the nature of the resealing, an independent forensic expert...made the evidential statement that tampering with the contents would be possible.'

David Mulcahy recalls that he was sometimes with his wife and young children at the time when John Duffy alleged that he committed the rapes and murders and that on another occasion his workplace gave him a cast iron alibi. On yet another occasion John Duffy said that David Mulcahy left his children with his (David Mulcahy's) two sisters. They had alibis showing that they were elsewhere so Mr Duffy then changed the dates of the attacks, explaining that his memory had let him down.

John Duffy had told his psychiatrist that Alison Day was

350 CAROL ANNE DAVIS

walking along the outside of the bridge with her hands on top, and that David Mulcahy prised her fingers off the bridge, so that she fell into the canal. But Mr Mulcahy notes that when video footage of the bridge was shown in court, it demonstrated that the reach from the ledge to the handhold of the bridge was well over eight feet tall and Alison Day was only five-foot six. John Duffy then changed his story to suggest that her hands were stretched out side to side.

Life sentences

John Duffy and David Mulcahy are currently incarcerated in separate Yorkshire prisons. John Duffy's parents have maintained contact with him and if he's eventually freed he may be repatriated to Ireland. David Mulcahy is unlikely to be released unless he can appeal successfully against his convictions. He has the full support of his family and friends, who believe wholeheartedly in his innocence.

16 A HOUSE DIVIDED
BRITISH COUPLES WHERE ONE PARTNER IS EXONERATED

Nowadays when a couple is charged with murder, society tends to assume that the woman has played a lesser role. But in the second case in this chapter the woman was found guilty and the man acquitted. In the first case, the woman – Alma Rattenbury – was found to be innocent, but the hatred of the British public ensured that she lost the will to live ...

Alma Victoria Rattenbury & George Percy Stoner

Alma was born in 1896 to a German father and an English mother with the surname of Clark. She was born in Canada and stayed there with her wealthy parents throughout her childhood. Her father worked as a printer (though other sources suggest he was briefly a gold prospector) whilst her mother put all her energies into turning Alma into a musical protégé. Indeed, the couple had originally called their newborn daughter Ethel but changed it to Alma because they thought it was a better name for a girl who they wanted to appear on the musical stage.

Alma's mother beat little Alma if she thought that the child wasn't giving her full attention to music. By eight, Alma – who was genuinely gifted – was playing the piano publicly. She enjoyed being in the limelight, a trait which would remain with her throughout her increasingly unhappy life.

The first husband
But she yearned for love and ran away in her teens with an older man called Caledon Dolling and married him. They travelled together, living first in Vancouver and later in England where she worked at the War Office and he joined the army. They were devoted to each other and she was devastated when he was killed in the First World War. Alma then became a nurse in Scotland and was herself wounded twice, receiving an award for bravery.

Though she was a very hard worker, she craved both sexual satiation and romance. Fortunately her appearance – large grey eyes and an exceptionally full lower lip – was attractive to men, and she had many suitors. Unfortunately, perhaps because her unhappy childhood had left her with skewed notions of love, she often made the wrong choice of man.

The second husband
She married in 1921 for the second time, choosing Captain Thomas Compton Pakenham, an officer in the Coldstream Guards. He was as handsome as Alma was beautiful so they made a striking couple. They had a son, Christopher, and the three of them eventually emigrated to the USA. There, he became a music critic and she gave piano lessons. But money was scarce, Thomas was often unemployed and Alma yearned for a more exciting life. She soon deserted her husband and travelled back to her native Canada with her toddler son.

The third husband
In Canada she met her third husband, an English architect called Francis Mawson Rattenbury. She was still in her

twenties whilst he was almost thirty years her senior. He was already married but was drawn to her beauty, her musical accomplishments and general good nature – though he wrote to his sister of the sadness in Alma's eyes.

Perhaps she saw in him a loving father figure who would help repair the damage that her over-ambitious mother had done, or maybe she just craved the financial security which he offered. Whatever her motivation, Alma married Francis in 1925 after he divorced his wife. Two years later she bore him a son, John.

The couple, John, and Alma's firstborn Christopher now relocated to England and rented a house, the Villa Madeira, in the seaside town of Bournemouth. Thereafter Frances Rattenbury opted for a quiet semi-retirement – but the much younger Alma revived her musical career, writing emotional song lyrics which earned her significant royalties. She spent these on expensive clothes and partying and often asked her husband for even more money, inventing reasons why she needed the additional funds. Sometimes she pretended the money was for various operations: either Frances was very naïve or he believed he had an increasingly sick wife!

Cracks soon began to show in the marriage as her husband worried about possible bankruptcy. His unhelpful response was to take to drink, sometimes consuming a bottle of a whisky a day. She tried to cheer him up by playing cards with him every evening but he remained maudlin and frequently threatened to commit suicide.

Despite her outwardly flamboyant nature, Alma was a very caring woman and she confided in her live-in housekeeper that she worried about Francis's moods. She asked him to accompany her to various musical evenings but he was happiest in his own company and invariably turned her down.

She watched his strength continue to decline – and in 1932 her own health failed and she was diagnosed with tuberculosis. She, too, now took to drink. One night the couple fought so violently that he gave her a black eye and she bit him. Both continued to rely on whisky to get through the long, lonely nights.

They stopped sleeping together – and she would later suggest that he made it clear she could go elsewhere for sex. Alma soon did just that, with ultimately fatal results...

George Percy Stoner

She placed an advert asking for a youth to do general chores and drive her to cocktail nights. The advert was answered by seventeen-year-old George Stoner and he was given the job.

George, the son of a bricklayer, had been backwards as a child. Unlike the educated Alma, he was barely literate. He had no male friends and had never had a girlfriend. But he was both easygoing and easy on the eye. Alma chatted to him as he cut the lawn and washed the windows, and the mutual attraction grew.

Three days after his eighteenth birthday, she seduced him. The pair of them now had sex as often as they could. Alma even persuaded George to leave his parents' house and move to the bedroom next to hers, and he would come to her bed late at night and leave early the following morning.

It's probable that Alma's husband knew about these trysts. His bedroom was directly downstairs and journalist Roger Wilkes, who later visited the house, says that it's sufficiently small that you can hear people walking from room to room. But the architect was now in his late sixties, partly deaf and further de-energised by maudlin thoughts and bottles of whisky. Perhaps he no longer cared about fidelity or sex.

The affair continued and was so selfish that George Stoner would come to Alma's bedroom even when she was sharing it with her youngest son John. (He went to boarding school during the week but came home at weekends.) Alma swore that the five-year-old slept through these amorous encounters which took place in the bed next to his. It was a strange arrangement as they could have easily gone to Stoner's bedroom which was just down the hall.

Alma's previous lovers had been superficially powerful men – men of war like her first two husbands or men of stature like her current husband, who had been given two very highly paid architectural commissions within days of their meeting. She was now determined to remake the teenage George Stoner in their image and bought him numerous expensive presents and encouraged him to dominate her. But the subtleties of a sexual powerplay relationship were lost on the well-meaning but out of his depth youth Stoner, and he turned into a bully determined to get his own way.

He became increasingly jealous of any time that Alma and Francis spent alone and she fuelled this jealousy by threatening to finish with him. After she made these threats, he produced an air pistol (some reports have wrongly said it was a knife) and said that he would kill her rather than accept the end of the relationship. A more balanced woman would have gotten herself a new handyman, but Alma had a love of the dramatic. She saw this as proof of the boy's intense passion so continued to sleep with him. She even told the live-in housekeeper about the relationship.

A pivotal moment

If Alma and George had simply remained lovers at the Villa Madeira, the murder might never have taken place. But Alma took her handyman to London with her for a four day holiday and introduced him to the hotel staff as her younger brother. For the first time, the awkward teenage boy was treated as a man of substance, a fabrication which Alma bolstered by buying him lavish gifts. Perhaps the boy began to see himself as a potential fourth husband or, at the very least, a full-time companion on subsequent trips.

But the honeymoon was over as soon as they got back to Bournemouth, finding Frances Rattenbury in a very black mood. He'd been reading a book about suicide and admitted that he once again felt suicidal. Alma, who still cared deeply for the older man, suggested that he and she go to Bridport together. George Stoner objected to this, terrified that the husband and wife would renew their sex life during a weekend away.

He began to shout at Alma, saying that if the Rattenburys went on the trip he would refuse to drive them. He clearly dreaded being reduced to the role of chauffeur when, only yesterday, he had been a man about town.

The teenager left her house in a rage and went to his grandparents' house where he borrowed a carpenter's mallet. He'd already decided to remove his rival...

The night of the murderous attack (24th March 1935)

Alma went to bed – and when her young lover joined her he was clearly upset and couldn't settle. Eventually he blurted out that he had 'hurt Ratz.' Alma went downstairs and found that Francis Rattenbury had sustained three heavy blows to the back of his head as he sat reading or dozing in his chair. The attack on the sixty-nine-year-old had been so brutal that it drove fragments of bone into his brain and made his false teeth shoot out of his head. He was unconscious so she screamed for the housekeeper to fetch medical help.

Alma had been drinking whisky earlier that evening and now helped herself to more. By the time the police arrived she was talking to herself and pacing the house and sometimes vomiting. She was so drunk that she even flirted with the constables and tried to kiss one of them. She told the police 'I did it. He has lived too long. I'll tell you in the morning where the mallet is.' (George Stoner had already told her that he hit her husband with a mallet and hidden it. Police soon found the weapon hidden in the garden under a bush.)

Medics took the injured man to hospital. Meanwhile a doctor arrived and gave Alma morphia but within two hours the police had woken her up again and taken a statement. Sleepless and still deeply drugged, she said 'I did it deliberately and would do it again.' She added that she had killed her husband because he wanted to die. (He was still unconscious in hospital.) She was arrested and sent to prison to await trial. Three days later a doctor would find that there was still enough morphia in her system to cause serious disturbance of thought. On the one previous occasion that her doctor had injected her with it she'd slept for twelve hours – but on this occasion she had only been asleep for two.

Meanwhile, George Stoner told the housekeeper that he was the one who'd bludgeoned Mr Rattenbury, using gloves so as not to leave fingerprints on the mallet. He said that the mallet belonged to his grandparents and that he'd used it to beat Mr Rattenbury because he'd found him having sex with Alma earlier that day. The sex was all in his imagination – a boy with a prodigious sexual appetite, he imagined that everyone else was equally passionate. Now, out of his depth, he started running drunkenly up and down the road shouting that he was responsible for Alma's plight.

He was soon arrested for the assault. Frances Rattenbury died of his injuries that day so the charge became murder. George confessed to the police that he'd bludgeoned his alleged rival and said that Alma wasn't to blame.

Alma was now visited in prison by her first-born son, thirteen-year-old Christopher. It seems that she decided her first loyalty was to both her children and she wrote to her housekeeper of the remorse that George Stoner must feel at 'what he's brought down on my head.' It was her first public admission that he was the guilty one of the pair.

The trial

There wasn't a vacant seat in The Old Bailey when the trial started on 27th May 1935. Public opinion had initially assumed that Alma Rattenbury was guilty of the murder – but that opinion changed as they heard her speak. She was clear and articulate and refreshingly honest. The adultery wasn't a problem, she implied, because her husband had told her to live her own life when it came to sex. She admitted that she had loved George and clearly still felt protective towards the youth.

He did not give evidence in his own defence, merely pleading guilty through his solicitor. He had tried to blame the attack on his being in a cocaine-fuelled state, but witnesses noted that he could not accurately describe cocaine. It was thought that he'd made up stories about taking drugs in order to appear more interesting to Alma Rattenbury.

The jury were out for less than an hour before they came back with their verdict. Alma was found not guilty but George was found guilty and the death sentence was passed. Alma came close to hysterics – and her mood was not helped when she was booed by the crowds outside the court. The newspapers also had a field day, painting her as the whore and George Stoner as a simple lad who had been led astray.

Suicide

The beautiful and talented Alma had always enjoyed public praise but now she was portrayed as a stupid, immoral woman. She had lost her husband and now her lover was about to be hanged. Her husband's relatives became so alarmed about her mental health that they booked her into a nursing home to save her from further press intrusion. She seemed to improve there and was allowed to go out alone on the third day after the trial.

Alma still had her two children but she decided they weren't enough reason to live. Determined to end it all, she went to Oxford Circus and tried to throw herself under a train but there were too many passers-by and she lost her nerve. Later that day she considered falling under the wheels of a bus but again the number of onlookers put her off. Finally she walked for many hours until she reached the River Avon at Christchurch and wrote a note which in part said 'it must be easier to be hanged than to do the job oneself... Pray God nothing stops me tonight.'

Nothing stopped her and she took out a knife and stabbed herself six times (three of the blows entering her heart) before falling into the river. George was heartbroken when he heard.

Ironically, his death sentence was reprieved after 350,000 people signed a petition calling for mercy and he served just seven years in jail, being released to join the armed forces during the Second World War. He later found happiness with another woman and married her. By then he had changed his story to suggest that Alma was the one who had attacked her husband and he had opted to take the blame. Whatever the true nature of events, the newspapers now left him alone.

But scandal again entered George Stoner's life when he was seventy-four and assaulted a twelve-year-old boy in a Bournemouth public toilet. The offence, for which he stripped nude, took place in 1990 and he was given probation for two years.

Deadlier than the male?

In retrospect, it's clear that George Stoner was more violent than Alma Rattenbury and that he was the one guilty of his rival's murder. Granted, she wanted excitement – and the occasional loud argument or jealous fight added to that excitement – but she didn't want anyone to die. In the next case, however, that of a murder for profit, there was more doubt about who did what but the judiciary ultimately found the woman culpable.

Louisa & Alfred Merrifield

Louisa May was born in 1909 to a Methodist minister and his wife in Wigan. Her childhood was strict and joyless. She was a physically unattractive and ill-educated woman who would fail in every one of her relationships.

She married an iron worker called Joseph and had four children by him, working throughout the marriage until his death from a diseased liver. It's likely that heavy alcohol consumption contributed to this. Louisa made it clear that she'd despised him – she'd go on to make similar comments about every husband she had.

Three months later she married her lodger, Richard Watson, who was aged seventy-eight. She herself was only in her thirties. He died two months later of a heart attack. Determined to enjoy a better quality of life, she committed ration book fraud, obtaining seven ration books by deception. In 1946 she went to prison for 84 days. The following year, her three youngest children were taken into care as she'd been neglecting them.

At forty-six she married for a third time, choosing Alfred Merrifield, a Blackpool-based pensioner in his late sixties who was very deaf. She told acquaintances that she married him because he kept pestering her to do so but it's more likely she thought that she wouldn't be able to tempt a younger and more vital husband, for by now Louisa was bespectacled, increasingly plain and several stones overweight.

She certainly hadn't married Alfred for his money because he didn't have any. From the start, the couple had financial problems so she did cooking and nursing work. But she was so difficult to get on with that she went through twenty jobs in just three years, couldn't earn enough to supplement his pension and took to pawning the few possessions they had.

On 10th March 1953 she spotted an advertisement in the West Lancashire Evening Gazette asking for a live-in housekeeper in Norbreck, a salubrious part of Blackpool. Mr and Mrs Merrifield went along and were given the job. It's unclear why this ill-matched couple were chosen as there were fifty eager applicants for the work. Their new employer was a seventy-nine-year-old invalid called Sarah Ricketts who wanted someone to do the chores, keep her company and provide the occasional cooked meal. Partially paralysed, she spent most of her life in bed and often ignored food in favour of cheering alcoholic drinks. She was known to be difficult and demanding and was forever changing her will in favour of various tradesmen and women, possibly as a way of emotionally blackmailing her daughters to bow to her often eccentric requests.

The day after answering the advert, the Merrifields moved in to Mrs Ricketts' cosy bungalow. Louisa cooked the meals and cleaned the rooms whilst Alfred cleared the overgrown garden. Sarah Ricketts was delighted with her new housemates and praised them to the skies. After all, she'd been living off cereal and jam and now they were providing her with nutritious hot meals. The Merrifields also sat by her bed for hours talking to her and she gladly handed over her chequebook so that they could pay the bills on her behalf. It's likely that during these long talks they encouraged her to think badly of her daughters, the beneficiaries to her estate.

Whatever the sequence of events, within days of making their acquaintance she decided to change her will in their favour. She told her solicitor that the couple were looking after her so now she was looking after them. The solicitor was surprised but it was clear that she wasn't senile so the changes to the will were duly made and signed.

That same month, both Mr and Mrs Merrifield travelled to Manchester where they bought rat poison. Mr Merrifield clearly wasn't concerned about getting himself noticed for he spoke to the shopkeeper about his leg ulcers and about being deaf. Buying rat poison was perfectly legal – but they had travelled fifty miles to buy a poison that they could have purchased locally.

By April, Louisa was complaining openly to tradesmen that Sarah Ricketts was difficult to nurse. The elderly lady often tried to get out of bed at night, constantly complained of the cold and sent back meals uneaten. She told the man who delivered her regular supply of alcohol that she thought the Merrifields were spending her money and that they'd have to go...

At this stage someone put rat poison into Sarah Ricketts' food and she began to complain of terrible stomach pains. She cried when she went to the bathroom and after four or five hours of suffering lost the power of speech. She died on 14th April 1953, five hours after the poison was administered. It was also less than five weeks after inviting the Merrifields into her home.

Poison was found in the old woman's body and immediately suspicion fell on the oddly-matched housekeeping couple. First, Louisa showed no sadness at her employer's death and boasted to anyone who would listen that she now owned the old lady's bungalow. She also told journalists that she believed her husband, now seventy, might have been tempted into bed by the partially-paralysed invalid. She clearly hated her husband

and described him as an idiot and a bore.

The couple were quickly arrested and went on trial that summer. Alfred Merrifield denied ever being in Manchester – but his general confusion clouded many of the issues. He also denied having any kind of sexual relationship with his elderly employer and cut a kindly – if somewhat self-pitying – figure in the dock. Meanwhile his wife repeated her suspicions that Sarah Ricketts had tried to cajole Alfred into bed. As a result, the judge described Louisa Merrifield as 'a vulgar and stupid woman with a dirty mind.' Her stupidity was such that she had told a woman at a bus stop that she'd inherited a bungalow. The problem was, she'd said this three days before Sarah Ricketts died...

The trial lasted nine days at the end of which she was found guilty and sentenced to be hanged. The jury couldn't decide about Alfred so the judge ordered a retrial. But before the retrial could take place the Attorney General decided that the murder charge against the old man should be dropped. He did not make his reasons for this public, something he was not obliged to do.

Meanwhile Alfred Merrifield gave an interview to a national newspaper, admitting that he was increasingly afraid of his imprisoned wife. He'd found out that she'd taken out seven insurance policies on his life and added that during their marriage she'd treated him so badly that his health had broken down. Nevertheless, he found the energy to visit her twice before she was hanged at Strangeways Prison, Manchester on 18th September 1953, the last woman to be executed at the jail.

Alfred's health continued to decline, not helped by the

fact that the courts eventually ordered him to give up the bungalow. He tried to make some money by appearing in local fairground sideshows but ultimately died in penury in a Blackpool hospital in 1962. He was eighty years old.

BIZARRE COUPLES WHO KILL

Most of the deadly duos in this book had a clear motive. That is, they were impoverished and killed to inherit wealth or they were deeply misogynistic and killed for sexual satisfaction. But the following cases have weirder elements.

Christine & Lea Papin

The Papin's double murder is strange because the violence used was so excessive and because one sister exactly copied the other in gouging and battering their victims to death.

Christine Papin was born near Paris in 1905, the second daughter of a deeply dysfunctional couple. Seven years later her parents gave her a sister, Lea. Their father was an alcoholic who sexually assaulted their older sister – and the girls fared little better with their mother who had a hysterical personality.

Eventually the family broke up, the oldest girl fleeing to a nunnery whilst Christine went to a convent school and Lea to an orphanage. They never again saw their elder sister after she became a nun. But they doubtless heard that their uncle had committed suicide and that one of their cousins was committed to an insane asylum until he died.

Christine and Lea grew up to look so similar, with their almond-shaped eyes, full mouths and wavy hair that they could have passed as twins. When the girls were of age they were reunited and found jobs together as live-in maids. They were hard workers but would frequently change jobs in search of better pay. They were wholly reliant on each other and never went to social events like other teenage maids did and it was suspected that they were lesbian lovers, a claim which both would later deny.

In 1927 – aged twenty-two and fifteen – the Papin sisters found employment at the beautiful home of retired lawyer Monsieur Rene Lancelin, his wife Madam Lancelin and adult daughter Genevieve. They were employed as housemaid and cook by the family and given a bedroom in the upstairs part of the house. They ate the same food as the Lancelins, earned enough to amass substantial savings and had a heater in their room, something that was unusual for servants in 1930s France.

But the girls' lot was not a happy one. After they had dusted, Madam Lancelin would walk around the house wearing white gloves and touching the surfaces in search of specks of dirt. And she would send notes of complaint down to the kitchen if she wasn't happy with the meals. In the six years that the Papins were to work there, she rarely spoke to them directly, communicating with glares and scribbled complaints. The girls sat in their room night after night and read religious tracts which promised that the meek would inherit the earth. But Christine, increasingly suffering from a persecution complex, was tired of being meek.

On 1st February 1933, the iron broke and Madam Lancelin deducted five francs from Lea's wages to pay for the repair. The following day the iron broke again, this time fusing the lights. The sisters were frightened as they waited for their mistress to return, unsure of what she would do or say.

A double murder

Within hours of the iron fusing, Madam and Mademoiselle Lancelin returned home, bringing a parcel of meat with them. For some unknown reason they were ascending the stairway with the meat when they were confronted by Christine who explained about the iron. Sensing that the older woman was going to hit her, she jumped – strangely – at her daughter Genevieve and gouged out her eyes. She shouted to Lea to do the same to Madam Lancelin and Lea immediately copied her actions, leaping onto the older Lancelin and pulling out her eyes with her fingertips.

Whilst the sightless victims blundered around in agony, Christine dashed downstairs and returned with a kitchen knife and a hammer. The Papins then took turns in bludgeoning the still-conscious women. Christine would stab one victim then hand the knife to her sister who would stab the other victim in the exact same way. Christine also grabbed a pewter pot from an occasional table and bludgeoned the screaming victims with that.

When the two women were dead or dying, the sisters pulled their fingernails out and partially undressed them. They pulled Madamoiselle Lancelin's knickers down and stabbed her multiple times in the buttocks and in the calves. During the assault they knocked out all of their mistress's teeth and some of Genevieve's teeth – one of her molars would later be found embedded in her scalp. Lea finished the mutilation by stabbing Genevieve's thigh tops as Christine had told her that the source of life was between the thighs.

Afterwards the sisters rushed to their room and stripped off their blood-stained clothes then got into one of the beds together and lay there waiting for the police to arrive.

The newspapers would suggest that they were naked but they had actually put on dressing gowns.

That day Monsieur Lancelin got no answer when he phoned home – and he returned to find himself locked out though he could see candle light shining from the maid's room. Alarmed that something had happened to his family, he contacted the police. They broke in and saw the half-naked corpses then found themselves staring at the disembodied eyes.

Trial

The trial took place on 20th September 1933. Both women moved slowly as they entered the courtroom, their faces betraying no emotion. They seemed unaware of the enormity of what they'd done and, when asked if they had any regrets, neither replied.

Christine said that she wasn't prepared to be hit by her employer so had struck first. Lea, clearly the passive one of the sisters, corroborated this. The sisters had such a poor defence that their appalling childhoods weren't referred to and psychiatric reports suggested that both young women were of sound mind. In reality, Christine had started to have holy visions whilst awaiting trial and had become so animated that she managed to extricate herself from her straitjacket, a feat previously believed impossible. Lea also acted oddly in prison, so distraught without Christine that she rarely moved or spoke. Both girls ceased to menstruate whilst in prison and Christine often went into sexual paroxysms during which she begged for her sister to be brought to her.

Eventually Christine went on hunger strike, at which point the authorities briefly reunited her with her sister.

But she fell on Lea so passionately that the younger girl began to choke. She tried to tear Lea's blouse off, begging 'say yes to me, Lea, say yes.' Lea remained completely passive throughout this show of combined lust and love.

When Christine received the death penalty she appeared shocked and collapsed – yet she'd previously told her jailers that she expected to be beheaded. Her younger sister was given ten years' hard labour as she'd clearly been dominated by the more forceful – and less rational – Christine.

Update

Christine Papin's death sentence was commuted to life imprisonment but in jail she very quickly showed signs of insanity. She was transferred to a psychiatric hospital where she died age thirty-two. Lea served her own ten year sentence then disappeared from the public record. Free of her sister's malign influence, she was not expected to offend again.

Teri Depew & Carole Hargis

This case stands out from many others because of the disturbing number of times – and the ways in which – the couple tried to kill their victim, a man who had done them no harm.

Carole and Teri lived next door to each other in an attractive part of San Diego. Carole, who was thirty-six, was married to David who was in the Marine Corps. They lived with her two sons from a previous marriage, and it was clear to everyone that David doted on his ready-made family and was deeply in love with his attractive blonde wife.

Unfortunately Carole soon fell in love with twenty-seven-year-old Teri and the two women decided that life would be much better without David. The fact that he had a forty thousand dollar insurance policy which named Carole as the beneficiary made his death even more attractive to them.

During the first attempt to kill him, Carole pretended to trip whilst drying her hair and threw her hairdryer into David's shower. He survived so she then drugged his food but he just thought that he had flu and was given medical treatment at his work. Incredibly, they then took the poison sac from Teri's pet tarantula and fed it to David in a pie but he noticed the foreign object and put it to one side of his plate.

The two sociopaths now tried even harder to kill the unsuspecting young man, drugging him then pushing a needle into his flesh in the hope of introducing an air bubble. But he jerked in his sleep and part of the needle broke off in his arm. The women got forceps and removed the telltale implement and when the drug wore off, David woke up and assumed he'd been bitten by a particularly ferocious ant.

On the last night of his life, 20th July 1977, he took Carole's children to a Boy Scouts meeting then spent time playing card games with Carole and Teri. He went to bed first and fell fast asleep, whereupon Teri hit him with a heavy weight. Horribly injured, he woke up and called his wife's name, his voice getting weaker by the second. But she merely urged her lover to return to the bedroom and bludgeon him again. Teri obliged, after which they tried to drag his body to the Hargis' truck. But he was bleeding so badly that they had to bandage his head and ears to staunch the blood.

Eventually Teri drove off with the body and dumped it over a bridge. Meanwhile Carole laundered the blood-soaked bedding. But she couldn't get all of the blood from the walls and resorted to repainting them.

The next morning Carole reported David missing, explaining that he'd gone out snake-hunting the night before and hadn't returned. But to her consternation his body was soon found beneath the bridge with the bandages still sticking to his ears and head. This clearly wasn't an ordinary mugging as it was apparent that someone had tried very hard to staunch the blood.

The investigators went to David's house and found blood under the wet paint on the walls and blood in David's truck. Now Teri told the police that she'd killed David in the truck after he made a pass at her – but they knew that he'd been killed in his own bed.

Teri went to jail awaiting trial and soon turned Carole in. Carole, in turn, now said that Teri had made her go along with the murder plot by threatening her children. Love, as it so often does with unstable people, had turned to hate.

In court during November 1977, Teri pleaded guilty and was sentenced to life imprisonment. Carole's trial followed a month later, during which she suggested that that her butch lesbian neighbour had terrorised her into covering up the murder. Carole sobbed throughout her testimony and sounded like a terrorised child. But the jury were allowed to hear the call she'd made to the police when she reported her husband missing, during which she'd wept, until they put her on hold – then talked calmly to Teri, not realising that the police tape was still recording. She'd cried some more as soon as the operator came back on the line.

Carole hoped to win a forty thousand pound life insurance policy and an Oscar, but – like Teri – had to settle for life imprisonment.

David Terence Sandman & Daniel Antonious Delker

This British case is out of the ordinary because the ingredients include so-called witchcraft and a victim who had previously been a rapist. And one of the killers had killed before ...

Daniel Delker was a twenty-three-year-old trainee machinist living away from home when his mother Melanie met witchcraft enthusiast James Bowman at a psychic fair. Bowman was living in a hostel for the homeless but soon moved into her house in Cornholme, West Yorkshire. Sadly, she doesn't appear to have had any psychic warnings about his past. For Bowman was a career criminal who'd served sentences for rape, indecent assault, abduction and robbery and had numerous failed relationships. Unsurprisingly, his latest love affair also failed.

Melanie threw him out but he set up a campsite in the woods behind her house, upsetting her and one of her sons who she lived with. So she asked Daniel and his friend David Sandham to stay for the weekend. Daniel was a rational young man who would later tell the police that 'I don't believe in spirits or anything like that. It's claptrap and I ignored it.' But he felt sorry for his mother who claimed to have seen Bowman outside her house casting a voodoo spell over a bunch of flowers.

On 14th September 2002, the young men went for a walk in the woods. They located James Bowman's campsite and began to reign blows upon him. They battered his head with rocks and stones at least twenty times, fracturing his skull and damaging one of his eyes. They stabbed him in the chest, shoulders, back, thighs and buttocks then left him to die, a fate which may have taken two hours.

Arrest and trial

When James Bowman's battered body was found, Daniel's mother, one of his brothers, David Sandham, and Daniel himself were arrested. But Daniel's mother was released due to lack of evidence and, though his younger brother went to court, he was also freed as the authorities weren't convinced he'd helped kill the self-styled wiccan priest.

The case against Daniel Delker and his friend David Sandham was tried in Leeds on 1st May 2003. A female friend had overheard Delker talking about kicking someone in the face near a campfire. But he continued to deny attacking James Bowman until he heard that Bowman's blood had been found on his boots. He then said he'd kicked the man in the face after finding him near his mother's property – but there was too much blood for it to have come from one glancing blow. Bowman's blood had also been found on David Sandham's trousers and the pathologist was convinced that Bowman's injuries came from more than one assailant.

The court heard that Daniel's mother had suffered a breakdown during her relationship with Bowman and that Bowman had resented looking after her. The men – now twenty-four – heard witnesses say that Daniel Delker was protective towards his mother and wanted her to find a man who had a job and prospects rather than the charity cases she tended to adopt.

The jury listened bemused as witnesses talked of how Bowman's wicca had offended their own religious beliefs. It was a classic case of 'my magic good, your magic bad.'

After two weeks of evidence, both Daniel Delker and David Sandham were found guilty and given life sentences. Only then was it made public that David Sandham had killed before. Six years previously – in 1997 – he'd been given a five year sentence for the manslaughter of his brother who he stabbed to death after a row about the washing up.

Magdalena & Eleazor Solis

Magdalena Solis lived in Monterrey in north-east Mexico. In the late 1950s and early 60s she made a living as a prostitute, her pimp being her homosexual brother Eleazor.

In 1962 the siblings joined a cult based around offering sex to the gods and goddesses. This involved Magdalena having sex with the females of the group whilst Eleazor had sex with the men. These rituals were supposed to appease the gods and make the harvest prosper, so the cult received money from religious farmers in the area.

Eventually the harvest failed and the farmers became disaffected – but Magdalena promised them renewed fortune if they sacrificed two human beings. She, her brother, and other members of the cult consequently stoned two men to death. This revitalised the farmers' interest and over the next few months eight more cult members were sacrificed, after which Magdalena beat her lesbian lover to death. Her brother participated when another cult member had his heart cut out, at which stage word got back to the surrounding villages that people were joining the cult and promptly disappearing, never to be seen again.

A police officer investigated and was soon hacked to death by the group. Angry at this death, one of the cult members then killed the cult's founder. Reinforcements went in and arrested a dozen murderous devotees, most of whom received appropriately long sentences. Magdalena & Eleazor Solis were both sentenced to thirty years' imprisonment, the maximum sentence that could be given in Mexico at that time.

Daniel & Manuela Ruda

Daniel Ruda began to lust for blood at the age of twelve, describing a metallic salty taste in his mouth which accompanied an urge to kill. He would later be diagnosed with a severe personality disorder and it's likely it began at this early age. Nevertheless, he found work as a car parts salesman in his native Germany and regularly partied with friends.

By his twenties he had become involved in the neo-Nazi movement, joining up with other skinheads and fascists to protest about Germany's ethnic minorities. By the time of the 1998 general election he was canvassing for the fascist National Democratic Party. Through this movement he met the more extreme members of the German Gothic community, young men and women who practiced Satanic rituals and who drank each others blood.

Some of these youngsters had been targeted by those in the extreme right who'd noted that it was possible to influence people politically through the entertainment industry. Unemployed young Goths, they could see, were searching for an identity and could be slowly persuaded to adopt an extreme right-wing stance. This started with persuading German Goths to wear neo-Nazi symbols as a way to shock their parents. The next step was to give them tickets to concerts featuring neo-Nazi bands. In this way, Daniel Ruda became involved in the extreme Gothic scene as well as with the far right. He lost friends because of his politics and became more and more alienated from society.

But the party did badly in the election (after which their very legality was called into question) and Daniel drifted away from them, turning instead to black metal music, a variant of heavy metal, and joining a band called the Bloodsucking Freaks.

When the freaks couldn't satisfy his longing for a special companion, he placed an advert in a black metal fanzine which read 'Black-haired vampire seeks princess of darkness who despises everything and everybody and has bidden farewell to life.' Needless to say, the girls weren't exactly queuing up for the vampire – but an equally alienated twenty-one-year-old called Manuela replied.

Manuela

Manuela was thirteen when she began to bite people in the street. She was sent to a psychiatrist but her problems continued. At fourteen she believed that the devil had contacted her – the mentally ill often have such religious hallucinations, as can others under stress. By her mid-teens she had dropped out of school and shortly afterwards took an overdose.

At sixteen she ran away from home and travelled to London, becoming more firmly involved in the vampire scene through people she met at a Gothic club in Islington. The male clubbers followed her about but she pretended to only be interested in their blood and would claim 'they were my blood donors.' It's more likely that she found she could keep their attention by playing hard to get.

At age seventeen she travelled to Scotland and met up with other alienated Goths. Soon she was cutting her arms and sleeping on graves: photographs taken at the time show a somewhat overweight and desperately unhappy teenager, her white flesh spilling over constricting fetish clothes. But even vampires have to earn a wage, so she took a job as a hotel chambermaid.

By now Manuela had read about a sixty-two-year-old recluse who called himself the leopard man and who lived on the Isle of Skye. She got in touch, telling him that she hated everything and everyone and when the hotel closed for the winter she moved in with him.

In 1998 she travelled back to Germany. There she re-established contact with a former friend who noted that she was always desperate to be the centre of attention and that she loved to be photographed. But her friend also saw her good qualities – that she was reliable and honest, though she didn't let people get too close.

Fewer people wanted to get close after she had two of her teeth removed and replaced with animal fangs which she later had sharpened to points, the better to pierce human flesh with. She pierced such flesh – and sucked the blood – of other so-called vampires and Goths. Most Goths are harmless individuals who simply enjoy the style of dress, the music: even those few extremists who suck blood don't usually kill. But most vampires also don't bite strangers in the street. It was eight years since Manuela had done so and she still hadn't received significant psychiatric intervention. Now the girl who was full of hatred was responding to an advert from a man who also hated everything.

Beast meets beast

In autumn 2000 the couple met up and it was love at first bite. They began to spend more and more time together, and their blood lust intensified. Manuela cut a chunk out of Daniel's flesh and ate it. She also carved a pentagram on his chest.

They moved in together and Daniel drank from Manuela's veins so often that she had cuts everywhere. She'd often worn outlandish punk haircuts in the past but now she shaved off most of her hair. More tellingly, she started to talk about other people as if they were vermin – and vermin is routinely destroyed.

Daniel's grip on reality also lessened during this time. He'd been good at his job and was so reliable that his boss was thinking of putting him in charge of a second-hand car showroom. But now he was often ill and absent, lying about at home listening to black metal lyrics. And when he and Manuela did go out it was to take part in a Satanic sect.

Manuela bought a coffin which she sometimes slept in and she began to avoid the sun which must have played havoc with her body's supply of Vitamin D.

The couple (he was now twenty-six and she was twenty-three) decided to marry at the Registry Office and chose 6th June 2001. It was the sixth day of the sixth month but they needed another six to make up 666, the so-called number of the beast. So they decided to kill someone on the 6th of the following month.

The murder
On 6th July the couple invited thirty-three-year-old Frank Hackert to their home in Witten, West Germany. They believed that Lucifer had told them to kill and that he would like a court jester, so they chose Frank Hackert, a colleague of Daniel's who made them laugh. They told Frank that they were having a party – but in truth he was the only guest.

The couple chatted and shared drinks with Frank for a while, then Daniel walked behind him and dealt him two heavy blows to the head with a hammer. After a moment the bewildered man stood up and Manuela began to stab him with a knife, believing that it was glowing. In total she stabbed him sixty-six times. She'd later say that she saw his soul leave 'for the underworld' and added 'we were empowered and alone.' The couple then mutilated his corpse by cutting the veins and pouring his blood into a bowl, which they drank from. They left a scalpel protruding from his stomach and cut a pentagram, the sign of the devil, into his chest. They also mutilated his face and his arms and stubbed out cigarettes on his back.

Life after death
After the murder, the couple took their car and went on a sort of pilgrimage to towns where Jewish people had been murdered. Before she left, Manuela sent a farewell letter to her mother which said 'I am not of this world. I must liberate my soul from the mortal flesh.' Fearing that her daughter had made another suicide attempt, Manuela's mother went to the police who broke into the couple's house and found Frank Hackert's mutilated body decomposing on the lounge

floor. The apartment was filled with knives, a hammer, scalpels and human skulls. The coffin which Manuela sometimes slept in was placed next to a radiator in the lounge.

More worryingly, there were names written on the walls next to the words 'be happy – you are next to die.' There was also a list of sixteen names which police believe were men and women who the Rudas wanted to kill.

Meanwhile the couple had travelled through Sonderhausen, on to Apold and, finally, Jena, which is where the police caught up with them. The Rudas had stopped at a petrol station because even people with a hotline to a supposed underworld run out of gas. They surrendered immediately, something police were glad of when they found a chainsaw in the boot of their car. The Rudas said that they'd tried to kill themselves several times whilst on the run, but it's unclear why they failed.

In custody, Daniel Ruda claimed to have no memory of the murder but his wife recalled every detail and happily described the killing to the police.

Whilst in custody, he bit the veins in his arm, then made the unvampire-like move of asking for a doctor. He told his lawyers that he wanted to be more famous than Charles Manson – but Manson's infamy partly arose because his followers targeted beautiful, rich and famous people. He also achieved fame because there were fewer known serial killers in his day. Numerous men have subsequently chalked up much higher body counts yet are barely known outside the states in which they killed.

The trial

The couple's guilt was a foregone conclusion. Neither denied the murder – they simply said that they were not accountable for the death as they were acting on a higher instruction. After all, some religions kill unmarried women if they aren't virgins and other religions mutilate their children's genitalia. They, the Rudas, had been told by their deity Satan to make a blood sacrifice and they had obediently carried this out.

During the trial, they repeatedly made Satanic symbols and stuck their tongues out at the spectators. A seventeen-year-old killer vampire profiled in *Children Who Kill* did the exact same thing.

The judge called for psychiatric background reports and these found that both of the accused were narcissistic exhibitionists. Such adults have often been ignored or abandoned as children and grow up with a desperate need for attention, even if it's negative. The judiciary noted that the couple would probably never have killed if they hadn't met each other. This is undoubtedly true – Manuela would have continued to seek attention through the transgressive club scene and Daniel would have maintained a grip on reality through his work, getting rid of his aggression at skinhead rallies and violent political events. It was only when they became a couple that they dropped out of society and completely immersed themselves in murderous plans.

Sentencing

On 31st January 2002 Manuela Ruda was sentenced to thirteen years in a secure mental facility and her husband was given fifteen years, also to be served in a psychiatric institution. The court ordered that they must never be allowed to meet again. Surprisingly, neither Ruda was resistant to the order (though they may have secret plans to defy it) and both are now seeking a divorce.

18   MY FAMILY AND OTHER ANIMALS
THE 'ABUSE EXCUSE'

Couples who kill tend to fit into distinct categories. That is, a small number who *kill for profit*, mainly those who murder babies then live off the child allowance or other adoption placement fees. Frances Schreuder (aided by her abused son Marc) also murdered for profit to enjoy her father's wealth and Louisa Merrifield killed to enjoy her employer's estate. Similarly, some of Archibald Hall and Michael Kitto's murders were motivated by the desire to enjoy the trappings of an upper-class life.

A second category *kill out of fear*, notably Amy Grossberg and Brian Peterson who killed their newborn infant rather than admit to their families that they'd had sex.

A third grouping *murder out of jealousy* – Diane Zamora and David Graham exterminated a potential rival whilst George Stoner murdered Alma Rattenbury's husband in order to have her all to himself. This, though, is a sub-category of fear, with the killers murdering to avoid being deserted, a fate which terrifies them.

A fourth and much smaller group suffer from *serious mental illness* – namely the Papin sisters and vampire killers Daniel and Manuela Ruda. There were also traces of mental illness (but not insanity) in the schizophrenic Leonard Lake and the obsessive-compulsive George Woldt.

But by far the biggest group *kill for power and thrills*. Bittaker & Norris, Bianchi & Buono, Corll & Henley,

Lake & Ng, Coleman & Brown all fit into this category. All made clear statements of their motivation to their victims, from Roy Norris's 'scream bitch scream' to Lake's explicit diary about keeping sexual slaves.

This power and thrills motivation also applies to many killer couples who aren't profiled here such as Raymond Fernandez & Martha Beck, David & Catherine Birnie, Judith & Alvin Neelley, Karla Homolka & Paul Barnardo, Gwendolyn Graham & Cathy Wood, Carol Bundy & Doug Clark. (All of the women apart from Martha Beck are profiled in *Women Who Kill*.)

What the individuals in these five groups have in common is that most were from abusive or deeply dysfunctional backgrounds. Lawrence Bittaker and Roy Norris had suffered emotional and physical abuse throughout their childhoods and Bittaker has spoken of being multiply sexually abused. Angelo Buono also endured a miserable childhood at the hands of his mother after which he hated women. His adoptive cousin Ken Bianchi fared little better, as his natural mother gave him to a childminder who abandoned the infant for hours at a time and only returned to treat him cruelly, then he was constantly spanked and scolded by his adoptive mum.

Dean Corll suffered in childhood at the hands of his authoritarian father and obsessive mother. Serial killers often have multiply-married mothers – and Corll's married five times. His co-killer Wayne Henley had endured poverty and abuse throughout his formative years and was addicted to alcohol by age fifteen.

The same formative deprivation holds true for Leonard Lake who was abandoned twice by his mother. Charles Ng suffered even more cruelly as a young boy, for his father –

hoping to turn him into an exemplary scholar – bound him and beat him frequently.

Such childhood suffering has been described by so many killers that it's become cynically known as 'the abuse excuse' – but most such killers accounts are backed up by eye-witness statements. Many were known by social services to be at risk, whilst others had relatives who knew that they were beaten, humiliated or starved of love. Psychotherapist Gaynor McManus has written that many of her clients in prison are 'men who were systematically ill-treated as children ... men who learned that violence works when they reached the age of sixteen or seventeen and hit their fathers back for the first time. It is only when they ask for therapy in their quest to change their lives that they learn to understand the reasons for their anti-social behaviour and to realise they have choices.'

The 2004 London Mayor's Report also noted that 'physical punishment of children breaches their fundamental rights to respect for their human dignity and physical integrity' and added 'research has shown that its use may cause behavioural problems in childhood and later life.'

This author has covered the link between so-called legitimate childhood punishments and later criminality and mental illness in previous novels and true crime books, so doesn't want to repeat the same information here – but readers who want an end to parents hitting children can send a stamped addressed envelope to Children Are Unbeatable, 94 White Lion Street, London, N1 9PF, requesting further information and a membership form.

One of the questions which crime writers are frequently asked is why one member of a family becomes a murderer and his siblings don't. The answer is that everyone deals with violence differently. I can recall one family where the father battered all three of his children on a regular basis. One of his sons ended up on an attempted murder charge, one became a wife-beater and the third child – a daughter – turned the violence inwards and became a compulsive self-harmer, getting through the day on recreational drugs and using increasingly strong prescription drugs to help her sleep. In another family I know which also endured life with a violent father, the son went on to humiliate and threaten his own children whilst the daughter had a nervous breakdown but recovered to devote her life to children's rights.

The final variable, of course, is choice. Many of us have violent urges when we are under duress – but we don't have to give in to them. Wanting to hit someone and actually striking them are two very different things. And these killers didn't strike out once in anger: most planned each murder in great detail, sometimes even customising an abduction vehicle or finding a safe house to imprison their captives.

People who make the best recovery from an abusive childhood are often those who eventually find something that they're good at, a career or leisure interest which builds their self-esteem. None of the killers profiled achieved this distinction: most settled for dead end jobs and were constantly bored. Their rage against society grew, but rather than seek help for their emotional distress, they preferred to capture innocent victims for deadly entertainment. The rest is history.